A Criminological Biography of an Arms Dealer

For many, the arms trade and its dealers are the root cause of regional wars and global terrorism. In both public and academic debates, arms dealers are considered immoral as they profit from conflict, due to their key position in the international arms trading business. Nevertheless, there seems to be little to no interest in the personal lives of those actively involved. In his criminological biography of a certified arms dealer, Yarin Eski provides an in-depth, interdisciplinary approach to and understanding of the global arms trade, revealing a deep insider view placed in a wider sociocultural context.

From early discussions of childhood and career choices, to reflections on becoming and being an arms trader, Eski offers a methodologically embedded approach and advances biographical writing in the field of Criminology. It is a unique and thought-provoking contribution to the fields of criminology, ethnography, sociology, critical security studies, policing studies, war studies and international politics and offers an unparalleled insight from within.

Yarin Eski is an assistant professor in Public Administration at Vrije Universiteit (VU) Amsterdam.

Routledge Studies in Crime and Society

Harm and Disorder in the Urban Space
Social Control, Sense and Sensibility
Edited by Nina Peršak and Anna Di Ronco

Serial and Mass Murder
Understanding Multicide through Offending Patterns, Explanations, and Outcomes
Elizabeth Gurian

Mass Shootings and Civilian Armament
Alexei Ansin

Criminalization of Activism
Historical, Present, and Future Perspectives
Edited by Valeria Vegh Weis

Elderly Sexual Abuse
Theory, Research, and Practice
Eric Beauregard and Julien Chopin

Desistance from Sexual Offending
The Role of Circles of Support and Accountability
Kelly Richards

Oppressed by Debt
Government and the Justice System as a Creditor of the Poor
Edited by Saul Schwartz

A Criminological Biography of an Arms Dealer
Yarin Eski

For more information about this series, please visit: www.routledge.com/Routledge-Studies-in-Crime-and-Society/book-series/RSCS

A Criminological Biography of an Arms Dealer

Yarin Eski

Routledge
Taylor & Francis Group
LONDON AND NEW YORK

First published 2022
by Routledge
2 Park Square, Milton Park, Abingdon, Oxon OX14 4RN

and by Routledge
605 Third Avenue, New York, NY 10158

Routledge is an imprint of the Taylor & Francis Group, an informa business

British Library Cataloguing-in-Publication Data
A catalogue record for this book is available from the British Library

Library of Congress Cataloging-in-Publication Data
Names: Eski, Yarin, author.
Title: A criminological biography of an arms dealer / Yarin Eski.
Description: 1 Edition. | New York, NY: Routledge Books, 2022. |
Includes bibliographical references and index.
Identifiers: LCCN 2021038851 (print) | LCCN 2021038852 (ebook) |
ISBN 9781138552586 (hardback) | ISBN 9781032189024 (paperback) |
ISBN 9781315148236 (ebook)
Subjects: LCSH: Eski, Yarin. | Arms dealers–Biography. |
Arms transfers. | Arms transfers–Law and legislation. |
Violence–Social aspects.
Classification: LCC HD9743.A2 E75 2022 (print) |
LCC HD9743.A2 (ebook) | DDC 623.4/4092 [B]–dc23/eng/20211013
LC record available at https://lccn.loc.gov/2021038851
LC ebook record available at https://lccn.loc.gov/2021038852

ISBN: 9781138552586 (hbk)
ISBN: 9781032189024 (pbk)
ISBN: 9781315148236 (ebk)

DOI: 10.4324/9781315148236

Typeset in Times New Roman
by Newgen Publishing UK

To all the unsung heroes that have fallen in countless wars throughout our time.

And lo, do I see my father
And lo, do I see my mother
And my sisters and my brothers
And the line of my people,
Back to the beginning…
And lo, they do call me,
In the halls of Valhalla
Where the brave may live forever!

From an old Viking war prayer (unattributed).

Contents

Acknowledgements

This biography has been, if anything, a long, often exciting and sometimes difficult road we have taken together, Constantine. Or 'my arms dealer' as I would often call you when talking to others. Since the beginning in 2016, you have been involved and committed yourself beyond my expectations. You have taught me numerous things about arms dealing and about the world itself. Also, and more than you may ever realise, I have learnt a great deal about myself. To you, Constantine, my sincerest gratefulness. It has been a true privilege to have written your biography. The biography that lies here in front of you is as much a result of your efforts as it is of mine.

I owe much debt as well to the reviewers of the proposal for this biography and your sharp feedback. I would like to thank here also Frank van Gemert, my criminological colleague at the Vrije Universiteit Amsterdam. Frank, your biographical work is second to none and your comments in the final stages of writing have truly improved this book. If anything, I owe you, big time! Of course, the faults that have remained are mine and mine alone.

Along the way, about five years now, a lot has happened. I have moved from the United Kingdom back to my home country, the Netherlands. And therefore I have left good friends and colleagues, but also made many new ones. Thank you for being there and having been patient throughout all of it. A few of you have played a very important role for me, so, in alphabetical order, Eva Blomme, Mauro Boelens, Hans Boutellier, Wietse Dijkstra, Clarissa Meerts, Peter Millward, Yvonne La Grouw, Ruud Leijten, Elizabeth-Jane Peatfield, Antony Pemberton, Ronald van Steden, Ingrid van Tienen, Christophe Vandeviver, Ben Vosse and Rick van Weelden; to you all, thank you being for a friend! This biography would not have come into existence without your support.

During the interviewing for this biography, frequently Constantine and I talked about his family, but sometimes also about mine. The conversations we had about them made me realise how fortunate I have been and still am. So, finally, to my parents, Yaşar and Diny Eski, and my sister, Sharise Eski; I do not think I can ever thank you enough! Forever and for everything, my utmost respect and gratitude.

Abbreviations

AK47	Avtomát Kalashnikova Model 1947 (Kalashnikov's Automatic Rifle)
AKM	Avtomát Kalášnikova Modernizírovannyj (Kalashnikov's Automatic Rifle Modernised)
ATT	Arms Trade Treaty
BAE	British Aerospace Systems
BSc	Bachelor of Science
CAR	Central African Republic
CIA	Central Intelligence Agency
DSEI	Defence and Security Equipment International
EUC	End-User Certificate
FN	Fabrique Nationale
FN FAL	Fabrique Nationale Fusil Automatique Léger (Light Automatic Rifle)
G3	Gewehr 3 (Select-Fire Battle Rifle 3)
ICBM	Intercontinental Ballistic Missile
ISIS	Islamic State of Iraq and Syria
IT	Information Technology
ITAR	International Traffic in Arms Regulations
M4	Model 4 Carbine
MA	Master of Arts
MAAWS	Multi-role Anti-armor Anti-tank Weapon System
MANPADS	Man-Portable Air-Defense Systems
MSc	Master of Science
MP5	Maschinenpistole 5 (Submachine Gun 5)
MPN	Myeloproliferative Neoplasms
NATO	North Atlantic Treaty Organisation
NGO	Non-Governmental Organisation
OSINT	Open Source Intelligence
PKK	Partîya Karkerên Kurdistanê (Kurdistan Workers' Party)
SALW	Small Arms and Light Weapons
SAS	Small Arms Survey
SIGINT	Signals Intelligence

SIPRI	Stockholm International Peace Research Institute
SOP	Standard Operating Procedure
T56	Type 56 Automatic Rifle
UAV	Unmanned Aerial Vehicle
UN	United Nations
UNODC	United Nations Office on Drugs and Crime
UNRCA	United Nations Register of Conventional Arms
WMD	Weapons of Mass Destruction
YPG	Yekîneyên Parastina Gel (People's Defense Units)

'My life is a ****ed up book!'
An introduction

> You have to make money to live and if I'm in this business to make money, then yeah, you have to make money. And if I make money out of it, then I make money out of it. People are gonna hate me for that statement. But it's just the way it is. I have no moral compunction, I have no moral, what shall we say [...] Pfff [...] I have no moral compunctions about worrying whether some of the equipment that I'm gonna sell or have sold is gonna kill somebody. Otherwise car dealers would go out of business as well. [...] More people are killed with cars on the road every day than with guns. [...] You have to have a certain outlook on life [...] a certain coldness, heartlessness, call it what you want.
>
> (Constantine)

This biography is about the legal arms dealer Constantine, who, at the time of writing, is in his 60s, thinking about retirement. If only, because 'business is slow', as he would often say about the worsening condition of his arms-dealing company. For more than 20 years, he has been brokering deals and is therefore a seasoned professional in the international arms trade. He is, if anything, a business man, as the above makes clear. But he is also a religious man and a family man. Born and raised in a strict catholic family with military-like discipline, Constantine is the oldest and has four brothers and a sister. He has had a diverse career path, having been a diving instructor, a social worker and now arms dealer. He is also a father, a grandfather and a loving husband. And he has pancreatic cancer for over 20 years, a severe illness he has been fighting ever since. It is one of the reasons why he committed himself to have his biography written, to pass on a legacy. So, if anything, he is many things and many people think many things about him. About himself though, he mostly thinks he is an outsider.

> Some people call me wonderful, some people call me an evil person. Some people say I'm fantastic. My daughter thinks I'm a little bit strange. My sister thinks I'm evil. People have varying opinions of me. This is the same with everybody. Nobody is ever liked and loved by everybody. [...] I wouldn't have done it any other way. If there are some things that I could

DOI: 10.4324/9781315148236-1

change, reflecting on them […] Yeah, okay, maybe. Maybe a better relationship with my parents, better relationship, a closer relationship with my siblings, but I wouldn't have changed anything. […] I did it MY way. […] When you're an individual you don't try to fit in with something else, because otherwise then there wouldn't be any individualism. It's like people having the same haircut, people following fashions, people wearing the same clothes, people liking the same music or certain genre of music. They consider themselves individuals. Well, I'm sorry, as far as I'm concerned hahaha they're not! So, to me, doing what I do and the way that I do it, puts me outside of the box of a lot of people that are in that shoebox that sell arms. The guys that do that are mostly […] they're a little bit like shoe salesmen. Shirts, ties, respective cars, first class travelling. I don't do that unless it's being paid for by the client. That's what I mean. […] I think I am an outsider to the normal society, let's put it that way, always have been. It's positive for me [being an outsider]. I can consider myself special, if you want another word for it. That's not right either, but it's the only word I can think of. It's like I would go to meetings at the XXXX. […] There would be generals, and admirals, vice-admirals, the head of the XXXX navy was there. I was quite surprised actually, because I didn't think we'd left them any fucking boats. He was there […] and there was little old me, an arms dealer. Sitting there, giving a talk on […] security. This is what I mean by outsider. I don't fit in, in a normal […] Nobody can put me in a shoebox. Nobody can say "He's this type of person and he fits in with these people". I don't fit in with anybody. I'm me. […] My life story is a story of a person that's lived on the outside of society in one way or another. […] People have preconceived conception of what arms dealers do. I can't go around […] Even my wife said to me: "If anybody asks you here in the village or in the town, what you do, for God's sake, don't tell them you're an arms dealer". […] A lot of people know what I do, but I don't make a big deal out of it. If people ask me what I do, I reply "I'm involved in military equipment". […] I mean there's nothing more than I would have liked to have been able to marry once, have lots of children, settle down, little nice white picket fence, and go to work from 9–5. No, that's not for me. I always wanted more from my life, even now at 60+. I want more from my life than what I've got at the moment, I'm always struggling to get better at what I do, make more out of my life, for me personally, not for anybody else. I'm not talking about just material things. I'm talking about personal development. […] I can live with the person I am at the moment and that's the main thing. […] I have to live with what I am, what I've done, who I've done it to, and trying to make the best of it. This is what I've done with my life, trying not to hurt other people, trying not to treat people other than ways that I'd like to be treated. That's my […] That's my.. motto on life, basically. Do onto others what you would have them to do to you. […] In my younger years I was a hell raiser and that was it. You can't change that. All you can do is change yourself. If you want to change the world around

> you, start with yourself first. [...] Sometimes I catch myself thinking; "You know mate, if I was 20 years younger, I'd thump you", but then I think: "Nah, poor guy, I don't know what he's carrying on his shoulders, I don't know why he's aggressive, I don't know why he's got that attitude, I don't why he's driving like a lunatic. Let him just get on with his life", because karma's a bitch and it will come around and bite you in the ass. [...] Yarin, you know, there was a time when I would not go out of my way, I would not move if I thought I was in the right, then woe betide anybody who got in my way. I was a very [...] I KNEW what I WANTED and that was the road I took, and if anybody said to me: "No you can't do that", I'd say: "Well, you know, fuck you because I'm gonna do it anyway". I'll do it the way I want to do it, and if it's wrong then it's my mistake, it's not yours. I have to live with it, not you. That's who I am, that's how I was, and that's probably how I will end up being, you know, when I slide into the pearly gates with a worn out body, I will scream "Yahoo! What a hell of a ride!".

Thus spoke Constantine. The above fragment is one out of many in this book that gives a look into the 'many faceted character today in the way that I think and feel about certain things', as he described. To do this biography, meant for him to have gone 'deep down the rabbit hole'. It is about how he sees his life as a conglomeration of the choices, events, mistakes and all the things he has ever done up to the point of interviewing. It all made him the man he is today.

Based on the life of one person, this criminological biography of an arms dealer is but a small sample compared to a large statistical sample about arms dealers. However, as will become clear, it is not about the numbers though as criminological research is usually about (Young 2016). It is about a person of flesh and blood, about his childhood, his teenage years, the lovers he had and who he left, about his children and grandchildren. Regarding these topics, he admitted he was

> not sure what this has got anything to do with arms dealing. I know you don't want to write about the arms dealing itself, you wanna write about the arms DEALER and his morality and his life. I get that [...] I got that from the beginning.

Constantine deals in small arms and light weapons (SALWs) that are considered the real weapons of mass destruction (Yihdego 2003). These include handguns and the world-famous AK47, for example. Arms, and weapons more generally, are made to kill, but they also scare, protect and have been fascinating us since the beginning of mankind. They have always existed and, quite literally, have been attached to the human body. The earliest weapons were 'the hands, nails and teeth, as well as stones, pieces of wood, flames and fire as soon as they known', as Roman philosopher Lucretius documented in his *De Rerum Natura V* (1708). Archaeological findings of stone tips indicate that arrows and spears were used to kill, already over 60,000 years ago (Lombard & Phillipson 2010). Due to the discovery by humans of fertile soil, such weapons were more and more used for farming, for example, as ploughing equipment. In biblical writings, Tubal-Cain – a descendant of Cain (the first murderer of the world) – has been considered throughout history the first artificer, a forger of iron and inventor of 'arms and instruments of war' (Jackson 1752: 207), demonised into an 'eater of flesh, would-be killer of Noah' (Shepherd 2017: 95). That demonisation, with its religious roots, has continued ever since those descriptions in the bible. Being one of the oldest trades, especially in modern history, arms and the arms trade reflect a part of our human nature, which is to solve conflict by armed violence rather than debate and understanding (Smith 2007). It shows that, whether as blades or bullets, nuclear or cyber, weapons have brought about enormous societal, global changes. Yet almost nothing is really known about those who deal in arms.

Constantine's biography is certainly unique because he is alive, not imprisoned, and still active in the legal international arms trade. In case Constantine would not have shown his willingness to do this biography, it would have been hard if not impossible to enter the international arms industry and analyse data – qualitatively – retrieved from within the trade, as it is a very closed off and tabooed domain, accommodating a global but hidden community (D'Ancona 1991; Nordstrom 2004). Despite not knowing a lot about a very closed off sector, his biography comes at a time when more than ever before, the arms trade and arms dealers are severely demonised in public debate, politics, the entertainment industry and academia (Bauman 2016; Bromley et al. 2012; Democracy Now! 2016; Hornaday 2021; Theodoulou 2009; Ummid 2016; UN Security Council 2019; Wechsler 2016). They represent and are presented as immoral and evil, depicted as the worst kind of human beings by making money out of death and destruction. To an extent, arms dealers could be considered as a new international folk devil that causes global moral panic (Cohen 2011; Edwards & Gill 2002); one that is sensationalised into blockbuster movies, such as the well-known *Lord of War* (Niccol 2005), *Iron Man* (Favreau 2008) and *War Dogs* (Philips 2016), as well as into bingeworthy series, such as *The Night Manager* (Bier 2016) and *Conspiracy of Silence* (Brandstrom & Danielson 2018). The fact the arms dealer is the new 'big baddy' seems to relate to the idea of an absence of classical imaginary enemies that divide us. In looking for a common enemy that unites globally and gives a sense of worldwide cohesion, the figure of arms dealer is then

> "[t]he invisible obvious" [that] has had the same effect in Hollywood, which, at least since the Cold War, has looked for the perfect all-utility villain. With "no-good dirty Commies" decommissioned since the 1990s, screenwriters and studio executives tried their best to find convincing personifications of pure evil that would not perpetuate noxious stereotypes

> or hoary clichés. Having been sensitized to the poisonous symbolism of trotting out yet one more Arab terrorist or African American drug dealer or pimp, filmmakers cast about for figures everyone could loathe: *arms dealers*, sex traffickers, garden-variety corporate greedheads.
>
> (Hornaday 2021 – online source, emphasis YE)

However, why are arms dealers hated to begin with? To even begin to answer that question, first it must become clear who the figure of the arms dealer is, as this criminological biography will aim to do so. It is a book on human nature, but not necessarily (only) about the violent, exploitative and evil sides of a person, but more so about the loving, caring and sometimes simply boring aspects of an arms dealer's life. What does it mean to be an arms dealer in these volatile times in which everything is possible instantaneously? To understand that, first this biography will go back to Constantine's youth and coming of age, looking at the difficult relationship he had with his father (Chapter 3), his years in boarding school, university and early career (Chapter 4). From there, this book will consider his arms dealing career, his offers, his glory days and desk-bound years, and how he treats his clients and rivals (Chapters 5 and 6). Given the ongoing logistical, legal and moral puzzles contemporary legal arms dealers are confronted with (Kruse 2016; Melé 2018), the legal, political and public opinion context of his work shall then be focused on elaborately (Chapter 7). After that, this book will shed light on his not so clear retirement plans, his current family life and his struggles with his health, as he suffers from cancer since the 1990s (Chapter 8). The last chapter (Chapter 9) will conclude this biography, followed by a bitter-sweet criminological aftertaste of this biography (Epilogue). However, before getting to the 'juice' of his life story, what will follow is, first, an overview of how arms dealers are imagined and why this biography shall work towards a criminological imagination of Constantine (Chapter 1) and, second, a methodological reflection on why biography as a method fits to do so and how it has been carried out (Chapter 2).

References

Bauman Z (2016) A few comments on the mis-imagined war on terrorism. From: www.socialeurope.eu/2016/03/comments-mis-imagined-war-terrorism/.

Bier S (2016) *The night manager*. London: The Ink Factory, London: BBC, and New York: AMC.

Brandstrom C & Danielson H (2018) *Ingen utan skuld (conspiracy of silence)*. Sweden: Brain Academy, United Kingdom: Twelve Town and Brussels: Umedia and uFund.

Bromley M, Cooper N & Holtom P (2012) The UN Arms Trade Treaty: arms export controls, the human security agenda and the lessons of history. *International Affairs* 88(5): 1029–1048.

Cohen S (2011) *Folk devils and moral panics: the creation of the Mods and Rockers*. London: Routledge.

D'Ancona M (1991) Britain: business before disclosure. *Index on Censorship* 20(10): 16–17.

Democracy Now! (2016) Pope Francis points at weapons industry behind Brussels attack. From: www.democracynow.org/2016/3/25/headlines/pope_francis_points_at_weapons_industry_behind_brussels_attack.

Edwards A & Gill P (2002) The politics of 'transnational organized crime': discourse, reflexivity and the narration of 'threat'. *British Journal of Politics and International Relations* 4(2): 245–270.

Favreau J (2008) *Iron Man*. Hollywood: Paramount Pictures.

Hornaday A (2021) While Hollywood looked for perfect villains, they were hiding in plain sight. From: www.washingtonpost.com/entertainment/white-supremacy-hollywood-villains/2021/01/15/515f5386-5696-11eb-a08b-f1381ef3d207_story.html.

Jackson J (1752) *Chronological antiquities*. London: Noon.

Kruse K (2016) What I learned from an international arms dealer. From: www.forbes.com/sites/kevinkruse/2016/09/12/what-i-learned-from-an-international-arms-dealer/?sh=1b929aeb54a0.

Lombard M & Phillipson L (2010) Indications of bow and stone-tipped arrow use 64 000 years ago in KwaZulu-Natal, South Africa. *Antiquity* 84(325): 635–648.

Lucretius TC (1708) *De rerum natura*. Paris: Chez Pierre Aubouyn.

Melé A (2018) So you want to be an arms dealer?. From: www.linkedin.com/pulse/so-you-want-arms-dealer-tony-mel%C3%A9/.

Niccol A (2005) *Lord of war*. United States: Lions Gate Films and Neuilly-sur-Seine: SND.

Nordstrom C (2004) *Shadows of war: violence, power, and international profiteering in the twenty-first century*. Berkeley, CA: University of California Press.

Phillips T (2016) *War dogs*. Indiana: Green Hat Films, Los Angeles: The Mark Gordon Company and Los Angeles: RatPac Entertainment.

Shepherd D (2017) Seeing is believing: Aronofsky's Noah and cinematic spectacle. In Burnette-Bletsch R & Morgan J (eds) *Noah as antihero: Darren Aronofsky's cinematic deluge*. New York, NY: Routledge, pp. 84–101.

Smith DL (2007) *The most dangerous animal: human nature and the origins of war*. New York, NY: St. Martin's Press.

Theoudoulou M (2009) The bizarre double life of Latif Yahia. From: www.thenationalnews.com/world/mena/the-bizarre-double-life-of-latif-yahia-1.571406.

Ummid (2016) Arms dealers, killing government behind Europe refugee crisis. From: www.ummid.com/news/2016/March/28.03.2016/behind-every-refugee-to-europe-stands-an-arm-dealer.html.

UN Security Council (2019) Small arms and light weapons: report of the Secretary-General. From: https://undocs.org/en/S/2019/1011.

Wechsler M (2016) 'Merchant of death' or victim of an international sting?. From: www.thebigchilli.com/feature-stories/merchant-of-death-or-victim-of-an-international-sting.

Yihdego ZW (2003) Small arms and light weapons-the real weapons of mass destruction: versimilitude and observations. *bepress Legal Series* 29. From: https://law.bepress.com/expresso/eps/29/.

Young J (2016) Voodoo criminology and the numbers game. In Ferrell J, Hayward K, Morrison W & Presdee M (eds) *Cultural criminology unleashed*. London: Routledge, pp. 27–42.

1 Arms dealers imagined

Towards a criminological imagination of an arms dealer

> I think that if the devil does not exist, and man has therefore created him, he has created him in his own image and likeness.
>
> (Dostoevsky 1992: 202)

This is what Ivan Karamazov, one of the main characters in Fyodor Dostoevsky's last novel *The Brothers Karamazov* (1992), explains to his younger brother Alyosha Karamazov about evil. The novel is set in 19th century Russia and is in many ways a philosophical piece of work on the deeper, more existential questions about the human condition in relation to religion, free will and morality. Evil is a central theme in the novel and narrates how people all have their own (group) images of evil, to the extent that they separate themselves from evil particularly by dehumanising people into evil or the devil. Arms dealers are also subjected to dehumanisation and demonisation, having led to images of them as morally corrupt, as pure evil and as merchants of death (Bauman 2016; Bromley et al. 2012; Byrne 2007; Farah & Braun 2007; Hamid 2006; Hornaday 2021; Mac Cormick 1965; Maitland 1998; Moine 2006; Orlovsky 2005; Potter 2012; Theodoulou 2009; Ummid 2016; UN Security Council 2019; Wechsler 2016; Wisor 2014). This chapter will elaborate on these and other dominant (taken-for-granted) imaginations that exist about arms dealers in statistics, politics, moral debates and sensationalising mass (social) media, in particular the movie industry. Afterward, it will be argued to aim for a criminological imagination of an arms dealer throughout this book and to be finalised in the concluding Chapter 9, based on Constantine's biography.

1.1 The statistical-factual imagination

Arms dealers, like any other human being, are culture-creating beings with a free will, 'albeit in circumstances not of their own making' (Young 2016: 13), logically making one assume there are various deeper understandings available of their human activity in the global arms trade. However, and despite in current late modern times 'such creativity and reflexivity becomes all the more

DOI: 10.4324/9781315148236-2

apparent', the opposite is truer and thus it is rather ironic that 'at precisely such a time of the cultural turn' (ibid.), most knowledge on arms dealers and their business remains first and foremost statistical – detached from any insight on their persona, motivations and humaneness. The arms dealer is, to a certain degree, just another variable in the numbers game and not even interesting as a quantity itself: type in 'amount [or number] of arms dealers in the world' in Google search, and you will get results on amounts of arms manufacturers but not on a specific total of arms dealers. In the statistical-factual setting, the arms dealer remains a dark figure, quite literally.

Instead, statistical-factual focus is almost entirely laid upon arms and ammunition, almost solely on what small arms and lights weapons (SALWs) are out there, how many and what market value they have. SALWs include revolvers and self-loading pistols, rifles and carbines, sub-machine guns, assault rifles, light and heavy machine guns, handheld underbarrel and mounted grenade launchers, portable anti-tank guns, recoilless rifles, portable anti-tank missile launchers and rocket systems, and mortars of calibres less than 75 mm (UN Register of Conventional Arms (UNRCA), 2018). Journalists sometimes approach Constantine to only ask information about wanting to know what sort of weapons are purchased and how they are used, what kind of ammunition is required and how much damage can be caused. Also research centres approach him for information in order to do analyses of the market. The Small Arms Survey (SAS), a project of the Graduate Institute of International and Development Studies in Geneva, Switzerland, is such a 'global centre of excellence' (2021 – online source). One that

> provides expertise on all aspects of small arms and armed violence [...] The Small Arms Survey generates evidence-based, impartial, and policy-relevant knowledge and analysis on small arms and armed violence issues for governments, policy-makers, researchers, and civil society.
>
> (Ibid.)

The SAS is one out of various indexes that try to capture the volumes of civilian, law enforcement and military SALWs. They list staggering amounts of registered, legal arms. Deeper understanding of arms dealers though is lacking. Not entirely strange, because arms and ammunition are things, they have a concrete function and they cost money; they can be counted and thus be easily grasped. That knowledge gives an easy but superficial, mostly numerical understanding of the arms trade. But what do statistics on arms show then?

Usually, the numbers indicate that an almost unfathomable amount of 'guns and powder' is floating around the world. The global arms trade encompasses an approximately 200 billion business in which the United States drives almost 80% of it (Macias & Rattner 2020).

> There are more than one billion firearms in the world, the vast majority of which are in civilian hands, according to new research. The Small Arms

> Survey estimates that of the one billion firearms in global circulation as of 2017, 857 million (85 per cent) are in civilian hands, 133 million (13 per cent) are in military arsenals, and 23 million (2 per cent) are owned by law enforcement agencies. The new studies suggest that the global stockpile has increased over the past decade, largely due to civilian holdings, which grew from 650 million in 2006 to 857 million in 2017.
>
> (Small Arms Survey 2018: 1)

Firearms are the most popular SALWs these days, as reflected in the 550,000 seized firearms between 2016 and 2017 worldwide, according to a recent study by the United Nations Office on Drugs and Crime (UNODC) (2020). The global seizures' figure is most likely much higher than the estimated, yet it sketches the trend of pistols becoming especially more frequently prevalent in the Americas, whereas in Africa and Asia shotguns and in Oceania rifles are popular. In Europe, there was an equal distribution between pistols, rifles and shotguns (UNODC 2020: 7–9).

Constantine explained it would surprise people how large the amount is of government surplus arms and is lying around all over the world, 'just waiting for people to buy it', he said. That ready-for-sale growing amount of arms has led to a fast-growing global arms trade. From 2015 to 2020, the number of international transfers of legal arms grew with 5% compared to 2010–2015, with the largest exporters being the United States, Russia, France, Germany and China, and the five largest importers being Saudi Arabia, India, Egypt, Australia and China (Wezeman et al. 2020). It is also a highly volatile market (SIPRI 2018 – online) continuously developing, changing its flows and to a certain extent uncontrollable and unfathomable, dominated by the United States and the United Kingdom, followed by Russia, China and France, as currently the biggest arms dealers in the world (Charles Koch Foundation 2018; Sheffield 2016; Stone 2016). These are official numbers compiling the registered SALWs, giving an idea of the volumes in the global legal arms trade that is financially valued at least $88.4 billion, although the true figure is probably higher (SIPRI 2018).

What about illegal arms then? There is not a clear statistical estimate of unregistered, illegal arms, both in terms of what kind of SALWs there are on the black market, as well as what the estimated financial value of it is. There are estimates that indicate approximately $400 up to $800 million annually (Kinsella 2014: 524). It is also estimated that there are billions of illicit SALWs circulating, in particular in Africa and the Middle East (UN Security Council 2019). Research done has been predominantly preoccupied with (comparative) legal and statistical conclusions on the *illicit* (small) arms trade, its (Cold War) origins, its effects and the possibilities for its control (cf. Arsovska & Kostakos 2008; Cook et al. 2008; De Kerchove & Höhn 2015; Ojakorotu et al. 2014; Ruggiero 1996, 1997, 2007; Stohl & Grillot 2009; Taylor 2015; Yihdego 2007). Other approaches to the complexity of the illicit arms trade include analyses focusing on the public health and gender(ed) dimensions of the trade (Cukier 2002a, 2002b), as well as analyses that scrutinise connections between state crime, corruption and the arms trade (Feinstein 2011; Feinstein et al. 2011; Holden & Van Vuuren 2011). Cook et al. have pointed out that '[i]n spite of the obvious links between the illegal firearms and drug trade, criminological understanding of the dynamics of illicit weapons flows, and their impact on the scope, scale and distribution of armed violence is limited' (2009: 266).

Despite large bodies of statistics and numbers-focused research on the arms trade, the synthetic scaling of the arms trade(rs) overlooks that we are nowhere close to fully oversee and truly understand the arms trade and its traders. It reflects what Young (2016) claims about voodoo criminology, the numbers game and how 'criminologists themselves are far distant from crime out there hidden behind a wall of verbiage and computer print-out, the barrier graphited with the Greek letters of statistical manipulation' (ibid.: 26). The statistical-factual imagination shows facts on arms, which categories there are, how to use them, which damage can be done, as well as statistics on the numbers of arms and reports on market values of the (il)legal arms trade. Yet an understanding of arms dealers remains absent. Instead, these 'facts and numbers' dehumanise arms dealers, making arms themselves matter more than their dealers, by concentrating on the what, how, when and where, but not necessarily on whom, and definitely not on why. The arms dealer is quantified away, not just as a human being, but also as a variable itself. There is not even statistical and factual interest in this actor; arms dealers are not counted and therefore do not count. Only what they trade in, consisting of things existing in unfathomable amounts. Consequently, demographic statistics of arms dealers do not exist: how many are men, how many women? How old are they generally? What's their income? It is actually rather remarkable that a 'voodoo criminology' of arms dealers is not readily available, given that legal arms dealers are registered and, for that matter, easily objectified into numbers. Yet also that has not happened, at least not in criminological research. All in all, arms dealers do not exist in the official numbers and remain uninteresting for criminologists. They remain a criminological nonentity. However, they do exist, but somewhere in the shadows, invisibly.

1.2 The political-moral imagination

The political-moral imagination of arms dealers is one in which they are perceived as indispensable cogs in the wheel of the international arms trade, because of their ascribed stealth and invisibility. Their profession forms the core of that trade, making arms dealers an essential part of international security that makes and solidifies alliances, influences governments and benefits economic stability, as much as that they play a key role for countries' national security, brokering arms deals to sell and supply weapons to and from military and police forces, as well as for civilian use (Stohl & Grillot 2009). The fact they broker arms deals and that 'conventional weapons transfers are not as visible or concerning to a general audience' (ibid.: 185) come in handy for governments to operate in the shadows of the wider military- and security-industrial complex (Dunne & Sköns 2010; Nordstrom 2004; Stockmarr 2015).

Nordstrom did an ethnographic study on what she defines as 'complex sets of cross-state economic and political linkages that move outside formally recognized state-based channels', where the 'illegal' and 'legal' blur, and activities 'cross various divides between legal, quasi-legal, and downright illegal activities' (2004: 34). She placed herself in networks that operate on the 'thin line between criminal traffic and government-inspired trade', as Castells put it (1998: 178). Those networks operating in the shadows consist of people 'who move goods and services worldwide—networks that broker power comparable to, and in many cases greater than, the power of some of the world's states', and are especially visible in warzones (Nordstrom 2004: 107). Featuring in the shadowy extra-state political economies and international markets, are a wide range of legal and illegal actors active that wield power yet are governed by specific 'rules of exchange, codes of conduct, hierarchies of deference' (ibid.). These are by definition international actors that have formal and informal bonds between

> corrupt commercial elites, religious leaders, international agency personnel, as well as international racketeers and their middlemen, smugglers, money-dealers, pirates, and slavers and abductors, not to mention soldiers in the warring armies and foreign troops.
>
> (Ibid.: 108)

Although the legal global arms trade complies with international rules and regulation, one way or another, legal arms dealers are supposedly confronted with intersections of informal, less compliant arms trading routes through which legal weaponry may also travel in conjunction with the fluid (il)legality of everyday products (ibid.). Therefore, legal arms dealers and their legal brokering cannot be easily disaggregated from their illegal counterpart or other criminal flows of illicit goods, or from the power structures of shadow networks in which these activities take place. At least, that is what is being imagined politically.

Then again, if it is something taking place in the shadows, remaining unseen, why bother? See no evil, hear no evil, speak no evil? Generally, people do not seem to care much about, whether legal or illegal, arms dealers are brokering SALW deals and what their geopolitical impact may consist of. Only when headlines speak of weapons of mass destruction there is an interest, whereas SALWs cause far more death and destruction (Stohl & Grillot 2009). Or when the topic of further disarmament and arms control reappears in the news, in particular regarding international arms (trade) treaties, arms dealers receive public and specifically political scrutiny. In that political setting they play the role of scapegoat, subjected to a perceived moral superiority of global peacemaking to legitimise further arms disarmament, which has been a trend since the beginning of the 20th century (Bromley et al. 2012; Erickson 2015).

The arms trade has played a major role especially in the last two 'centur[ies] of total war', showing that '[t]he arms trade is morally serious for many reasons' (Williamson 1998: 252). In fact, 'the arms trade has been the object of moral contempt' in which '[t]he foundation for this moral stand, [is] that private profit is made from providing the instruments of war, as well as its double-standards' (Brzoska 2004: 162). Right after World War I, the League of Nations pushed for the St. Germain Convention for the Control of the Trade in Arms and Ammunition, primarily motivated 'by the European powers' desires to keep weapons from falling into the hands of "problem actors" in areas of colonial influence' (Erickson 2015: 49) and the public's 'moral criticism of the role of arms dealers in fomenting the First World War' (Bromley et al. 2012: 1032). Since that convention, many more arms trade agreements followed. It is remarkable how morality influences these agreements, whereas they 'do not have to be grand moral projects [...] but when they are, the lesson of history is that they are more likely to succeed when the security subjectivities of policymakers and ethical ideals of campaigners are complementary' (ibid.: 1034).

In that political-moral setting of arms control as moralising projects and public demonisation, arms dealers fulfil the role of global folk devils (cf. Edwards & Gill 2002) by brokering deals on SALWs that are considered to be

> key driver[s] of human suffering. Their production, including craft manufacture, is a lucrative business and an attractive means of sustaining the activities of terrorist and criminal groups. Stockpiles of weapons and ammunition are increasing, including in areas affected by conflict.
>
> (UN Security Council 2019: 3)

Arms dealers are behind 'the primary cause of death in the violent conflicts raging today' (Kinsella 2014: 523), benefitting from 'a problem that impacts every country in the world, and civilian populations bear the brunt of human rights violations associated with this trade' (Arsovska 2014: 295). In particular, illegal arms dealers are active 'in areas afflicted by armed conflict, violence, and organized crime, where the demand for illicit weapons is often highest' that not only fuels ongoing civil warfare but also 'stocks the arsenals of terrorists, drug cartels, and other armed groups' (Small Arms Survey 2015).

Not just civil warfare or genocidal prone areas are 'attractive' for the arms trade; more and more also the link between terrorist attacks and the arms trade is made in political-moral debate. Emphasising the worldwide prevalence of arms and vilifying the exploitative nature of the arms trade, Pope Francis made the following statement:

> Three days ago, there was a gesture of war, of destruction, in a city of Europe [Brussels] from people who don't want to live in peace. Behind that gesture there were arms manufacturers, the arms traffickers who want blood, not peace, who want war, not brotherhood.
>
> (Pope Francis, Rome, 24 March 2016 – Democracy Now! 2016)

In (the war on) terrorism, neither terrorists nor the 'allies of the free world' are triumphant, 'except perhaps the producers, sellers and smugglers of murderous weapons [that] may emerge victorious [...] [t]he global arms trade [...] has by now transformed the planet into a minefield' (Bauman 2016, online source). The Director of the Transnational Foundation for Peace and Future Research, Jan Oberg, connected the refugee crisis in Europe with the arms dealers and stated: 'Stop the bombing, stop the wars, it is all a consequence that behind every refugee stands an arms dealer and a killing government' (Ummid 2016, online source).

In the political-moral imagination, arms traders stand accused of wielding their fortune by preying on conflict, feeding off of a fear-based felt necessity of people and countries to purchase arms to secure themselves; an exploitation that makes the trade and its merchants look immoral and inhumane, if not, pure evil (Byrne 2007; Maitland 1998; Wisor 2014). Arms dealers, as Cohen (2011) would have framed it, are then targeted by a moral panic about them as a 'group of persons [that] emerges to become defined as a threat to societal values and interests' in which 'the moral barricades are manned by editors, bishops, politicians and other right-thinking people' that will resolve the issue (ibid.: 1).

So, whereas the role of arms dealers in the statistical-factual setting is one of being non-existent, in the political-moral imagination, their role is rather bipolarised: while their existence is vital to move around arms in the invisible political domain of shadow economies where governments use arms trading to turn surplus weaponry into mass income, in public debate their existence is disapproved of and politically used to control arms. The way the arms dealer is politically utilised – practically necessary in secret yet demonised in public – is typical for the late modern, bulimic society (Young 2007), 'where both inclusion and exclusion occur concurrently' and 'where massive cultural inclusion is accompanied by systematic structural exclusion' (ibid.: 32). The arms dealer, however, is structurally included but culturally (and morally) excluded. The cultural exclusion is reflected in public debate of the international community, predominantly focusing on arms dealers as heartless, cold, rational, empty creatures merely motivated by financial gain from conflict, war and genocides; 'creatures' who commodify the violent human nature and a will to kill. They are condemned as exploitative individuals, inhibiting an evil nature; that 'nature is presented in a stylized and stereotypical fashion by the mass media', Cohen notes on folk devils (2011: 1). That folk devil role of arms dealers is in turn sensationalised in the third and last imagination, namely, the sensational imagination.

1.3 The sensational imagination

Not necessarily known for his arms dealing, but one of history's richest men and most influential arms dealers was Basil Zaharoff. He was a Greek industrialist and referred to as a 'Merchant of Death' (Mac Cormick 1965) and gained that infamous status at the end of the 19th and beginning of the 20th centuries. He and many more arms dealers would be ascribed evil nicknames – in particular as merchants of death, as will become clear – and stigmatised by especially pacifist-inspired discourses, stereotyping arms dealers as having 'an unlimited thirst for power and lucre and a quasi-demoniacal capacity for nuisance', turning them into almost phantasmagorical, rather macabre individuals; an image that criminalises the socio-economic position of the wider arms industry and trade (Moine 2006: 139). It fits the overall moral panic about arms dealers being publicly condemned as the root of all evil, confronted with disapproval and disgust, and being held (solely) responsible for using conflict, war and terror for their business (Orlovsky 2005).

The sensational imagination consists of especially depictions coming from investigative journalism and the wider entertainment industry that use imagery of arms dealers with their 'evil characters', which often blurs the lines between sensationalism, criminalisation and moralisation. Perhaps the most well-known sensationalisation of illegal arms dealers is the movie *Lord of War* (Niccol 2005), a movie in which Nicholas Cage plays Yuri Orlov, a Ukrainian-American illegal arms dealer. The movie has been accused of 'emulat[ing] other big-budget message movies by making a fuzzyheaded and unspecific argument that amounts to something like: "arms dealing is bad"', depicting an arms dealer who is placed in a 'world in which he operates [that] allows him to choose no sides and to retain no moral compass' (Hamid 2006: 53–54). Also in *Iron Man* (Favreau 2008), the more recent BBC series *The Night Manager* (Bier 2016) and the movie *War Dogs* (Phillips 2016), the emphasis lies on the exciting, the adventurous, the deviant and evil of arms dealers, (re)affirming certain stereotypes that dominate and are amplified in the public debate through especially post-9/11 Hollywood filmmaking (Castrillo 2020), in this case, about the arms trade and arms dealers. An exception to the sensationalisation of arms dealers as immoral, empty and evil 'creatures' is the Swedish political thriller series *Conspiracy of Silence* (Brandstrom & Danielson 2018) about a former arms dealer who takes revenge against an industry he was once part of. The series puts an emphasis on how the arms dealer is but one of the guilty in a chain of guilty actors, including politicians, inspectorates and other state and corporate actors, as the original Swedish title *Ingen Utan Skuld* captures perfectly: *No one without guilt*.

It is known that sensational storytelling has always been influential in how morality is shaped – an influence that has been problematised since Ancient Greece. Was it not Plato who asked in *The Republic*:

> And shall we just carelessly allow children to hear casual tales which may be devised by casual persons, and to receive in their minds ideas for the most part the very opposite of those which we should wish them to have when they are grown-up?
>
> (Plato in Bronfenbrenner 1970: 4)

Sensational storytelling on the arms dealer is nowadays especially undertaken by the entertaining industry. It functions as a source for shaping norms and values – our collective conscience (Durkheim 1964) – using morality as a plot device to construct dramatic tension and inviting audiences to think about what is (im)moral (Gillet 2013). Although usually less known for its sensation-appetite, investigative journalism has changed over time and is not entirely immune to thrill-seeking temptations anymore (De Burgh 2005). That change is reflected in how reporting is conjoined with a high moral tone with sensational description (ibid.: 44) to satisfy the audience's desire for pleasurable indignation (ibid.: 48), due to financial and commercial pressures existing in the domain of investigative journalism, making seductions to sensationalise or vivify content quite strong (ibid.: 166). Investigative journalism too tells us sensational stories, also about arms dealers.

Such sensationalising of arms dealers being pure evil, opportunistic, self-interested, egotistical, hyper-masculine, fame- and fortune-orientated, seductive, apathetic, and fearless, morph arms dealers into taken for granted caricatures; it leads to a (re)affirmation of arms dealers as the morally corrupt Other, and thus, audiences maintain a morally right Self – it is textbook othering (Said 1978) in which moral panic feeds into sensationalisation which in turn feeds into further othering and moral panic (Cohen 2011). This continuous othering feedback-loop where the (moral) setting is mediatised, and media sets (moral) reality is referred to as 'the street scripts the screen and the screen scripts the street' in which 'there is no linear sequence; rather the line between the real and the virtual is profoundly and irrevocably blurred' (Hayward & Young 2004: 259). It is a feedback-loop that must be confronted with by a criminological imagination.

1.4 Why towards a *criminological* imagination?

To know how to criminologically imagine anything, it is important to give some sort of – and most definitely not exhaustive – idea of what criminology 'is' in order to make it relevant for this criminological biography of a legal arms dealer. This has to do with the fact that criminology is largely regarded as the study of crime, whereas 'legal arms dealer' implies there is nothing criminal or deviant about the arms trading business the biographee is working in: his profession is fully allowed by law, and which he fully complies with. Yet, when we think of arms dealers, the connection with violence and war is easily made, and these are most definitely themes that have been researched by criminologists (cf. Jamieson 2017; McGary & Walklate 2019).

In reality, the idea that criminology merely attempts to study criminality by converting it into definite analysable – preferably statistical – and homogeneous categories is an outdated one (Young 2011). Crime, and therefore criminology, comprises much more than that. Admittedly, over time, criminology had a tendency to become predominantly a collection of perspectives that crystallised crime into a purely measurable phenomenon of lawbreaking behaviours; a tendency through which criminologists got distanced from the heterogeneous realities of crime instead of getting closer to them (Ferrell &

Sanders 1995). Such criminology pushes researchers into delivering positivistic knowledge-criminology that usually leads to harsher policies on and policing of crime but not necessarily better understanding of crime (Ferrell et al. 2004; Garland 1992). It is a type of policies and policing that is legitimated by 'tough on crime'-rhetoric and frequently politically exploited (Simon 2007).

However, criminology does take into account as well the complexities of crime policy and policing themselves, including analyses of public perspectives on crime and victimhood, state and corporate crimes and war, human rights violations and genocide (cf. Green & Ward 2000; Slapper & Tombs 1999; Walklate & McGarry 2015). Moreover, in studying crime as something more than a thing-in-itself, but also as a thing-for-itself (Crewe & Lippens 2009) which implies to understand crime in a perspectival and relativist manner as criminalisation, criminology incorporates a wide range of disciplines, doing so for many more audiences than just the state (Bosworth & Hoyle 2012). Criminology is, if anything, an umbrella, or rather, a hybrid discipline (Pease 2021) that may lack a strong coherence of scientific dogma, theory and method; yet because of that incoherence, it is dynamical and it has the capacity to understand harm, deviancy, crime and control from a kaleidoscopic perspective. Meaning, a robust criminology may also account for harmful acts that remain legal (cf. Mol 2017; Tombs 2018).

This is where this biography fits in perfectly, as it delves into the life of a person that made a career in the legal arms trade; a profession that monetises on weapons with which people cause conflict and often lethal harm. The connection between personhood, profession, legality and violence is biographically focused on here, thus making this biography criminologically relevant. The politically correct and public opinion about arms dealers, though, is not immediately that of them being legal economic actors that make an income legitimately and pay their taxes. Instead, arms dealers are considered to be the lowest of the lowest, even evil 'creatures' exploiting death and destruction (Irondelle et al. 2015). A criminology that would merely undertake research that would target the criminogenic aspects of such evil without paying serious relativist attention to how and why arms dealers are perceived as evil would be a problematically limited one.

The quality of criminology to consider the relativity of crime in studying has been done so by one of the founding fathers of criminology: Cesare Beccaria. He is famous for his work *Dei Delitti e Delle Pene*[1] (2009 [1793]) in which he laid out the groundwork for the proportionality principle (crime and punishment must equate) in many national legal systems to this day. He emphasised that 'the history of nations, and their laws, will generally find, that the ideas of virtue and vice, of a good or a bad citizen, change with the revolution of ages' (ibid.: 31). This means that how crime and control are considered by us, differs over time and per location and tells something about society itself. In fact, crime is needed because it forms a violation of strongly held moral sentiments that reaffirm a larger collective conscience of what is considered good and evil (Durkheim 1964). In that sense, 'an act is "criminal" because it shocks the collective conscience; it does not shock the collective conscience because it is "criminal"' (Machalek & Cohen 1991: 217). Crime, or for that matter anything considered a violation, insults society and effectuates strong emotional responses, such as outrage and disgust (ibid.). This means that crime and society's responses to it expose something about the social and cultural context, as well as about ethics and morality (Boutellier 2019). It is exactly that dialectic between crime and society that is interesting to consider in relation to legal arms dealers. Their business is not a legal violation; however, arms dealers do incarnate some sort of moral violation according to society, which depicts Constantine as a legal evil.

The criminological imagination of an arms dealer should become one that attempts to provide, along the lines of Mills' sociological imagination (2000 [1959]), an understanding of arms dealers while being aware of dominant perceptions about arms dealers, and what these perceptions tell about society. Meaning, Constantine can only be understood biographically in relation to an understanding of the socio-historical of society itself, through which is acquired 'a set of viewpoints that are simple enough to make understanding possible, yet comprehensive enough to permit us to include in our views the range and depth of the human variety' (ibid.: 133). A criminological imagination must not get lost in theory nor in empirical-statistical detail but should remain somewhere in between. This means that any criminological imagination ought to perceive (crime) statistics as social constructions themselves, while remaining aware of how deviance is not an inherent quality and that meaning depends on context. A criminological imagination is therefore about seeing the context of contestation, diversity and unequal power relations in which 'human subjects are creative actors' (Karpiak 2013: 390). To go about in this manner leads to a criminological imagining of arms dealers, only to be disciplined by biographical fact while remaining attentive to the biographee's meaning-giving and identity, and, eventually, to the intrinsic humanity of him despite that he is considered 'evil' or 'deviant' (cf. Young 2011).

Young's explanation of the criminological imagination (2011) emphasises to use the ethnographic 'view from below' when researching the many criminalised and often marginalised powerless (e.g. migrants, homeless and drug addicts) to give them a voice, in order to criticise the few powerful (e.g. state-corporate crime). It seems, thematically, he solely focuses on the marginalised, and methodologically, predominantly on ethnography. However, it is as important to research those who are in power from their own perspective, their own humanity, perhaps without state-funding (Walters 2013) in order to escape 'the criminological straitjacket' while staying close to (legal) social harms that are laid upon those unheard (Barton et al. 2013: 208–209). Moreover, it is then as important to do such research also with the use of biographic studies.

Approaching an arms dealer in that manner could lead to an understanding of an arms dealer's humanity and the banality of his life (choices). It is an understanding that may scare people, because it brings arms dealers closer to ourselves than we might want to (admit). Therefore, this biography – undertaken without any state or corporate funding, by the way – brings forward a type of deviant knowledge (Walters 2003) that 'speaks truth to power' *and* to its reading audience, also to those who prefer to dehumanise and demonise arms dealers. In other words, the deviant biographical knowledge delivered here, and the criminological imagination emerging from it, may pose a rather inconvenient truth. It is so, exactly because this biography shall not portray the arms dealer as a demon or as exceptional evil, but as a human being, much like Hannah Arendt did with her study on the banality of evil regarding Adolf Eichmann, the high Nazi official who organised the train logistics of the Holocaust (2006).

In line with an expansion of Young's criminological imagination (Barton et al. 2013), it is then also important to imagine the arms dealer not necessarily as part of a marginalised, dehumanised group, nor as part of specifically inhumane powerful group, but rather as someone somewhere in-between. To understand him is to understand his 'personal troubles and problematic behaviours within their socioeconomic and political contexts' (ibid.: 210). To complete that task, this biography attempts to remain both deconstructive and reconstructive in writing down his life's story (ibid.). The more so, because (social scientific) scholars tend to deliver (sometimes empirical) critiques that leave from simplistic pro-war or anti-war positions, whereas it is '[f]ar better that [studies] are conducted with an intention in mind to inculcate change, even where that seems on the face of it to be unlikely, than not at all' (Rech et al. 2015: 56). This means that the criminological imagination that will be developing throughout the remainder of this book and concluded in Chapter 9 should let 'go of our comfortable beliefs that we already know who is resisting war and militarism and how they are doing it and be brave enough to remain open to alternative possibilities form people and places we least expect' (Brownfield-Stein 2017: 68), in this case being, an arms dealer himself.

The criminological imagination that will emerge from this biography has already begun by having critically considered the specific statistical-factual, political-moral and sensational imaginations of arms dealers that already exist. Through these, it is possible to sensitise oneself (Blumer 1954) in order to be(come) critical of certain taken-for-granted 'truths and realities' that shape and are shaped by a collective consciousness (about arms dealers). Meaning, for this biography, the criminological imagination that will emerge *while* reading Constantine's life story is not meant to strictly test a theory or to become a theory on arms dealers. As a matter of fact, that would even damage a life's story in a biography (Van Gemert 2011). The emergent criminological imagination may confirm or fix certain imaginations that exist but will not blur Constantine's life lived in flesh and blood into the background. Instead, the criminological imagination aimed for should be appreciated next to, or perhaps even against, the considered (stigmatising) narratives, stereotypes and demonisations about arms dealers.

1.5 Conclusion

In the interrelated and interacting statistical-factual, political-moral and sensational imaginations, the imagination of the arms dealer as a human being fades away. Or actually, it never existed. It remains rather unclear and unknown what their banal – all too human – life and their experiences consist of, and how these are informed by their own choices and (personal) morality. Meaning, an actual *understanding* of arms dealers as human beings and the understanding of their everyday, unexcitable and banal life is lacking. However, in developing a more holistic and criminological imagination of Constantine the arms dealer, it is important to realise that the ideas about arms dealers do focus on them as statistical-empirically non-existent, and that they do not seem to matter in the political-moral imagination and debate where only illegal arms dealers are mostly accounted for. If there is a keen interest, it is in the perceived 'exciting' part of their lives; then they *do* exist as abominable and evil, from which some sort of guilty pleasure and excitement can be gained. So, given that there is no interest in the statistical-factual and secret versus open political-moral roles of arms dealers, but only in the sensational, this biography is set to comprehend an arms dealer *himself*, from his *own* perspective. Together with the aforementioned (distorting) statistical-factual, political-moral and sensational imaginations, while reading about the life of an arms dealer seen through his own eyes, a criminological imagination about Constantine the arms dealer will emerge and concluded in Chapter 9.

Note

1 Translation from Italian: *On Crime and Punishment*.

References

Arendt H (2006) *Eichmann in Jerusalem*. London: Penguin.

Arsovska J (2014) Introduction: illicit firearms market in Europe and beyond. *European Journal on Criminal Policy and Research* 20(3): 295–305.

Arsovska J & Kostakos PA (2008) Illicit arms trafficking and the limits of rational choice theory: the case of the Balkans. *Trends in Organized Crime* 11(4): 352–378.

Barton A, Corteen K, Scott D & Whyte D (2013) *Expanding the criminological imagination*. London: Routledge.

Bauman Z (2016) A few comments on the Mis-Imagined war on terrorism. From: www.socialeurope.eu/2016/03/comments-mis-imagined-war-terrorism/.

Beccaria C (2009 [1793]) *Dei delitti e delle pene*. Lyon: ENS Editions.

Bier S (2016) *The night manager*. London: The Ink Factory, London: BBC and New York: AMC.

Blumer H (1954) What is wrong with social theory?. *American Sociological Review* 19(1): 3–10.

Bosworth M & Hoyle C (2012) *What is criminology?*. Oxford: Oxford University Press.

Boutellier H (2019) *A criminology of moral order*. Bristol: Policy Press.
Brandstrom C & Danielson H (2018) *Ingen utan skuld (conspiracy of silence)*. Sweden: Brain Academy, United Kingdom: Twelve Town and Brussels: Umedia and uFund.
Bromley M, Cooper N & Holtom P (2012) The UN Arms Trade Treaty: arms export controls, the human security agenda and the lessons of history. *International Affairs* 88(5): 1029–1048.
Bronfenbrenner U (1970) *Two worlds of childhood*. New York, NY: Russell Sage Foundation.
Brownfield-Stein C (2017). Gender and visual representations of women combatants. In Woodward R & Duncanson C (eds) *The Palgrave international handbook of gender and the military*. London: Palgrave Macmillan, pp. 475–491.
Brzoska M (2004) Taxation of the global arms trade? An overview of the issues. *Kyklos* 57(2): 149–171.
Byrne EF (2007) Assessing arms makers' corporate social responsibility. *Journal of Business Ethics* 74(3): 201–217.
Castells M (1998) *End of millennium, vol. 3 of the information age: economy, society, and culture*. Malden, MA: Blackwell Publishers.
Castrillo P (2020) The post-9/11 American political thriller film: Hollywood's dissident screenplays. *Journal of Screenwriting* 11(2): 191–206.
Charles Koch Foundation (2018) How America supplies the world with weapons. From: https://bigthink.com/charles-koch-foundation/how-america-supplies-the-world-with-weapons.
Cohen S (2011) *Folk devils and moral panics: the creation of the Mods and Rockers*. London: Routledge.
Cook PJ, Cukier W & Krause K (2009) The illicit firearms trade in North America. *Criminology & Criminal Justice* 9(3): 265–286.
Crewe D & Lippens R (2009) *Existentialist criminology*. Abingdon: Routledge.
Cukier W (2002a) Gendered perspectives on small arms proliferation and misuse: effects and policies. Farr VA & Gebre-Wold K (eds) *Gendered perspectives on small arms and light weapons: regional and international concerns*. Bonn: Bonn International Center FOR Conversion (Internationales Konversionszentrum Bonn), pp. 25–39.
Cukier W (2002b) Small arms and light weapons: a public health approach. *Brown Journal of World Affairs* 9(1): 261–280.
De Burgh H (2005) *Investigative journalism: context and practice*. London: Routledge.
De Kerchove G & Höhn C (2015) 'The fight against terrorism in the EU's broader neighbourhood. In Gstöhl S & Lannon E (eds) *The European Union's Broader Neighbourhood: challenges and opportunities for cooperation beyond the European Neighbourhood Policy*. London: Routledge, pp. 81–104.
Democracy Now! (2016) Pope Francis points at weapons industry behind Brussels attack. From: www.democracynow.org/2016/3/25/headlines/pope_francis_points_at_weapons_industry_behind_brussels_attack.
Dostoyevsky F (1992) *The Brothers Karamazov*. New York, NY: Vintage Books.
Dunne JP & Sköns E (2010) The military industrial complex. In Tan AT (ed) *The global arms trade: a handbook*. London: Routledge, pp. 281–292.
Durkheim E (1964) *The division of labor in society*. New York, NY: Free Press.
Edwards A & Gill P (2002) The politics of 'transnational organized crime': discourse, reflexivity and the narration of 'threat'. *British Journal of Politics and International Relations* 4(2): 245–270.

Erickson J (2015) *Dangerous trade: arms exports, human rights, and international reputation*. New York, NY: Columbia University Press.

Farah D & Braun S (2007) *Merchant of death: money, guns, planes, and the man who makes war possible*. Hoboken, NJ: John Wiley & Sons.

Favreau J (2008) *Iron Man*. Hollywood: Paramount Pictures.

Feinstein A (2011) The shadow world: inside the global arms trade – an address at the Los Angeles World Affairs Council On November 14th, 2011. From: www.lawac.org/speech-archive/pdf/1631.pdf.

Feinstein A, Holden P & Pace B (2011) Corruption and the arms trade: sins of commission. In *SIPRI yearbook 2011*. Oxford: Oxford University Press.

Ferrell J, Hayward K, Morrison W & Presdee M (2004) *Cultural criminology unleashed*. Cavendish: Routledge.

Ferrell J & Sanders C (1995) *Cultural criminology: an invitation*. Lebanon, NH: UPNE.

Garland D (1992) Criminological knowledge and its relation to power. Foucault's genealogy and criminology today. *British Journal of Criminology* 32: 403–422.

Gillet P (2013) *Film and morality*. Newcastle upon Tyne: Cambridge Scholars Publishing.

Green PJ & Ward T (2000) State crime, human rights, and the limits of criminology. *Social Justice* 27(1): 101–115.

Hamid R (2006) 'Lord of War' film review. *Cinéaste* 31(2): 52–55.

Hayward KJ & Young J (2004) Cultural criminology: some notes on the script. *Theoretical Criminology* 8(3): 259–273.

Holden P & Van Vuuren H (2011) *The devil in the detail: how the arms deal changed everything*. Johannesburg: Jonathan Ball Publishers.

Hornaday A (2021) While Hollywood looked for perfect villains, they were hiding in plain sight. From: www.washingtonpost.com/entertainment/white-supremacy-hollywood-villains/2021/01/15/515f5386-5696-11eb-a08b-f1381ef3d207_story.html.

Irondelle B, Mérand F & Foucault M (2015). Public support for European defence: does strategic culture matter?. *European Journal of Political Research* 54(2): 363–383.

Jamieson R (2017). *The criminology of war*. London: Routledge.

Karpiak K (2013) Jock Young: the criminological imagination (book review). *Critical Criminology* 3(21): 389–391.

Kinsella D (2014) Illicit arms transfers to Africa and the prominence of the former Soviet bloc: a social network analysis. *Crime, Law and Social Change* 62(5): 523–547.

Mac Cormick D (1965) *Peddler of death. The life and times of Sir Basil Zaharoff*. New York, NY: Holt, Rinehart and Winston.

Machalek R & Cohen LE (1991) The nature of crime. *Human Nature* 2(3): 215–233.

Macias A & Rattner N (2020) Global arms trade is a nearly 200 billion business and the US drives nearly 80% of it. From: www.cnbc.com/2020/02/04/global-military-expenditure-and-arms-trade-report.html.

Maitland G (1998) The ethics of the international arms trade. *Business Ethics: A European Review* 7(4): 200–204.

McGarry R & Walklate S (2019) *A criminology of war?*. Bristol: Bristol University Press.

Mills CW (2000 [1959]) *The sociological imagination*. Oxford: Oxford University Press.

Moine JM (2006) The arms dealer Basil Zaharoff (1849–1936). *Ethnologie française* 36(1): 139–152.

Mol H (2017) *The politics of palm oil harm*. Newcastle upon Tyne: Palgrave Macmillan.

Niccol A (2005) *Lord of war*. United States: Lions Gate Films and Neuilly-sur-Seine: SND.

Nordstrom C (2004) *Shadows of war: violence, power, and international profiteering in the twenty-first century*. Berkeley, CA: University of California Press.
Ojakorotu V, Kelechi JA & Kamidza R (2014) Response of the international community to terrorist attacks in Africa and Europe – a focus on Nigeria and France. *Africa Insight* 44(3): 15–28.
Orlovsky K (2005) International criminal law: towards new solutions in the fight against illegal arms brokers. *Hastings International & Comparative Law Review* 29(3): 343–380.
Pease K (2021) Commentary to "how international are the top ten international journals of criminology and criminal justice?". *European Journal on Criminal Policy and Research* 27: 179–182.
Phillips T (2016) *War dogs*. Indiana: Green Hat Films, Los Angeles: The Mark Gordon Company and Los Angeles: RatPac Entertainment.
Potter M (2012) *Outlaws Inc*. London: Pan Books.
Rech M, Bos D, Jenkings KN, Williams A & Woodward R (2015) Geography, military geography, and critical military studies. *Critical Military Studies* 1(1): 47–60.
Ruggiero V (1996) War markets: corporate and organized criminals in Europe. *Social and Legal Studies* 5(1): 5–20.
Ruggiero V (1997) Criminals and service providers: cross-national dirty economies. *Crime, Law & Social Change* 28: 27–38.
Ruggiero V (2007) War, crime, empire and cosmopolitanism. *Critical Criminology* 15: 211–221.
Said E (1978) *Orientalism*. New York, NY: Pantheon Books.
Sheffield H (2016) Arms trade: one chart that shows the biggest weapons exporters of the last five years. From: www.independent.co.uk/news/business/news/arms-trade-exporters-importers-weapons-transfers-sipri-a6891491.html.
Simon J (2007) *Governing through crime: how the war on crime transformed American democracy and created a culture of fear*. Oxford: Oxford University Press.
SIPRI (2018) Financial value of the global arms trade. From: www.sipri.org/databases/financial-valuc-global-arms-tradc.
Slapper G & Tombs S (1999) *Corporate crime*. Harlow: Longman.
Small Arms Survey (2015) Weapons and markets: transfers. From: www.smallarmssurvey.org/weapons-and-markets/transfers.html.
Small Arms Survey (2018) Small Arms Survey reveals: more than one billion firearms in the world. From: www.smallarmssurvey.org/fileadmin/docs/Weapons_and_Markets/Tools/Firearms_holdings/SAS-Press-release-global-firearms-holdings.pdf.
Small Arms Survey (2021) About the Small Arms Survey. From: www.smallarmssurvey.org/about-us/mission.html.
Stockmarr L (2015) Security fairs. In Abrahamsen R & Leande A (eds) *Routledge handbook of private security studies*. London: Routledge, pp. 187–196.
Stohl R & Grillot S (2009) *The international arms trade*. Cambridge, MA: Polity Press.
Stone J (2016) Britain is now the second biggest arms dealer in the world. From: www.independent.co.uk/news/uk/home-news/britain-is-now-the-second-biggest-arms-dealer-in-the-world-a7225351.html?amp.
Taylor MB (2015) Law, guns and money: regulating war economies in Syria and beyond. In NOREF July 2015 Report, pp. 1–11.
Theoudoulou M (2009) The bizarre double life of Latif Yahia. From: www.thenationalnews.com/world/mena/the-bizarre-double-life-of-latif-yahia-1.571406.

Tombs S (2018) For pragmatism and politics: crime, social harm and zemiology. In Boukli A & Kotzé J (eds) *Zemiology*. Newcastle upon Tyne: Palgrave Macmillan, pp. 11–31.

Ummid (2016) Arms dealers, killing government behind Europe refugee crisis. From: www.ummid.com/news/2016/March/28.03.2016/behind-every-refugee-to-europe-stands-an-arm-dealer.html.

UNODC (2020) Global study on firearms trafficking, 2020. From: www.unodc.org/documents/firearms-protocol/2020/2020_REPORT_Global_Study_on_Firearms_Trafficking_2020_web.pdf.

UN Register of Conventional Arms (2018) The global reported arms trade. From: www.un-register.org/SmallArms/Index.aspx#.

UN Security Council (2019) Small arms and light weapons: report of the Secretary-General. From: https://undocs.org/en/S/2019/1011.

Van Gemert F (2011) *Van prison gang tot tbs; Biografie van een gewelddadig man*. Meppel: Just Publishers.

Walklate S & McGarry R (2015) *Criminology and war: transgressing the borders*. London: Routledge.

Walters R (2003) *Deviant knowledge: criminology, politics and policy*. London: Routledge.

Walters R (2013) Critical criminology and the intensification of the authoritarian state. In Barton A, Corteen K, Scott D & Whyte D (eds) *Expanding the criminological imagination*. London: Routledge, pp. 27–49.

Wechsler M (2016) 'Merchant of death' or victim of an international sting?. From: www.thebigchilli.com/feature-stories/merchant-of-death-or-victim-of-an-international-sting.

Wezeman PD, Fleurant A, Kuimova A, Lopes da Silva D, Tian N & Wezeman ST (2020) SIPRI trends in international arms transfer. From: https://sipri.org/sites/default/files/2020-03/fs_2003_at_2019.pdf.

Williamson R (1998) Moving in vicious circles: the moral dilemmas of arms transfers and weapons manufacture. In Anderson MB et al. (eds) *Hard choices: moral dilemmas in humanitarian intervention*. Oxford: Rowman & Littlefield Publishers, pp. 251–268.

Wisor S (2014) The moral problem of worse actors. *Ethics & Global Politics* 7(2): 47–64.

Yihdego Z (2007) *The arms trade and international law*. Portland, OR: Bloomsbury Publishing.

Young J (2007) *The vertigo of late modernity*. London: Sage.

Young J (2011) *The criminological imagination*. Cambridge: Polity Press.

Young J (2016) Voodoo criminology and the numbers game. In Ferrell J, Hayward K, Morrison W & Presdee M (eds) *Cultural criminology unleashed*. London: Routledge, pp. 27–42.

2 Talking arms

A methodological reflection on biography

'Talking arms' is the English translation of the French 'armes parlantes' that historically refers to heralds in France who would sound out the name of the armigers, the arms-bearers (Uden 1968). Whereas heralding someone or something is usually done to praise that person or item, the heralding of the biographee in this book will comprise a careful tale of someone's life, in which I as biographer have tried to stay as close to his story as possible during the process of sounding out his life in writing. Constantine is neither praised nor judged by me in this biography, which is *his* biography. That is, I have tried to be as understanding and non-judgmental as possible. Still, as with any social scientific method, whether quantitative, qualitative or mixed, this biography too has its inherent advantages and disadvantages that significantly influence the biographer, the biographee and the process of writing a biography. Although this chapter is the main reflexive one, throughout this biography such reflection took place. But first Constantine himself will tell how he experienced the making of his biography with me.

> This interaction between myself and my author? How did I find it [...] it's like chatting to a friend. That's all. I don't see anything wrong with it. I certainly don't find it in anyway compromising of information. I know that you and I have signed the paperwork for the university and that you're bound by certain ethics. I mean, I haven't told you anything that I wouldn't tell anybody else, to be quite honest. Obviously we've gone into some subjects a little deeper than I would go into with other people, obviously. Apart from that, I think it is a good way of talking to somebody when you can't actually interview them face-to-face! It's just not possible. This way you have the possibility of interviewing people all over the world. [...] So, you know, there's nothing wrong with interviewing via Skype, as far as I'm concerned. [...] You know [in real physical life], we would drink too much coffee! Or beer! Too much coffee or beer and if we were in the Netherlands, we'd probably smoke too much marihuana as well. The coffee shops! I don't think it makes that much difference. I mean I can see your facial expressions, I take it you can see mine as well. [...] There's obviously pros and cons to this sort of interview over

DOI: 10.4324/9781315148236-3

> long-distance but I don't see anything wrong with it as far as interviewing for a subject or a topic is concerned. That's just my opinion, obviously there could be learned colleagues who would disagree, obviously because they got nothing better to do and they probably can't operate Skype anyway [referring to old, jealous professors] [...] they're probably all jealous that you got access to somebody they can't get a hold of haha [...] I can imagine your colleagues being extremely peeved, green behind the gills. [...] [In real life] we would have to be in an office somewhere. An office or a coffee shop, or a hotel, or wherever. I mean, okay, it's 20 interviews. I don't know how long it has taken us, about a year, possibly? I mean, can you imagine if we did weekly appointments and I had to come to XXXX, or you had to come to XXXX? We never would have finished. It would be too expensive. [...] You pay me for the tickets and all the expenses to come over and I will come, yeah sure, why not? [...] You're going to get the same results over Skype as over a live interview. Well, this is live, we are [...] together real-time in the virtual world. [...] I don't have any surprises. I mean, it's a biography, you're writing my biography. There were some questions I must admit, you perhaps could have gone deeper with [...] I don't remember now, to be quite honest. I don't remember, but no disappointments. No real surprises. I mean, you asked me questions and I answered. Then we had a general conversation. From that you extracted information. That's normally how an interview works. [...] I would have answered [the questions] in the exact same way if we've been face-to-face in a room, we're in the same space and I would've answered them here. It's the same thing for me. I don't make a difference. [...] I mean I've done interviews with [an academic], I've done interviews with the XXXX, I've done interviews for XXXX, I've done interviews for XXXX where I was interviewed for a job there, that was on camera. It's nothing strange to me. [...] Could [I] have done it with someone else? I would have had to develop a certain amount of trust and there would have had been the initial, sort of, friendly connection so to speak. I mean, you're a sympathetic person, there are lots of things that I find about you interesting. I think that there's a good relationship that's been built up [...] I don't know whether I could do it with somebody else. Like I said, there would have to be somebody, they would have to win my trust for me to speak so openly about personal things as well as business matters. [...] They would have had to win my trust and that is not an easy thing to win.

This chapter will reflect on the abovementioned important aspects of at-a-distance interviewing, its advantages and disadvantages, and about gaining trust. It will also consider what the role is of biography in criminology and what to take away from other biographies on arms dealers. Afterward, it will be explained how Constantine and I met, which sources were used and how, the mechanisms of understanding and reflecting and what it meant for me to carry out a criminological biographical study of a person who belongs to a population that is usually hard to find, all done so in a digital age.

2.1 A criminological neglect and necessity of biography

Although considered necessary for theoretical building blocks regarding crime and control (Van Gemert 2011), however, biography has been mostly avoided by criminologists, and despite a revival of the biographical approach in criminology (Goodey 2000; Van Gemert 2011, 2015b), criminological research seems to favour a more reductionist approach to crime, missing out on a holistic understanding of the person behind the crime (Van Gemert & Van Swaaningen 2012: 10). In fact, most criminologists, often without any reflection on the outcome of research results, apply 'natural scientific methods [...] to human action, [convinced] that behaviour is causally determined, that incontestable objectivity is attainable and that precise quantitative measurement is possible, and indeed preferable' (Young 2016: 16). Applications of natural scientific methods spawned forward a widespread positivist belief of criminologists that they can even predict crime by measuring risk factors and explain it in terms of causality. Such belief reflects a 'zealous search for "laws" presumably comparable to those imagined to be found by natural scientists' (Mills 2000 [1959]: 17–19). Such a positivist criminological enterprise, also referred to as 'voodoo criminology', nested its crystallised perceptions of deviance and crime in the core of criminology (Ferrell et al. 2004).

Along comes the pressure on criminologists to search for the *new* (Filmer 1978; Reiner 2007; Rock 2005). Criminological work has to be cutting-edge and covering all the most recent literature on the research topic, rather than older, perhaps even more relevant material. One of the reasons to merely (over-)reference novel work has to do with the fact 'the new has its own self-conferring legitimacy' (Reiner 2007: 481). Decades ago, the social sciences were criticised as they shunned offering new directions but actually portrayed 'unreflective neophilia' (Filmer 1978: 136). Due to obsession for the new, criminology integrated a high level of inner circle self-reference that is not benefiting critical academic spirit and interdisciplinary intellect in criminology. The criminological neglect of biographies reveals criminology's 'unhealthy intellectual suspicion of what "the individual" or, more damningly, "the personal" has to offer' (Goodey 2000: 474). The fear of the individual, personal, indeed, the very human part of crime is strange and apparently 'uncriminological'.

One of the founding fathers of criminology, Cesare Lombroso, already realised though that explanations of criminal behaviour require biographical insights. As a criminological positivist, he principally left from a physiognomic point of view and spoke in terms of the criminal man as the atavist (Gaakeer 2005; Lombroso et al. 2006). Yet, he recognised that in order to fully grasp criminal behaviour of prisoners, one has to pay attention as well to 'prison walls, and the songs they write about their own crimes' (Gaakeer 2005: 2346). Lombroso's positivist criminologies incorporated individually orientated, biographic approaches to crime in order to understand it more fully. Centuries later, also Michel Foucault emphasised the importance of biographic relevance in understanding people and their deviant, criminal behaviour, exactly because the penal system changed into a (purely) disciplining exercise, in which understanding the everyday of the individual has become less and less important:

> To be looked at, observed, described in detail, followed from day to day by an uninterrupted writing was a privilege. The chronicle of a man, the account of his life, his historiography, written as he lived out his life formed part of the rituals of his power. The disciplinary methods reversed this relation, lowered the threshold of describable individuality and made this description a means of control and a method of domination.
>
> (Foucault 1977: 47)

Whereas criminology may have delivered dehumanising descriptions of criminal individuals as tools for control, and while biographies remain unpopular in criminology, contradictory enough, (auto)biographies about and by (ex-) criminals draw a very large audience. As spectators we cannot seem to get enough of 'true crime stories' that are made by journalists and documentary makers but not by criminologists (Van Gemert & Van Swaaningen 2012).

What is also quite interesting to mention here are the biographies *of* criminologists and criminal justice reformers, such as that of Dirck Volkertszoon Coornhert and his role in the abolition of capital punishment (Bonger 2004), of the Lombroso family (Dolza 1990), of crime statistician Adolphe Quetelet (Lottin 1912), of the creator of the panopticon, Jeremy Bentham (Warren Everett 1966) or that of Herman Bianchi, who questioned the cruelty of modern criminal justice (Sluys 2016). These biographies have in common that they herald these individuals' benevolent aspirations to improve criminal justice systems and criminology itself (Fijnaut 2010: 11). What these biographies on white males in criminology by white males in criminology expose, is the unconscious gendered and racialised hegemonies that linger in criminology, whether that is positivist or critical and cultural criminology (Burton 2019; Groombridge 2006; O'Neill & Seal 2012; Saleh-Hanna 2020).

Compared to the lauding through and of racial(ising) and gendered biographical literature on criminology and criminal justice's heroes, the canon of criminological biographies *by* criminologists *on* crime is as big. Shaw's (2013 [1930]) *The Jack-Roller* is one of the most familiar criminological biographies on crime. There is also the, for its time, pioneering biography of Chic Conwell, *The Professional Thief* by Sutherland (1937). Other pivotal works include J.R. 'Yellow Kid' Weil's autobiography on being a con man (1948), Klockars' *The Professional Fence* (1974) on a man who made a career out of knowingly buying stolen goods and reselling them for profit, Carlen's collection of autobiographies in *Criminal Women* (1985), Bovenkerk's *La Bella Bettien* (1995) about a Dutch female criminal and Howard Marks' autobiographic work *Mr Nice* (1997) telling the tale of a criminal entrepreneur who smuggled tons of marijuana. There is Peeter's *Gerrit de Stotteraar* (2002) about a repeat offender. Noteworthy and more recent criminological biographies are Van Gemert's biography of Jan Hoolwerf and his career of violence (2011) and Van Gemert's biography of Saïd Bensellam, a fearless bouncer and once the 'uncrowned king of Amsterdam-West' turned youth worker (Van Gemert 2015a). The criminological focus in these biographies is almost entirely laid upon male, working-class, white offenders committing violent crime but not so much on female offenders, nor on victims (McGarry & Alker 2018). Whether there exists specifically a criminological biography of state crime or corporate crime offenders and victims is unknown, which may have to do with the political influences and cultural practices involved in the state as the main subsidiser of criminological research (McGarry & Walklate 2015).

This biography too is about a male, but contrary to the abovementioned criminological biographies, the focus is laid on his legal activities as an arms dealer professional. An arms dealer who is white and could be considered to be of working-class descent yet has (higher) middle-class income. Moreover, it is a biography written by an author who is male, yet not white but biracial. As will be reflected on more in depth later on this chapter, hopefully this biography will be an example of a less-narrowed criminology on white males by white males towards a more diverse criminology, also through writing increasingly more criminological biographies.

2.2 What is biography and why was it chosen?

'Perhaps the simplest accurate definition of biography should read: "the story of a human life"', as Garraty stipulates (1957). And perhaps it is 'just' that: a story that aims to capture the, by definition, complex phenomena of a person, very carefully connecting 'the individual biography with the global, structural characteristics of the given, lived, historical situation' (Ferrarotti 1983: 62). This makes biography inherently genealogical as it is set out to understand lives in its broader historical, sociocultural roots and contexts, about which a single story is written that, preferably, includes autobiographical material, archival studies and analyses (O'Neill et al. 2015). Due to the genealogical nature of the biography, one does not focus on the linear history of a phenomenon or phenomena, nor do you occupy yourself with 'erecting of foundations [of a phenomenon – added by author]: on the contrary, it disturbs what was previously considered immobile, it fragments what was thought unified, it shows the heterogeneity of what was imagined consistent with itself' (Foucault 1977: 147). So, what one does when writing a biography is focusing on the individual and heterogeneity of phenomena that may seem undisputable but ought to be considered 'effects of certain historical, social, cultural, political and economic configurations' (Tamboukou 2013: 88). It is in writing about the biographee's life that makes that life invested in with significance, that is to say, 'the life becomes an exemplary instance of the strong narrative in which it resides' (Greene 2007: 729).

The story of our time is told through the life story of Constantine. So, to write a biography is about restoring somebody's life textures as they have been lived. This way, the reading audience is able to identify and empathise with, even reconnect history with life (ibid.). That history is reconnected with, to the extent that a biography shares specific knowledge about the intersection of cultural, political, economic and wider social developments in a certain time and location, in which somebody's motives, ideas, events and (world)views are integrated in the life and mind of a single subject (ibid.: 730). A biography is then *a* – but definitely not *the* – documentation of a person's character interactions with society, rebuilt by the biographer. Writing about character then means writing about the (narrative) identity of somebody (Atkinson & Silverman 1997; Denzin 1989; Goodey 2000; Roberts 2002; Van Gemert 2011). Moreover, identity is intrinsically tied to one's own, personal morality, meaning I must account for that connection, because 'it is an untenable position to separate issues of self and morality' (Punzo & Meara 1993: 36). This means that this biography will provide 'a more complete understanding of the moral life as it is experienced in daily life and the acknowledgement that the moral voice is not stilled when one departs public life for the private realm' (ibid.: 38).

Transferring one's life into a biography always entails the creation of a textual *afterlife*. By the time a biography is written and published, and the biographee is still alive, that life has changed. It is then about the arms dealer's textual afterlife that is construed and is imbuing the written with his own identity. This ensures that whenever his biography will be read that his life story, character and identity of a certain point in time is invoked in the mind of the reader, delivering a fragment of a certain time and place. That is any biographee's legacy (Head 2016). Thus, from a methodological advancement point of view, the biography ought to be considered a vessel for a textual afterlife that is 'a paradoxical strategy of self-preservation and, at the same time, selfdissolution – the very being of the [biographee] inscribed in text, inscribed as text, in a life beyond life' (Bennett 1999: 19). Such biographical recreating and rebuilding it into a textual afterlife of someone produced a variety of data about thoughts and behaviour from which fundamental (theoretical) building blocks can be retrieved for criminology (Gemert 2011; Goodey 2000; Maruna & Matravers 2007), and for that matter, for any social science. A biographical approach thus enables the biographer to explore and understand the impact of the intrinsically complex fabric of our heterogeneous social realities on an individual, and from which the individual should not be disconnected (Gemert 2011).

By exploring, biographically, 'the complexities, the conflicts, the contradictions, the insecurities and the confusions that all of us struggle with as vulnerable, sensitive emotional beings' (Maruna & Matravers 2007: 430), it becomes possible for criminology to 'recover social processes and social structure, networks, social change, and so forth, for people are located in a social and cultural environment which constructs and shapes not only *what* we see but also *how* we see it' (Stanley cited in Goodey 2000: 475 – emphasis in original). So, I aim to produce an individual account of an arms dealer's life that will be understood within contemporary cultural and structural settings (cf. Ferrarotti 1983; Merrill & West 2009) and not merely at some broad social level (Roberts 2002).

When writing a criminological biography, it is not about the celebration, but the recognition of 'the real' of 'the defiance, the anger, the resentment, the loneliness, the love, the fun, the warmth of an individual life [...] as a lived life', documented by a biographer who 'transforms lived life into a linguistic form that becomes the object of study' (Presdee 2004: 44). It is about truly wanting to understand. To avoid delivering a positivist criminology and because we have lost our will to understand crime biographically and instead turned into a unreflective discipline that is disciplining itself (Foucault 1977), this criminological biography is based on a strong will to understand and reflect. This way, an emic perspective of an arms dealer could be collected self-critically. That emic perspective is important, because existing biographies about arms dealers only exceptionally included such emic perspectives.

2.3 Investigative biographies of arms dealers and the curious cases of Viktor Bout and Samuel Cummings

This biography is not the first biography of an arms dealer. Several investigative journalists have delivered investigative biographies of arms dealers that exist, exploring the lives of notorious arms dealers and their remarkable lives (cf. Austin 2002; Collins & Pujol 2015; Karskens & Smits 2018; Kessler 2017; Mac Cormick 1965; Van Amerongen 1968). This genre of biographies portray the gunrunning careers of a couple of infamous international illegal arms dealers, describing how most of them profited vastly from surplus arms derived from the collapsed Soviet Union in 1990s and sold them to warmongering dictators ruling conflict-torn areas such as Afghanistan, Argentina, Angola, Ecuador, Liberia, Palestine and Sierra Leone (Farah & Braun 2007). Especially, the AK47, also known as the Kalashnikov, as well as the portable rocket-propelled grenade (RPG), were easily sold by, for example, South Florida's Jean Bernard Lasnaud, the Ukrainian Leonid Efimovich Minin, the Dutch Guus Kouwenhoven and Paul Wilking a.k.a. 'Pistol Paul', the Syrian Monzer Al Kassar and the Armenian-Lebanese Sarkis Garabet Soghanalian. These are all illegal arms dealers who are not active anymore, because they are either retired, imprisoned or dead. There are also more recent accounts of arms dealers, including legal ones. Kevin Kruse, CEO of LEADx, interviewed an international arms dealer for the popular American business magazine Forbes to talk about business successes and strategies, to be inspired and retrieve tips and tricks which can be applied to other businesses and sectors (2016). He points out how he initially considered arms dealers to be people who engage in 'surreptitious deals, exotic locales, and high stakes negotiations with evil warlords', assuming that they 'look and act like Nicolas Cage in the movie Lord of War' (ibid.: online source). He was surprised when he met his first former arms dealer, Dave Chesson. Chesson, a 33-year-old man, actually made deals that had 'nothing to do with dark smoke filled rooms and a lot do to with navigating the complex puzzle of international relations, legal regulations and coordination of multiple government agencies' (id.). It is a rare example of considering arms dealers as 'normal' and not as deviant entrepreneurs, as they usually are, in particular, the most infamous of them all, the Russian-Tajikistani Viktor Bout and a less known but as influential arms dealer, the American Samuel Cummings. They deserve some further exploration.

2.3.1 Viktor Bout (1967–present)

Of the little number of arms dealer biographies, the most well-known would be that of Viktor Anatolyevich Bout, a.k.a. the 'Merchant of Death' (Farah & Braun 2007). Born on 13 January 1967, in Dushanbe, Tajikistan,[1] Viktor studied at the Russian Military Institute of Foreign Languages. It has been claimed he speaks over six languages fluently, which made him a valuable asset in the Soviet army where he may also have served in military intelligence as a translator (Potter 2012). Next to his military service, he founded 21 freight transport companies (that are known of) that were registered in a wide range of countries. These 'safe havens' consisted of countries such as Belgium, Bulgaria, Gambia, Ivory Coast, Democratic Republic of Congo, Kazakhstan, Moldova, Rwanda, Uganda, the United Arab Emirates (UAE) and the United States (OCCRP 2010). After an international warrant that went out with his name on it, Bout was arrested in Thailand, 6 March 2008, after being lured into a deal over which he would be paid a $5 million commission; Bout still claims he was on a holiday (The Economist 2008). After his arrest, two years later, he was extradited to the United States where he was charged with conspiracy to deliver weapons to the (deemed) terrorist organisation, the *Fuerzas Armadas Revolucionarias de Colombia* (FARC). He was also charged with conspiring to murder American citizens and conspiring trade in anti-aircraft missiles (Raab & Milward 2003). Official UN reports claim that Bout violated weapons embargoes in Angola, Sierra Leone and Liberia (Anders et al. 2006). Eventually, the Manhattan Federal District Court convicted and sentenced Bout to 25 years (Weiser & Moynihan 2012).

The Bout case has received significant legal and scientific scrutiny. A variety of sources report that he sold to any party, whether to paramilitaries that would weaponise child soldiers to commit genocidal acts or to the counterparty that needed weapons for protection against such genocidal insurgencies (Collins & Pujol 2015). Especially wars that took place in West Africa have been saturated with former Soviet Union armoury transported by Bout's companies that comprised 'a fleet of sixty battered Antonovs and Ilyushins', flying-in 'weapons, poison, chemicals, operatives, and cash' that were also delivered to Hezbollah, Taliban and Al-Qaeda (Raab & Milward 2003: 427). He supplied through air cargo in cunning ways; the planes were frequently (re)registered via the companies he owned, of which some have, allegedly, been complicit with other arms dealers and legitimate organisations. He was known for supplying rebels of the Sierra Leonean Revolutionary United Front (RUF) with weapons, free of charge; weapons that were given to child soldiers to wage an atrocious war against civilians, killing and amputating them (Farah & Braun 2007).

The US government have been accused of using Bout's services to ship American arms during the Gulf and Afghan wars (OCCRP 2010). Those operations required many resources and manpower, and Bout 'is believed to [have] employ[ed] at least three hundred people in his operations, including pilots and brokers' (Raab & Milward 2003: 428). Some of these people included other infamous arms dealers, such as Sanjivan Ruprah, on whom Bout relied logistically (Anders et al. 2006: 4–6). Ruprah and Bout were complicit as they accepted blood diamonds for their services; diamonds that were supposedly laundered in Antwerp (Raab & Milward 2003). Andrew Smulian was another one of Bout's business partners and also arrested during the 2008 Bangkok Bout Bust. After his arrest, Smulian cooperated 'with the authorities against Mr. Bout, meeting regularly with prosecutors and agents, and pleading guilty to supporting terrorism, among other charges' (Weiser & Moynihan 2012 – online source).

On trial, Bout has pleaded not guilty and, to this day, still being imprisoned in the United States, he insists on his innocence, arguing he has been framed by US authorities. Alla Yurievna Bout, his wife, awaits his return to Russia where she champions his innocence (Potter 2012). As he is a vegetarian, he faces difficulties in prison, as fruit and vegetables are unavailable, by which Potter (2012), who observed Bout, sketches an image of an ordinary man, worried about mundane, everyday things:

> [T]he man seems somehow smaller than the industry giant glowering from the UN reports, articles and indictments. He cuts stoical, sympathetic figure, enduring separation from his family and country, solitary confinement and the slings and arrows of a hostile administration.
>
> (Ibid.: 345)

That sympathy is apparent in his donations to the Congolese National Park and the fact that he financially supported the Russian expedition to the North Pole (OCCRP 2010).

The most recent development regarding Bout is that he, together with pilot Konstantin Yaroshenko who is imprisoned in the United States because of his alleged drugs trafficking,[2] were going to be exchanged for the Ukrainian pilot Nadiya Savchenko who was convicted by a Russian court for being involved in the murder of the Russian journalists Igor Kornelyuk and Anton Voloshin (Quinn 2016). On 25 May 2016, Savchenko got released, indeed in a prisoner swap deal between Russia and the Ukraine, however, unexpectedly, not in exchange for Bout and Yaroshenko, but for the two Russians Yevgeny Yerofeyev and Alexander Alexandrov who were accused by a Ukrainian court for conducting aggressive warfare (Litovkin 2016). On that same day, Savchenko was flown back to Kiev, together with the Ukrainian president Petro Poroshenko, who addressed the media at the Presidential Administration about her heroism and imprisonment (Klikushin 2016). Media directly following the prisoner swap did not mention Bout or Yaroshenko *not* being exchanged, as seems to have been the original plan. Why is the United States so strong on keeping Bout and Yaroshenko on their soil? This is a question that feeds into ongoing suspicion about political interests, secrecy and deception surrounding the Bout-case (Collins & Pujol 2015).

Due to Bout's insistence on being innocent, the non-existence of some facts and the existence of (assumedly) fabricated facts, as well as the suspected political involvement at the highest level of the US administration, the Bout case has been criticised. It has been argued that Bout's trial is being used by the United States to distract the public and political attention away from his connection *to* the US government (e.g. delivering armour to US-backed rebel troops) (ibid.). It is an indicator of how governing the arms trade can (deliberately) focus on the criminal individual rather than trying to tackle the wider structures that sustain the illegal arms trade of which the US government itself is part. It makes the Bout case serve 'as a reminder of the hyperindividualistic nature of neo-liberal crime control policies' (ibid.: 105). Thus, Bout's immoral crimes may have assisted the United States' moral agenda. This, while the United States may be as, if not more so, responsible for having created the conditions for structural illegal arms trading (ibid.). Still, is Bout

> clean or dirty? Is he the Merchant of Death or, as he contends, the ideal modern businessman? Entrepreneur, criminal, misunderstood visionary, or a puppet? Innocent, cunning, or in denial? Or maybe something altogether truer, if less certain; maybe something in between. Something between black and white, just like the arms business he followed.
>
> (Potter 2012: 344)

2.3.2 Samuel Cummings (1927–1998)

Potter's observation on the in-betweenness of Bout's arms dealing business may be even truer regarding Samuel Cummings, born on 7 February 1927 in Philadelphia during the Great Depression. Although less known and not as elaborately written about, Cummings was an arms dealer extraordinaire (Brogan & Zarca 1983). In realising the American dream by making his fortune through his multinational company dealing in specifically American small arms, the International Armament Corporation (also known as Interarms) in 1953, for decades, he dominated the global arms trade (Isikoff 1986). Over 30 years, Cummings' company operated in the shadows of global arms trading, having sold 'an estimated $80 million worth of pistols, submachine guns, rifles, hand grenades and other weapons each year' (ibid.: 24).

On 29 April 1998, he passed away in Monaco due to several strokes (Brogan & Zarca 1983; Weiner 1998). Cummings enjoyed high-quality education, having gone to Oxford University, something he was very proud of; he was a hard worker and had an entrepreneurial spirit. Altogether his arms dealing did not only bring him millions of generated income, but he also gained celebrity status through his company and rather outspoken, often controversial, points of view and public appearances; he was 'a genial man who was an unabashed merchant of death' (Weiner 1998: 29).

Cummings' fascination for arms began during his youth, when his father passed away when he was only eight years old, a most traumatic event for him. Nevertheless, the event that was 'most decisive for his future occurred three years earlier, when he was five' and 'found a machine gun, a German Maxim M08/15, brought back as a trophy from the First World War and abandoned by a post of the American Legion in Philadelphia' (Brogan & Zarca 1983: 40). As a matter of fact

> [h]ad he not taken to guns at so early an age, he might have made a career as a distinguished lawyer, whose hobby was taking cars apart. But it happened that he acquired a gun, a real one, not a toy, and his family's poverty meant that he had few other toys to play with. So he taught himself to take the Maxim apart and put it together again at an age when other small boys play with toy pistols, take them apart, and discover that they cannot be reassembled. He never found a belt for it and so, when he was allowed to fire it, could only fire single shots. It was enough to inspire a lifetime's passion for firearms and a career. As the child became a boy, he acquired other guns. He had no money, so he traded objects to get them, books or anything else he could lay his hands on. Guns, too, were worth very little in those days.
>
> (Ibid.: 41)

When he just turned eighteen years old, he had his first stock of fifty arms, through which he 'had acquired an invincible self-confidence, ambition, and industry' (ibid.: 39). Other important influences that made him the way he was as an arms dealer was the role of his mother, a strong, resolute woman who as a single mother raised him, sent him off to good school and universities and showed the importance of hard work. He went to the American military and also worked at the Central Intelligence Agency (CIA) before he founded Interarms.

Next to being the leading supplier of military surplus firearms and ammunition to the US commercial market during the 'glory days' of the mid-1950s to late-1960s, Cummings was known for also being an arms broker for delivering guns to illegal arms smugglers and dictatorships, such as Somoza in Nicaragua, Batista in Cuba and Trujillo in the Dominican Republic (Isikoff 1986). Perhaps the most telling arms deals he did, were brokered deals for Fidel Castro who spearheaded a popular revolution in 1959 against the then Cuban dictator Fulgencio Batista, to whom Cummings also delivered arms (Brogan & Zarca 1983: 147). His arms dealing business went very well until the passage of the Gun Control Act of 1968, a first attempt of a country to have a disarmament law.

> The Gun Control Act was Cummings's greatest challenge since the firm was started fifteen years before, but he was in a strong position to confront it. Thanks to the large stocks of surplus Interarms had in its warehouses when the 1968 Gun Control Act was passed, there was no drop in profits. By the late 1970s the company was the leading importer of sporting arms. By 1982 Interarms was selling well over 200,000 guns a year, a quarter to a third of them American-made, the rest imported.
>
> (Ibid.: 289)

He went to Europe with his business, but he always stayed on the legal side of things, apparently. Due to the Balkan wars and UN embargos, Cummings had to stop dealing with Bosnia where there was 'no shortage of weapons and prices [were] rock-bottom', however, he said, 'the Serbs had made sure they inherited most of the former Yugoslavia's arms industry' (Bellamy 1992 – online source). Meaning, Interarms could not import from that surplus armoury as hunting rifles anymore to the United States. Still, despite the 'avalanche of surplus from the whole eastern world, including China' (ibid.), as Cummings said, Interarms managed to stay healthy. It was only when Cummings passed away, Interarms almost died as well, if it was not for the High Standard Manufacturing Company of Houston, Texas to have resurrected the Interarms name in 2000 (Gun Digest 2021).

If anything, he should be considered nothing other than a successful and up-front businessman, 'always tak[ing] the long view […] In his view, he doesn't sell death, he sells small pieces of machinery, sort of like sewing machines' (Isikoff 1986: 24), and perhaps he could be considered, like his biographers saw him, 'as a pleasant and law-abiding merchant of death' (Weiner 1998: 29).

So, there are several merchants of death that are more 'normal' than is usually considered. What the biographical depictions of Bout and Cumming's life do, as most biographies on arms dealers, they provide a certain image of arms dealers that cover up their 'dirty' arms dealing business – whether illegal, legal, or somewhere in between – to keep their operations going in a shadowy world (Feinstein 2011; Marsh 2002). The investigative biographies are based on, predominantly, archival research and court observations. This had to do with the fact that either the arms dealer passed away, quit his profession or was imprisoned. Direct interviews with them were often not possible to conduct.

The investigative biographies were written as non-scientific work but could not resist the journalistic temptation to chronicle their lives with entertainment and romanticising them, as well as trying to uncover larger conspiracies of the shadowy world of the global arms trade (Atkinson & Silverman 1997; Bennett 1999). Such investigative biographical writing has made biography

> as much a journalistic genre as a literary one; indeed, in the realm of popular culture it has become solely journalistic. Biography in this sense exists not to explain and understand but to eviscerate and exploit, and its methods have less to do with literature than with guerrilla warfare [...] What the genre now demands are a ferret-like determination to dig up facts, or factoids; a nose for the sensationally newsworthy; a talent for innuendo and selective interpretation; an insensitivity to nuance or human ambiguity.
>
> (Yardley in Weinberg 1992: 3)

That is not the type of biography delivered here. This criminological, biographical exploration of an arms dealer's daily (international) life will focus on the grey of arms dealers (whether legal or illegal), while it advances criminological theory about (the greyness of) the arms trade, because 'what theory lacks is an understanding of the ways in which shadow networks function in daily international life' (Nordstrom 2000: 51).

The criminological biography of a legal arms dealer here will, therefore, provide an understanding of an individual's life on the international stage of arms dealing, by focusing on how his own experiences are interpreted and narrated by him (cf. Roberts 2002: 5). However, whereas Bout resided on predominantly the illegal side and tried to stay out of the spotlights but clearly failed doing so, and whereas Cummings ran his business somewhere amidst the illegal and legal spheres yet enjoyed the attention, this biographee's life story and professional career is different. He is someone who operates entirely legal and wants to tell his story, but without getting public credit for it – he wants to remain anonymous. His willingness to deal in arms, the way he does his business and his overall life path though are not that different from Bout's and Cumming's, which could in turn tell us something about how to think about the wider topics of illegality and legality. That, altogether, required a strong will to understand and be understood, especially because understanding of the human side of things usually fades away in much criminological research (cf. Ferrell 1997; Young 2016) but is important and achieved by biography (cf. Van Gemert 2015c).

2.4 A will to understand and be understood

> Unless there is a will to understand, it is quite useless for us to present the facts that could be an antidote for prejudice.
>
> (Bartlett 1946: 163)

In considering Constantine as an agent of his own life, identity, morality and meaning-giving to it, and in comprehending why and how he performs his acts on the everyday international stage in his role as an arms dealer against the backdrop of larger social and cultural contexts, I tried to interpretively understand him (Bartlett 1946; Ferrarotti 1983; Ferrell et al. 2008; Martin 2000; Piacentini 2005; Weber 1980). In doing so, the performing of a Verstehende Soziologie ('interpretatively understanding sociology') proved to be useful (Ferrarotti 1983), because then a person's meaning-giving to life is chronicled and comprehended from that person's point of view. Verstehen then comprises the attempt to understand and explain the world of, in this case, the arms dealer, by letting the phenomena speak for themselves through the participant's narratives about those phenomena (Ferrell et al. 2008; Piacentini 2005; Weber 1980). According to Weber, one must 'interpretively understand [verstehen] social action and thereby causally explain its course and its effects' (Weber 1980: 1). Verstehen, therefore, requires 'extra emotional capacity in researchers' (Piacentini 2005: 193), a capacity that is stimulated by the use of 'existential frameworks, which reject distance in favour of connection and which involve thinking with the body as well as the mind', providing crucial understanding of 'how emotions and melancholia can create rational social meanings' (ibid.). Subsequently, biographers ought to immerse themselves in the participant's world without judging and by seeing through the participant-as-narrator's eyes to, eventually, understand participants through their perspectives (whether these are 'false' or 'true'). This is called obtaining the *emic perspective* that sheds light on a 'self-reported sense of meaning' and attaches less importance to 'linear causation' (Druckman 2005: 10), which was crucial for this biography of Constantine.

Such an appreciation and evaluation of narrative is in line with the growing body of literature on narrative criminology that prescribes and theorises to treat narratives not as sources of data on causes; rather, narratives themselves should considered causal, as they promote or facilitate (desistance from) offending (Presser & Sandberg 2019), and thus narratives are also causal for moral and immoral behaviour. However, critiques have been made against this rather linear explanation of narrative as causal (Fleetwood 2016). Meaning, narratives communicated through and by the arms dealer in stories on his life history do not only feed his arms trading and moral morality but his narratives are also fed by arms trading and morality. This leaves behind a more dialectic and dynamic approach of narrative (criminology), in line with Mill's 'insistence that the sociological imagination occupies the intersection of biography, history and social structure', which is one of the key roots of narrative criminology (Carrabine 2016: 579). Understanding narrative criminologically and biographically in this manner made me stay closer to (auto)biographical writing (Atkinson & Silverman 1997; Bourdieu 1986; Denzin 1989; Goodey 2000; Roberts 2002; Van Gemert 2015c).

Some reflective considerations are necessary to account for such interpretive understanding of narrative (Roberts 2002), in particular so, because understanding social phenomena in general depends on what social scientists are interested in to understand, on the questions that are being asked and on describing the phenomena by the biographer (Gelderman 1996; Martin 2000). Leaving out a consideration of these elements and staying insensitive to a reflection on it, makes any social scientific study unwarranted (Martin 2000: 249–251).

Especially because this biography disputes what seems undisputable – the inhumanity of arms dealers – that is considered to exist as an immobile form that precedes an 'external world of accident and succession' (Foucault 1977: 142), I must take the biased, changing and interactive existence of Constantine and myself into account. It requires acknowledgement of how 'auto/biographical narratives as sources revealing how human subjects constitute themselves through practices interwoven with power/knowledge relations' (Tamboukou 2013: 88). This means I – almost continuously – contrasted his and my own ways of reasoning along each other, trying to reflect on what I think I may have read into his narratives (ibid.).

So, I immersed as much as possible myself in Constantine's narrated world by attempting to see through the biographee-as-narrator's eyes to, eventually, understand him through his own perspectives (whether these are 'false' or 'true'). I aimed to interpretatively understand the arms dealer Constantine and his normal, banal everyday (work) life that he lives like any other individual; an ordinary life that is embedded in an extraordinary trade. Central was, therefore, the discovery of where, when and how coherence was ascribed by Constantine to his life story, while staying off my own assumptions and understandings. Also, because biographers get personally invested by sharing stories, build trust and establish credibility and solidarity (Roberts 2002), meant I influenced the construction and shaping of the story of Constantine's life, making me a biographical participant as well. I collect, present and interpret the narratives, as well as that I become personally invested by sharing stories, in building trust, and establishing credibility and solidarity (Roberts 2002). It has been argued 'that biographers tell certain life stories because they are somehow seeking themselves in others' lives [...] slowly discover[ing] that their subjects' lives echo their own' (Gelderman 1996: 328). On top of that, a biography could tell us 'more about the biographers and their times', also because biographies are 'a kind of mirror of the cultural Zeitgeist', than about the biographees themselves, making a biography an 'oblique self-portraiture' (ibid.: 329). Thus, a part of my self and the cultural Zeitgeist I share with Constantine are revealed. That share comprise not as much as that of the biographee, but a construction of my own narrative is implicitly present in this biography. Put differently, a part of my own everyday life echoes in the background of Constantine's life story.

This also means it was impossible to stay an objective outsider (if that is even possible at all), unintendedly influencing and being influenced by the biographee, which is integrally part of writing biographies (Cohn 1987). Actually, the biographer who 'impersonates a neutral, absent ghost' is performing a type of 'wizardry', because a biographical interview's consistency *is* social interaction (Ferrarotti 1983: 68). Biographies are not monologues that are spoken out to an observer; every interview conducted for a biography 'is a complex, social interaction, a role system, a system of expectations, orders, norms and implicit values, often also of sanctions [that] hides tensions, conflicts, and power hierarchies' (ibid.). Meaning, the interviews I had with Constantine reflect our relational interaction. As matter of fact, to enact such an illusion of objectivity disrupts and affects the interactional quality of a biography (Ferrarotti 1983: 68). It is because of my humanity and thus subjectivity, we got to the topics discussed, also sensitive ones; topics that may have never been talked about if I were to be a cold, distant and falsely neutral interviewer. Not only during interviewing, but throughout the process of the biographic study, this non-neutrality occurred, in which subjective interpretations and judgements let new issues or insights arise (Badiou 2008: 14). That way I also did not accept his life story as reflections of some sort of 'real' objective reality, by which I avoided what Bourdieu (1986) has defined as the biographical illusion. So, instead of perceiving the participant's life as coherent, it is about how Constantine perceives his life and how he gives coherence to it (Denzin 1989).

Although subjectivity plays a major part in studying an individual biographically, this does not mean, as said at the beginning, a biographee should be heralded, or demonised for that matter. It is important to avoid romanticising the participant's life (story), also referred to as the temptation of the 'Romantic impulse' that may occur (Atkinson & Silverman 1997). Such temptation can pull the biographer unconsciously into becoming too sensitive 'to the narrative organization of everyday life [of the interviewee]' that 'result[s] in an unauthorized and uncritical endorsement of personal narratives themselves' (ibid.: 322). Giving into the seduction of romanticising participants' lives is not uncommon to (particularly cultural) criminologists who engage in in-depth qualitative research (Tierney 2010; Zaitch 2002). This means that in comprehending and communicating the 'deviant knowledge' (Ferrell et al. 2008) this biography will retrieve about the arms dealer has been met with caution, my *subjective* caution. Meaning, I tried to push myself as much as possible not to give into a romanticisation of the abnormal, the exciting and the exceptional. The tendency to romanticise generally comes along though when 'researchers and journalists are ready to accept or even push forward their sensational versions' of 'interviewees guarantee[ing] professional prestige and commercial success'; it can make criminologists blind to 'more complex and contradicting aspects of organised crime', for example (Zaitch 2002: 8). At the same time, I also pushed myself to look not only for the trivial and banal. If anything, it is about what Constantine himself told by sensationalising or downplaying his life story. It was from the first contact until the very writing down of these words in this book about understanding

> processes at the individual level in societies where traditional ties and ways of thinking no longer have the same relevance as in earlier times [...] in that each person must explain and underpin their actions and choices by "rational" arguments rather than by referring to "traditional" ways of doing things.
>
> (Nilsen & Brannen 2013: 92)

As much as I wilfully wanted to understand Constantine, he wanted to be understood. That will of his became clear when he explained why he was motivated to talk with me about his life for this biography. He is always honest, he explained, as that is the most important feature in doing arms deals. There is a strong code of honesty that runs through the arms trade, because the arms dealer is there

> to give arms to all men who offer an honest price for them without respect of persons or principles: to aristocrat and republican, to Nihilist and Tsar, to Capitalist and Socialist, to Protestant and Catholic, to burglar and policeman, to black man, white man and yellow man, to all sorts and conditions, all nationalities, all faiths, all follies, all causes and all crimes.
>
> (Shaw cited in Cahn 1979: 125)

As long as it is legal, an arms dealer should not discriminate in making deals. This trademark was important for Constantine to do this biography, and to participate in it as honest and transparent as possible, he told me:

> It would be very easy for me to sit here and draw honey from my tongue so that you could say: "This is perfect, what I want for my article, oh yeah I could make so much money, and fame and fortune as a professor, I will have ALL those speaking engagements". But [...] that's not what I am here for, and that's not why you asked me to do this. [...] I don't stand for bullshit. [...] There's only one thing I have in my life, and that is my word. [...] When a man gives his word, it is his word. I don't have anything in my life apart from my word. My word is my bond, which means I don't put honey on my tongue to drip socially acceptable bullshit to somebody who wants to write a book. [...] You're gonna get a lot of flak for this [book], for sure, especially from people who are, shall we say, more, higher than your peers. Everybody is gonna try and knock the wind out of you, but I wouldn't. [...] I've dealt with professors in my time. In fact, there aren't many that I like. I would count you as one that I do. You're not the normal run of the mill.

Having considered Constantine's willingness to be understood and my will to understand, and having reflected on the subjectivity of striving towards such a will, throughout this biographic study, a number of practical challenges emerged. First of all, how does one meet an arms dealer?

2.5 Gaining access, trust and trustworthy data

How did I gain access to such a, generally, hard to reach actor who is uniquely positioned as he is alive, not imprisoned, and still active in the trade? Many arms dealers, in particular illegal ones, are usually not available and also not aware of their biographies being written. In fact, apart from the Dutch Pistol Paul's authorised biography (Van Amerongen 1968), most biographies about arms dealers are unauthorised and predominantly based on secondary material such as police files, court cases and other indirect data (cf. Van Gemert 2015c). This biography is most definitely authorised as Constantine fully cooperated. In case he would not have shown his willingness to do the biography, it would have been hard if not impossible for me to enter the international arms trade and talk with an arms dealer in-depth. This is because of the fact that the arms trade remains unchallenged by impertinent questions and the public retrieves only occasional glimpses into that closed world of the global arms trade (cf. d'Ancona 1991). Still, we did meet, but we met for something completely different. Meaning, I was not necessarily interested in doing a biography on an arms dealer and I also was not looking for one. The first contact was not entirely random though, because I got his name from a contact to approach him on security studies-related matters in January 2015. We spoke for the first time and immediately we connected through our shared sense of dark humour.

> Come on, you get my black humour yeah? It's a sign [...] so I've been told [...] black humour [...] A study by, I suppose, clever people, who said that black humour is a sign of dementia. I mean, dementia, well, in that case I'm fucked yeah? [...] I like black humour. Although it takes a lot of people [who] don't understand it and they hate me for it, "How can you say it? you offend me". [...] They don't have to laugh. I'm not a politically correct person, I say what I want. If somebody is offended, well, you know, you're a grown up. Deal with it.

It is because I could 'deal with it' and also because he could deal with mine, we could commence the biography. This was the very first start of us building trust in each other. The ice was broken.

It surprised me that I felt this trust building straight away, because it made me realise I had something in common with a person whose line of work I disagree with. Yet I felt very quickly rather comfortable talking with him. This is what Kadar (2014) refers to as adapting to new grey-zone knowledge, for which the biographer ought to explore and embrace 'the possibility that the tender, poignant ambiguities of life writing' implies that we must confront 'repressed material in the stories we tell ourselves about evildoers and the "the enemy among us", about their difference from us, about our national purity and/or safe borders, and about humanity' (Kadar 2014: 112), and vice versa. Constantine had certain stories he told himself about academics, thinking we sit in our Ivory Tower and write about an arms industry that we know almost nothing about, he explained. In fact, where he trades in arms, I trade in knowledge, he sometimes confronted me with. Meaning, given how we may all contribute and benefit from commodification, in Constantine's case monetising on violence, c.q. arms dealing, and in my case commodification of knowledge, c.q. the neoliberal university (cf. Ball 2012), revealed his and my genuine interest in each other's life. He, therefore, was amazed that I undertook the biography in my spare time, unpaid. Immediately he said to me that 'if you're doing it in your free time, what right does the university have? [...] it shouldn't have any hold over what you do'. Constantine and I thus were confronted with our repressed ideas of each other and our lines of work, and that we actually have similar thoughts about life and the world in which we live:

ME: Do you think we think alike?

CONSTANTINE: Yeah of course we do, which is probably why we have this special rapport. [...] Let me put it this way, Yarin, I've not met ANY, or let me put it this way [...] I can count them on one hand. There are very, very few people that I can look in the eye and say "We're on the same wave length".

After our first contact, we started to not only converse more frequently over the phone but also via Skype, which gave us 'a face' for each other, but at a distance. More and more we both talked about professional as well as personal matters. Having told him about a couple of important personal, rather tragic events that happened in my life, we ended up in deep conversations about life and death. He also opened up more about his own life and the tragic as well as positive events that made him the man he became. In a way, the sharing of our feelings about our lives provided me 'access' to his life, and him to mine, nourishing willingness to talk and comradery. The access to him was actually established before my interest in writing his biography. As I heard very personal things about his life, it made me eventually say to him: 'You should write an autobiography of your life!', to which he replied in all seriousness 'Why don't you do it? I have a good feeling about you'. It established trust and openness from the very first moment that resulted in the process of setting up and eventually writing the biography of Constantine. Although heavily delayed by the ethics committee review (see Section 2.6 in this book), eventually I could start interviewing Constantine from January 2016 onward, for which he has allowed me to explore his personal and professional life. From his childhood until now, from specific persons, such as his (former) partners, parents, siblings, grandchildren and friends, to specific topics, such as (personal) morale and ethics; these topics were covered and often repeatedly discussed in multiple interviews.

As a biography is a story always told by a biographee, and always afterwards, the data retrieved from the interviews always provided a retrospective account, but one that is something more than just a memoir (Tierney 2010). Next to risks of romanticising a biographee, which distorts fact (Bennett 1999), biographical data itself is often challenging to validate, making its validation depend on the adequacy of the interpretative analysis of a second, perhaps even third, party (Frankfort-Nachmias & Nachmias 1996). It is recommended to complement interview transcripts with available archive material and interviews with relatives and friends, if possible (Morrison 2001: 785; Rosenthal & Fischer-Rosenthal 2004; Van Gemert 2015c: 359–360). So, on top of the 20 planned interviews, ranging from an hour to sometimes five hours, as well as several spontaneous Skype calls of a few minutes, text messages and emails were included to form a document of over 300 pages of primary data. It was complemented with several other sources, including online websites of Constantine's registered companies, social media profiles and other types of relevant online material. Moreover, he shared in confidence different documents with me such as but not limited to: lists of arms and ammunition he deals in, his licenses, quotes, end-user certificates (EUCs) and letters of intent that his clients have to negotiate with him. It supported and visually enriched his stories, as much as it deepened my understanding. Interviews with relatives or friends, for example, did not take place. This means only Constantine's own tale of his life story came under narrativist analytical scrutiny, in which a distinction was made 'between life as narrated and life as lived' in the reconstruction of his stories into this biography, by making use of both sides of the distinction and relating them to one another in a process-oriented way (Rosenthal & Fischer-Rosenthal 2004: 261). This concretely led to, first of all, a chronological collation of the data, leading to Chapters 3 and 4 about his past up to the point of when his arms dealing career started. From there a thematic collation of data led to Chapters 5–7 (also with chronological organisation within them) on arms dealing, to eventually ending at another chronological and thematic collation of data resulting in Chapter 8 about his past love life and current state of affairs of his family life. Considering this written biography as a collection of 'formulations of results [that] are always of a provisional character', it means this biography, like any other, is merely valid 'until further information is available' (ibid.). If anything, biographical data turned into a readable biography, also this biography, are always a 'result produced by analytical reconstruction [that] sets up concrete expectations and possibilities in the framework of the structure, but these do not necessarily come about; it could also turn out differently' (ibid.). To increase validation, not only were all transcripts member-checked by Constantine himself (cf. Buchbinder 2011; Koelsch 2013), but he also read the entire manuscript several times, as well as that the manuscript was read and commentated on by a trusted criminological biographer and whose comments have been taken into account during the finalisation of this biography. Next to these challenges of gaining access, trust and trustworthy data, there were specific challenges in how the interviews took place online, through Skype, often on quite personal matters.

2.6 Biography-by-Skype and digital challenges

CONSTANTINE: You can see how hot it is in my office today. Here I am. I'm talking to you half-naked. Actually, I'm not wearing any shorts either, so, I'm not going to stand up hahaha!
ME: That's more than enough information haha!
CONSTANTINE: Too much information, too much information!

The abovementioned chit-chat between Constantine and myself, just before an interview was going to start, captures in a laughable way a few key aspects that were practically and ethically challenging. The fact he was sitting half-naked, the top half, had to do with the fact he was in his home office. Where he lives, there is usually quite warm weather, whereas I was living in Liverpool at the time, in another country. We, therefore, had to Skype to do the interviews, and it was also the only way we did the interviews. As you can pick up from the cited material, we were already being quite friendly with one another.

The fact I have been biographically interviewing the participant via Skype posed all sorts of trivial practical advantages and issues but has led as well to interesting questions with regards to doing a biographical study, and doing so *in* and *on* digitalised life of the 21st century. What worked and what not so much? Which nuts and bolts-practicalities were involved and what did it all mean in terms of the deeper methodological, epistemological and ethical questions that are involved in doing a digital biography via Skype (Arthur 2009; Deakin & Wakefield 2014)? Let's begin with some practical matters that cannot go unmentioned. These were predominantly of a technical nature, as is common in Skyping with a participant (Hanna 2012). It was assumed both by him and me that we had the necessary hardware and software installed, as well as proper user-understanding of them, in order to do the interviewing. Constantine was not put off due to a lack of 'digital capital' (Ragnedda 2018). In fact, he possesses more digital capital than most of us do, given how he implied at one point that he has tracking and infiltrating software, and highly advanced cyber-skills that

> if you suddenly call me from a different room, I'll know what's happened. […] You'd be surprised about the tools I have available to me. Listen, I don't follow anybody on the internet, don't worry. If I wanted to I could dig out, I could drill into your computer and could dig out lots of things but I'm just not interested in it. It's just not worth my while to be quite honest.

And I had to trust him, as much as he had to trust me in dealing carefully with the recorded and written raw data. All the Skype interviews were recorded through recording software I installed on my laptop, of which he was made aware when we would start an interview. Sometimes the internet connection would be poor, Constantine or me were inaudible (mostly due to wrong settings), or the video was blurred or pixelated. Rather funny were the moments when Constantine cursed and struggled with getting his webcam and headphones functioning correctly. He was muted but I could see him getting angry. He laughed about me having similar struggles with technical hitches as well:

CONSTANTINE: At the moment, my camera isn't working due to the back-up, which I still have running and which should finish, because I had a problem with the hard-drive. Because I have two hard drives separately bootable, unfortunately, I've lost the one. There was a boot-sector corruption on there so I had to re-install the whole thing again from a back-up. At the moment I'm still in the middle of that, and that's probably why the camera is not working although I don't really know why.
ME: It's okay, I don't necessarily HAVE to see you, Constantine.
CONSTANTINE: I've got a face for radio, you know that.

Such moments are all too human responses to digital limitations that are more and more seen in our Zooming society (Lahiri 2020: 48). Perhaps more than ever we are alone, yet also connected exactly because of the digital advances, and maybe even more so because of our shared struggles with them. For example, Constantine and I were connected through an online platform, but we had to stop our connection there, because a single 'like' or comment by me on his posts and vice versa would uncover his identity. Also, my contacts could cross-reference through our contact lists. These were, for me at least, new challenges around participant protection, privacy and confidentiality in an online environment (Schrooten 2012). We had and still have to look digitally disconnected to the outside world, whereas we connected very much in-depth through the personal stories he shared with me and I sometimes with him.

What has been pointed out by much research utilising Skype are the concerns about the easiness for participants to not 'show up' and stop the interview if they feel uncomfortable (James & Busher 2016). Simply not logging on or leaving Skype is literally only a mouse-click away, especially when things get tough or awkward (Deakin & Wakefield 2014). Moreover, as Constantine was interviewed while being in his home office, he sometimes would receive work-related calls on potential deals or deals that were already taking place. Sometimes his wife would walk in, or he would be called to come for dinner. I would sometimes receive phone calls from family or friends, which was not strange given that we did the interviewing after work, in our own time. These 'interruptions' that naturally flow from our own private lives confronted us with our own mundane, human everyday life and brought us closer to one another.

Generally there is a concern about the decreased interpersonal quality of doing social research on and with real human beings through Skype. The idea that 80% of language is non-verbal in particular seems to be a much-heard argument for keeping Skype interviews to a bare minimum, as not being physically co-present with participants, makes it more difficult to use interpersonal skills to access and interpret social worlds (Janghorban et al. 2014). You only see a 'talking head'-shot, making you miss out on crucial in-person communication; when we are quiet, non-verbal cues are communicated but those are not necessarily registered when video calling. Fidgeting or inhaling, for example, helps retrieve a holistic picture of what is being conveyed and what is expected in response from the researcher. Instead, you become more focused on merely words instead, while you frame a participant only from the shoulders up and that makes it virtually impossible to observe hand gestures or other body language (Sklar 2020). Other typical video call-related issues involve digital eye strains due to glaring at a screen and poor sitting postures (Bhattacharya et al. 2020), as well as becoming tired from continuously not looking each other straight into the eye – you look at a screen in which a person looks at you in a screen. True eye-contact cannot be made, which makes the brain correct itself in what it is observing and what we are presented to be thinking to see. Although mutual gaze is a key conversational resource, it is difficult to overcome the disparity between the position of the camera and the position of your eyes on the screen (Grayson & Monk 2003). An interesting energy-consuming element of video calling is that of emoting, in which we look to ourselves while interacting with the other, making us 'act' more than in other non-digitised settings – it makes the interaction perhaps even more less natural (Sklar 2020). Altogether, and especially since the COVID-19 lockdown, video calling leads to what is referred to as 'Zoom fatigue' (Wiederhold 2020). Constantine and I experienced such a fatigue pre-COVID-19 with Skyping, as often we both would be exhausted after a Skype conversation.

These practical challenges of using Skype for biographic interviewing, and video calling in general, are part of the shift in social sciences from the interpretation of 'life online' to researching 'mediated life', because life itself has become interpenetrated by digital data, also that of researchers and research itself. And also of arms dealers. The almost total digitalisation has led to 'new questions, concerning the roles of infrastructures and expertise, the shaping of personal relationships, the public visibility of private life, and the continuous surveillance of people, things and transactions' (Hand 2014: 2). Regarding the survivability of biography and any 'traditional' method for that matter, within a computer-mediated setting, depends on its 'capacity to be utilized and adapted to the technology that mediates human interaction online' (Stewart & Williams 2005: 396).

For this biography, Constantine and I engaged in an online, computer-mediated setting, in which we also talked about his life, specifically his later life as an arms dealer, for which he professionally engages online as well. Therefore, the online interviewing was also focused on his online life itself. Of course, even in the global lockdown due to COVID-19, life is not just an online life. Our lives are intertwined with other aspects of our actions and experiences that do still take place physically. Whereas some things are taking place entirely online such as websites for eating disorder communities, there are actions that may be primarily online and could lead to possible offline interactions, like cybersexual relations leading to real-life sexual contact. Or think about multimodal on- and offline social life, such as your interaction with friends, family and co-workers through email, Facebook or WhatsApp for example. Altogether, it defines the field or research setting (Garcia et al. 2009). The biography took place entirely online, as well as non-planned, short interactions with each other, like chatting about something that happened in the news, or sending each other links during and in-between interviews. It encouraged spontaneous interactions and the creative use of interactive visual and audio stimuli.

There was one night where I just got back from the gym, which was the reason why I looked exhausted, I explained to Constantine. He understood and told me he was the one who postponed the meeting to begin with. He also told me he posted something on his social media about the ongoing conflict in Syria. He wondered if I was a member of the specific group within the social media venue, which I was not. I was offered to become a member of that group and that I should start following them, which I did. This is an example of how the immediacy of being online and 'connected' helped enrich the interviews as they happened. Not only relating to the arms dealing world and its role in present conflicts, but also regarding the more personal matters we covered in the interviews. For example, we discussed our taste in music and shared YouTube and Spotify links with each other, or if we discussed something regarding newspaper of scientific articles, we Googled simultaneously. Also, not for an interview, but to simply catch up with each other was done online, mostly with video calling through Skype, but sometimes also without video and just sound. Meaning, we engaged asynchronously in non-real-time through emails and sharing links in a chat box, as well as that interacted synchronously in real-time through online (video) calling and textual in a chat box, or by 'instant threading'. However, the lines between organised interview moments and spontaneous interactions online did blur. It made it possible for us to overcome time and financial constraints, geographical dispersion and physical mobility boundaries. We had instant flexibility, as well as that it was convenient because we remained in trusted environment, namely, our homes and regular work space (cf. James & Busher 2016). Constantine said about such flexibility that 'if we had to meet in person to do this interview, this book would never get written. We are using the internet for something positive'.

Perhaps doing it all online may amplify the earlier mentioned unconscious autobiographic input of the writer into another person's biography. The question rises to which extent that becomes problematic? It is still Constantine's biography, not mine. It also raises the question to which extent digital interaction, as distant it may feel because of the non-physicality (and in the case of biography), may bring people closer in an abstract manner due to sitting in one's own familiar setting? It is then important to reflect on the effects of such proximity between biographee and biographer and possible other related distortions.

2.7 Distorted narratives, narrating distortion

Next to the digital and the more technical challenges encountered in retrieving access and doing the biographic interviewing online, there were a couple of key aspects that have influenced. To an extent, they distorted the stories told by Constantine. These were in particular his reasons for doing the biography, talking about personal, sensitive matters and becoming friends, conflicting morals, pseudonymisation and doing biography ethically.

2.7.1 His secret legacy

It did not really matter to him what we talked about during the interviews, as he argued that I was the one doing the writing and bringing it all together to a story. He wondered 'why on earth you want to write about my life story anyway?', and he did not 'hope for anything good to come out of this book apart from a few pennies, a few shekels'. Perhaps someone would read it and consider his life is interesting enough and perhaps motivate the reader to become an arms dealer, he explained: 'that would be terrible. In the foreword of this book it should be written "do not become an arms dealer" and sign it with "Constantine"'. The book contract was important to him:

> Are they gonna give us an advance on the book? [...] First of all they have to cover their printing costs. [...] To cover the costs they'd need to sell 70% of those books just to cover the printing costs. [...] Anyway, you know what you're doing, you get on and deal with it. [...] Just keep me in the loop, as to what you send them. So that if I see that it's not going the way that it should or the way I feel that it should, at least we have an open channel for communications. [...] It's not just the money, it's not just the money, it's about the facts that are going to be in that book.

He also wanted to have a separate contract between him and me, about what happens if one of us dies, where the money goes to and, most importantly, who will be benefitting from it:

CONSTANTINE: I trust you man, I trust you. Let's not make the thing [our own contract] too complicated, yeah?

ME: Because it's, what, 7 GBP a year?

CONSTANTINE: Well, who knows, who knows. They might decide in 5 years to make a film about it, who knows. Or in 50 years they might decide to make a film about it. In 50 years there's gonna be no world anyway.

He did not necessarily want to just make money for himself, but also for his daughter. Another important motivation was that his daughter would get a copy:

CONSTANTINE: The only thing that you and I have to work out is where the royalties of my share go. That's all. I still haven't decided whether they'll go to my wife or my daughter. I'd like to get them myself to begin with and if anything happens to me then they probably go to my daughter. [...] You and I will make an agreement that my half of the royalties will go into my bank and if at any time something happens to me, then the contingent payment should go to, and I will give you the name and bank details of this person. My only daughter, who's in XXXX.

[...]

ME: I think you may be doing this biography for your daughter.

CONSTANTINE: That's possibly true.

There is more to this than letting his biography being written for money and his daughter. He wants some sort of recognition for his life and the choices he made, which is observed more often in biography (Bennett 1999; Head 2016). In a way, he was looking for solace, or atonement, for how he has lived his life by telling his story anonymously:

> Obviously, I will die one day. At the moment, I don't have the intentions in doing so, but you know, the good Guy up there. Is he still gonna keep me around for a few more years, hopefully, until I can pay off the bills so that the kids don't get saddled with them. [...] I wanna go out owing nothing to anybody. I wanna go out with a good name, I wanna go out with my boots on, so to speak. [...] I want to go out with a good name, because that's all that's left afterwards. People don't remember the bad guys. Unless you're really bad, Mussolini, Hitler, Pol Pot. [...] I don't put myself in those brackets. No, no, I just want to go out and being remembered as one of the good guys who tried to be as, as straight as possible, and as, what shall we say, morally correct in all of his dealings. That's what I wanna do, that's how I would like [it]. On my headstone I would like "He was a good guy". "He sold guns but he was a good guy". [...] If [the biography] gets published, and if people actually get to read it, not just criminologists, "Who is this, what's this? arms dealer? legal arms dealer? Talking about the bad laws. Let's have a quick gander at that". Then they just say "Oh yeah that's interesting" put it on some [...] I like my life's work to be [...] even if it's only leftover for my kids, yeah, especially for my daughter, and my family obviously, and my siblings. [...] Setting the facts right!

He wants to leave behind a clean slate, a reset perhaps, being able to 'say to myself with my last dying breath, "at least I didn't fuck anybody up with the work that I've done"'. In admitting that he 'may have fucked people up in my private, personal life', he did not do so work-wise. So he is conscience of how some people have been hurt by the things that he has done in his life. Still, he told me that they should get over it: 'Grow a pair, man up and get over it'. What was important for Constantine was that he wanted to tell his story as a *legal* arms dealer, 'especially since I'm not a criminal!', as he once shouted. It made him want to read the entire manuscript before submission only because he would not let somebody write about him from a criminological point of view just like that. He explained that by making it criminological, the wider audience would automatically think they would read about 'a socio-psychopath who is morally corrupt', as he jokingly said. For him, and this biography, it is more about showing why he thinks he is 'always right, it's my morals that count, not anybody else's'.

2.7.2 Dealing with a sensitive past

This biography provides snippets of someone's life, not just about the professional aspects of his arms dealing work, but even more so about his personal life. His private sphere has been turned inside out while interviewing him, during which a very wide range of sensitive matters emerged. From his rather problematic childhood, his sometimes complicated love life to his difficult relation with his daughter; these were all heavy topics that gave me as a researcher a unique access to someone's emotional and even traumatic experiences. More importantly, it brought me closer to another person and that person to me, as I also shared sensitive matters with him, both negative and positive ones. Through each other, we spoke 'to the broken halves of all our selves and tell them to embrace, loving the worst in us equally with the best', as writer John Maxwell Coetzee once poetically wrote (2017: 38). It was these poetic moments specifically that made our life's biographies overlap and it provided a deeper insight into each other's past and present, the wonderful, the traumatic and the trivial, as well as hopes for and anxieties about the future. Our lives merged to an extent, letting me put in some of my own life in the biographee's biography. Such a merger is hard to avoid but does lead to more trust and that trust leads to richer and fuller understanding of the biographee (Ferrarotti 1983; Gelderman 1996; Roberts 2002).

These moments of sensitive matters often led to difficult interactions between us, mostly awkward and long moments of silence, or simply outbursts of frustration about how his life went the way it did. Especially regarding his relation with his father in the past could get Constantine aggravated:

> I don't respect him now either. I never knew my father. I can't say I know who my father was. [...] He's too old for me to sit down now and have a deep conversation with him because he's a little bit "dotters" and he would never [...] and even if he did remember, he would NEVER admit to remembering the things that he's done when he was younger. [...] I don't

> see them very often and they're getting older and older and I'd certainly wouldn't want to open up a can of worms by saying "I forgive you for beating the shit out of me as a young kid".

I asked him what it does to him, digging in the past and bringing up difficulties and the sometimes traumatic experiences:

> There's a lot of things I've done in my life that I'm not particularly proud of, don't get me wrong [...] Were all of them traumatic? To whom? To other people? No, to me, myself. [...] Traumatic experiences for me, basically, I just forgot about them, especially the ones from my childhood. Like I said, it was only after talking to my brother and being reminded or gently nudged in that direction that it came back to me. [...] All this reflecting on the past and why am I like I am, it will only fuck your head up to be quite honest, because you get so involved in what's been going on, you'll miss what's going on out there. [...] Don't get me wrong, I don't say I don't reflect sometimes on things that have happened in the past, but from my childhood, I've blocked most of it out. You know what happens when you have an immense shock? You tend to shove it on the side and forget about it. When a person has a traumatic experience, they block it off and they push it on the side and don't remember it. It was only after talking to my brother that a lot of this came back to me, I just shut it all off.

For him, this blocking off was and remains a way to survive; he explained to me that it was a way of protecting yourself. There is much he has (deliberately) forgotten. He

> put them in a box. Lock 'm away. That's it. You can call it a cooking pot with a lid on the top. But I don't think so because I don't think about them. [...] That's in the past. There's the past, the present, and the future. The past I can't do anything about. What's gone is gone, what's happened has happened. Move on, which is how I've lived my life.

The biographic interviews were for him, therefore, not always pleasant. As a matter of fact, and despite despising to reflect, he did do so on several occasions. He called it 'soul searching' instead:

> I had to do some soul searching, to give you the right answer. I had to do some soul searching to tell you what you wanted or rather what I wanted you to hear or to tell you "That's none of your fucking business, man". [...] Soul searching is where you look into your soul and say "Do I want to answer this truthfully?". I always answer truthfully anyway, but "Do I want to give him [Yarin] the whole truth or do I want to give him just a little bit?". It was always [...] Yeah I can put my hand on my heart and

> say it was always the whole truth. There was never anything in there that didn't fit.

The soul searching exercises led to him admitting he has done a lot of things in his life he is not particularly proud of, he explained, and asked me 'were all of them traumatic? To whom? To other people? No, to me, myself. [...] These things I'll never forget'. Those matters that happened in his childhood, as Chapter 3 will explore, have been traumatic for him and have consciously been pushed away. What this reveals is how conscious forgetting and presenting the truth as it is according to Constantine may distort a 'true' story about his life. Then again, it is about how he has experienced his life and the sensitive, personal and sometimes life-changing events.

Due to discussing sensitive matters and personal events in his life – sometimes also those of mine – we became closer and eventually, friends. Although we focused on his life, his family and friends and how he was doing, sometimes these rolls reversed and he would say to me he notices something was up with me:

> By looking at you, I can feel there's something wrong. [...] I've known you for quite some time now, it's obvious when I see you I notice your face, because that's all I see of you, and sometimes your hands and your eyes. The eyes are the mirror to the soul. So, just looking at your eyes I can tell there's something's wrong or not. Alright man, you have a good one, whatever's left of the Sunday [...] You take care now, yeah? Cheers now, bye!

I sometimes talked about my job and being micromanaged, to which he responded with a genuine interest, asking empathetic questions and giving advice. It cheered me up. At several instances, Constantine would also ask how my sister would be doing and he always gave his best wishes to her. This had to do with the fact she had a near-death accident from which she, miraculously, recovered fully. What happened, logically, is that my sister thanked him for his wishes and she wished him good luck back in dealing with his cancer, which I would then communicate back to him. The following was after my sister's accident happened:

> Thank you very much, I hope she is a lot better than what she was and I hope she continues to keep getting better, and I hope that she is very happy, and thankful for her second chance in life. [...] If you really want to give her a good surprise, and I'm sure you can get it there, is Powers 12 year old Irish whisky. Don't get the 3 year old, get the 12 year old, it's special. It's very, very good whiskey. In fact, if I drink, which I don't under normal circumstances, but if I do, I take a very, very small nip of that.

It depicts the strong rapport we built up, which intensified by the more informal, short interactions through Skype-chat: 'You're also sending me rainbow smiley's, Jesus Christ! When I saw that, I thought to myself: "What the fuck?" Hahaha! Sending me fucking unicorns next!'.

2.7.3 Moral and ethical clashes

Constantine pointed out to me that he and I 'are basically on the same wave length and our outlook on life'; however, 'you and I might disagree on torture and other things'. And we did and still do, because as much as we could have funny, friendly and personal moments shared and could agree on many things, we also had several frictions and a couple of moral tête-à-têtes with one another. Almost always, he would compare his business with that of another market area of consumable items:

> Ehm […] Yarin […] it's like […] pfff […] ttss. Okay, some people sell fruit, I sell weapons. Some people sell cars, I sell guns. Yeah? A cigarettes salesman [while he was smoking], yeah […] I mean, let's take it statistically, cars and cigarettes kill more people in a year than my guns.

During these clashes, it became clear that we did not agree morally, mostly about his line of work despite my wilful attempt to be as open and understanding as possible. In particular, at the beginning, when we still did not know each other as well as at the end of the interviews, I would explain to him it was hard not to let my own morals and convictions have a say in writing his biography about his life and work as an arms dealer. I told him during the third interview, for example, that my researcher part says I have to explore his life as interested and invested as possible. I also told him that I think of him as a very insightful and smart human being who anticipates conflict and human suffering, and right before that happens, does what any salesman would do: selling your product. That aspect of it, I did not understand as a human being; he would knowingly sell to a party that is about to be embargoed, which implies that party is doing something wrong and that misery is going to come out of it, such as human rights violations and genocide. Partially made possible by his arms deals. As long as it is legal, he wondered 'what do you have a problem with?', he asked me. He pointed out to me several times that I am selling knowledge, making me, therefore, not that different from him. Thus, whenever I would utter my personal or moral discontent

> it would just be your point of view against mine, that's not the idea behind it. […] you're gonna try and convince me that what I'm doing is morally wrong […] because you won't be the first one and you won't be the last, I'm sure.
>
> (Constantine)

Next to moral clashes between Constantine and myself, which will be topically explored in-depth throughout this book, there were vital ethical clashes between me and the ethics committee that had to approve this biography.

Anticipating that this arms dealer biography would trigger all sorts of ethical alarm bells in the ethics committee, I proactively approached two members of the ethics committee via email. Immediately, one of the ethics committee members replied, acknowledging it sounded like a great but challenging opportunity and that I was right to flag it with them. After a meeting with one of the committee members, it became clear this was the first time the ethics committee had to deal with a biography on an arms dealer. It was also the first time they suggested to a researcher, being me, to come in during a committee meeting and do a personal defence in front of them. After the ethical drilling exercise was over, and I survived the defence, I had to make sure that I emphasised in the ethical approval form that I had relevant experiences and qualifications, required detailed information, and that I would state I will report 'anything criminal mentioned' and any illegal activity by Constantine. I would have to make sure that I would consult with anyone else to help you me if something should be reported. And if reported, I would have to stop the research. In the participant information sheet, I had to state:

> to report any disclosures, e.g. threats to persons or ongoing damage to persons. So, by agreeing to participate in this research and by giving your informed consent, you agree to the fact you know I will go to the authorities in case of any disclosure of illegal activities you may be involved in.

For Constantine and me, it was all common sense, yet the ethics committee wanted to have it stated as such. Also, they wanted to see how secure the data was stored, as there may be 'information interesting to governments'. They also were worried about the 'risk that there may be a danger to either party from these sources', and whether I considered this risk. It happened throughout the interviewing that Constantine talked about his 'business intelligence' that comprises geopolitical information drawn on intelligence from operatives he would have in a country or from people he knows that are working in that country that could give insight into the geopolitical situation there. The ethics committee asked whether the government could retrieve access to such data, if it would be of interest to them. Here it was meant whether intelligence services could access the secured data without having to go through highly sophisticated firewalls to retrieve potentially interesting geopolitical information. It made me somewhat insecure about how safe and secure I should store my data, which I eventually did as safely as I could do. Other points the ethics committee wanted me to guarantee involved the reliability of the information provided by Constantine and whether one person's life story suffices to understand the phenomenon of the arms. For this, I had to explain biography as a method to a member who had a background in the beta-sciences, which was a difficult thing to do, as social scientific research methods, of which the biography is one (Van Gemert 2011), are generally not known to professionals in the 'hard sciences', and vice versa. Moreover, there were concerns about the publication of materials, making the ethics committee 'strongly recommend' a contract should underlie the project as it 'ensures safety for the researcher and for [the university]'. By 'contract' was meant a book contract, for which I had not yet approached a publisher as I awaited institutional ethical approval, as I clarified to the ethics committee. It then raised the issue of how the project would be funded at all, and they wondered if the publisher was liable and how much say would a publisher have in the final product. The ethics committee wanted me to state that the contractual terms should state clearly that the book could not be edited after agreement, as well as that Constantine cannot expect remuneration in exchange for his participation. Basically, the ethics committee was shaping the contractual conditions between Constantine, me and a potential publisher, and they also suggested I should 'seek some legal advice regarding contract and also with regards to publication'.

What became clear to Constantine and me is that the ethics committee wanted to have absolute guarantees that any liability of the university is taken out before the ethics application could even be formally submitted. Particularly worrying was the attention for the security of the data and if it could be breached by a government if it wanted to, as well as the far-going interference in the book contract. Eventually, the ethics application was approved more than eight months after the ethics application procedure was started. During all that time, I risked losing Constantine's interest and had to make sure he stayed 'hooked'. I often explained to him what was going on and we discussed the somewhat contradictory suggestions by the committee, but he always understood: 'Don't ruin your future because of that. If you feel that the job is worth it, well okay, we'll redo it [ethics application], but we have to get Routledge on board as well'. If it was not for his understanding of the ethics application procedure itself, the biography would not have happened at all. Like myself, he believed more in the ethics we ourselves had and still have regarding this biography, or, for that matter, him doing his arms dealing and me doing my research.

> Crusty old professors, that have been stuck in their position for so long, they don't really know what to do anymore. These are the guys you're gonna have to watch out for. Like I said, if somebody comes up and gives you a comment rather than ask you a question, I would ask "Would you like to rephrase your question please, or what exactly was your question again?". Everybody will know in the room what the fuck you're talking about, because they have all seen this jerk make his own statement. He has not asked a question, he just made a statement. I would stand up and say: "thank you very much for your comment, but what was your question again, or was there a question in there?". I mean, I'm sorry […] "I am sorry, but I have my ethics", this would be from your side, "I have my ethics, and if I had the slightest idea this guy was dripping honey into the conversation just to be socially and morally acceptable, then I would not do it".

What unfolds itself here is the bizarre situation in which a participant, with a unique story that has provided rich insights into controversial issues, has to have an understanding towards a researcher's struggle with an ethics committee that would rather see controversial research not taking place, or at least, under severe control. There is a clear mismatch between ethics applications and 'doing the right thing' (Winlow & Measham 2017), as illustrated by the above. Ethical branding (Singh et al. 2012) in academia requires a type of bottom-up methodological resistance against the 'ethics creep' in the environment of neoliberal academic capitalism (Haggerty 2004), as ethics committees seem to become more and more the very unethical element in research itself while producing 'ethical propaganda' that limits especially critical criminologists' qualitative research (Armstrong 2020; Scott 2018). Resilience is necessary against such ethics that serve the powerful status quo by subjecting qualitative researchers to the reign of unethical ethics committees that cause organisational deviance, crime even, within universities (Faria & Eski 2018; Hedgecoe 2014), a type of resilience this biography has tried to build.

2.7.4 Pseudonymisation, anonymisation and contextual integrity

I took doing the right thing seriously with regards to ethical challenges, especially regarding pseudonymisation, if only because the ethic committee questioned whether anonymity could be guaranteed if the arms trade was approached from a biographical study point of view. The ethics committee implied that perhaps a different method could be considered to study explore the arms trade. Which method, however, was not suggested. I had to explain to them that it is about the rich experience of Constantine rather than about specifics of his story such as times, locations, specific people or a brand of a gun. Still, there would only be agreement from the ethics committee to sign off the ethical approval form if 'the subject [Constantine] would give consent on the definitive last draft of the book before anything is shared. Because only he would know if anyone is identifiable'. Of course I would require his final okay – this was always clear to Constantine and to me. It is about the fact that the real concern of the ethics committee was primarily getting written consent, and secondarily (perhaps even not necessarily) the protection of Constantine through pseudonymisation itself.

He and I spent a significant amount of time on agreements on pseudonymisation and how to go about it. It reveals he wanted hidden fame. On several occasions, Constantine checked the transcripts of interviews as well as the entire manuscript. I was allowed to use the transcripts and the licenses and examples of arms deal contracts he wrote, as long as all names and titles have been removed. It is interesting what the story of pseudonymising this book and his eagerness to do so tell us.

As much as he wanted to bequeath his life story to his daughter and the world, for money, he also wanted to make sure pseudonymisation was done thoroughly. His non-claim to fame stems from his fear to get a target on his back, which he has always been careful about. He has been approached by journalists before that he distrusted. Usually, they want information about various subjects and specific information on, for example, what type of weapons were used in a certain conflict and what kind of damage the ammunition does. 'One thing I don't really like is my name being thrown around in those sort of circles', because if press leaks his name, he

> could very well be charged, under XXXX law, for spying, or passing on classified information, even though the information I would be giving him would be open source. [...] The last thing I need is to be made [...] a scapegoat for a government organisation's failings, in front of a XXXX court system.

During his career, he has always been protective of his own life in relation to media and the press, because

> the deeper you get involved, the more your name is banded around as being a "subject matter expert", the more you want to make sure that what you're doing or rather what the information that you're giving out [...] doesn't include anything to put you in a dangerous position. [...] Media is a whore that sells itself to the highest bidder. It's true.

When he is approached, first he wants to have his safety guaranteed, and second he wants payment: 'Obviously, I don't work for nothing and I have to eat, I can't live on air. I have a wife and three unemployed kids, wait, two unemployed kids, sorry. Two students that don't work, and one employed'. Also, he would have to support the cause that a journalist can advocate.

> If a journalist from an activist news site, what is his name, XXXX from XXXX. I wouldn't work with XXXX anyway, bunch of tree hugging pussies. But if a respectable, activist journalist came to me and said: "Okay, I got this great idea, we'll give it to WikiLeaks or something" then possibly. Then again, how's WikiLeaks gonna pay me? They run on their donations. [...] No, if somebody wanted me to spill the beans, they would have to make it worth my while.

That is why he goes to conferences he is invited to speak at, because it pays. Also, talking about his specialty separates him from 'illegal arms dealers [who] don't get these kind of opportunities', stressing he is always operating legal.

Occasionally, he mentioned he did not give me 'any state secrets or anything', because he cannot give me any specifics.

> Yarin, the thing is, there are only certain people with the knowledge that I have so it would be quite an easy matter afterwards to be able to say okay "Which asshole told him this?" and then they would look at dates,

> times, destinations, "Who has licenses for these countries, and who sent?" and then go back and check "Who sent what where?", so, 100% anonymity is never guaranteed. This is why we are not mentioning actual deliveries. I could give you hundreds of examples.

Yet, the fear of his case-based information being cross-referenced would lead up to a record of his deals and eventually his licenses: 'I'd be putting myself at risk there if I gave examples', he warned me. Therefore, he mentioned during almost every single interview that he 'will go through with big black marker pen [marking] "censored, censored"', despite that he also told me he did not say anything and would not be going to say anything that could possibly implicate himself in anything that could possibly be construed as being illegal.

Pseudonymisation and anonymisation, therefore, were done thoroughly in this book and in continuous agreement with Constantine. Names of family members are pseudonymised, but places, organisations and specific dates are anonymised – they are not mentioned as these could lead to the risk of becoming cross-referenceable, and thus, discoverable. So, we both took into account the maintaining of balance between retaining context and protecting him, his relations and myself as biographer by using pseudonyms and selectively deleting particular passages if they were cross-referenceable (cf. Thomson et al. 2005: 12). It meant that the pseudonymisation and anonymisation applied in this biography is done with contextual integrity which 'couches its prescriptions always within the bounds of a given context' rather than applying it universally (Nissenbaum 2004: 154).

The pseudonym, or 'nom de plume' for himself as he phrased it, had to be 'Constantine' after Constantine the Great, the first Roman Christian emperor in Byzantine times who erected Constantinople (current-day Istanbul). He owns a coin on which Constantine the Great and his mother Helena are depicted. The reason why he wanted his pseudonym to be Constantine had to do with the fact that he lauded how Constantine the Great fought several victorious wars, brought about many rigorous political and social reforms to the Roman empire, introduced a new coin and he was the first Roman emperor who converted to Christianity. After we agreed on his pseudonym, I often called him Conny, which he did not appreciate.

The greatness is something he admired in Constantine the Great and wanted to imagine himself into by having this pseudonym. At the same time, it also shows something about how he wants hidden fame for himself and protection of a close circle of people, while sharing his life's lessons to a wider amorphous audience to which he wants to remain unknown.

2.8 Lessons learned, guidance given

> Hang on just a sec, let me just close the door and turn the video camera on, so you can see this ugly mug, haha!

In this chapter, I have reflected on writing Constantine's biography. What becomes clear is that I have tried as much as possible to see beyond his 'ugly mug' and see *him*. In doing so, I have, first of all, explored why criminology has neglected the biographical method and then explained what biography entails and why it was chosen for the study of an arms dealer. Then, this chapter discussed and retrieved insights from predominantly investigative biographies on other arms dealers, in particular of Viktor Bout and Samuel Cummings, and what (not!) to do. Attention was paid as well to the will to understand and being understood, and why that really matters in doing biography. How access, trust and trustworthy data was gained for this biography, as well as what it means to do a biography by Skype and what that all tells about writing a life story in this digitised age have been considered. Finally, the internal and external challenges of biographic interviewing and writing have been dealt with, including a consideration of morality and ethics involved in doing this biography, and what pseudonymisation means while keeping contextual integrity of Constantine's story intact.

If anything, it becomes clear that doing biography is about being personal, sympathetic, empathetic and confronting, all the while both the biographer and biographee uphold integrity and mutual respect *and* self-respect. Biography is then about making yourselves available, about opening up and, to an extent, about establishing trust and friendship, something that altogether is well captured by Constantine in his reply to my question whether discussing his pancreatic cancer was difficult for him.

> If it's a very harsh question I would just tell you to "fuck off Yarin" haha! I think we're close enough for me to be able to say that to you and you to me as well.

Perhaps that is the most important methodological lesson from having done this biography: it has been about letting in as method and method as letting in. Building rapport and comradery in that sense is as much a goal of a biography as it is (just) a means towards a biography.

Leaving from that key lesson, and for what remains of this book, I will give some sort of reading instruction for Constantine's biography. It is important to understand that what is to be taken from his life story is not fully reflective, or for that matter, a 'real' or 'true' depiction of his life, also given what has been discussed in this chapter. To be clear: this biography is not an objective 'truth' about his life. It is an as honest as possible recollection of portions of his life, given as candid as possible by him, gathered by me as reliable as possible and then put down in writing as consistent as possible. Still, despite all that aimed for truth and truthful handling, this biography is, if anything, but a fragmented story and, therefore, not a complete reflection of the entirety of his life. As has been pointed out before about biographees who share their life story, they crave to tell a coherent story about themselves and their life, but their lives are very complex (Van Gemert 2011). Eventually, a biography is a retold, rebuilt and much shorter story-version of an original and much richer, incoherent and longer 'life [that] is not a straight line, the chapters of his biography are not easily in [a chronological – YE] line with each other' (Van Gemert 2011: 209–210). It is filled with contradictions, paradoxes and detail that simply cannot be reduced to a book. This biography, like any other, will never be as comprehensive and encompassing as Constantine's life has been in reality.

Nevertheless, once this biography was started and now that it is available to the wider audiences in writing, at the same, the biography itself has become part of the biographee's life, my life and its readers. To an extent, in having some of Constantine's life components written down in this book, he still remains fundamentally the same person. And at the same time, that life is enriched by the biography and the path towards it. His life story is metamorphosed into the written biography which comprises the textual afterlife the biographee shared with its readers (Bennett 1999; Head 2016). Meaning, it is because of the biography that the arms dealer's textual afterlife is construed, by imbuing the written with his own identity, ensuring that whenever his biography will be read, that his life story and identity is invoked in the mind of the reader, through which the all too human, banal aspects of his life and arms dealing are dispersed as the biographee's legacy (Head 2016: 205). In this sense, this biography functions as a vessel for his textual afterlife that is 'a paradoxical strategy of self-preservation and, at the same time, selfdissolution – the very being of [Constantine] inscribed in text, inscribed as text, in a life beyond life' (Bennett 1999: 19). The textual afterlife of Constantine aimed for here, much like Arendt's biographical report on the banality of Adolf Eichmann's evil (2006), is a criminological biographical report on an legal arms dealer, exploring his relations, key life events, motivations and reflections on them. Altogether these have shaped him as an arms dealer; a shaping that is a process which has been attempted to be captured in this biography as a textual afterlife. It all may very well spark a sympathetic understanding of him, of not only his 'evil' but also his 'good'.

Notes

1 It is not with certainty to claim this, as it has been presumed that he was born on 13 February 1967 somewhere in the Ukraine (OCCRP 2010).

2 It has been indicated that Yaroshenko got convicted for these drug charges after (and perhaps because) he refused to testify against Bout (Cole 2016).

References

Anders H, Cattaneo S, Vines A, Wood B & Yankey-Wayne V (2006) *Developing a mechanism to prevent illicit brokering in small arms and light weapons: scope and implications*. Geneva: UNIDIR/UN.

Arendt H (2006) *Eichmann in Jerusalem*. London: Penguin.

Armstrong EK (2020) Political ideology and research: how neoliberalism can explain the paucity of qualitative criminological research. *Alternatives* 45(1): 20–32.
Arthur PL (2009) Digital biography: capturing lives online. *a/b: Auto/Biography Studies* 24(1): 74–92.
Atkinson P & Silverman D (1997) Kundera's immortality: the interview society and the invention of the self. *Qualitative Inquiry* 3(3): 304–325.
Austin K (2002) Illicit arms brokers: aiding and abetting atrocities at gunpoint: the small arms and light weapons trade. *Brown Journal of World Affairs* 9(1): 203–216.
Badiou A (2008) Philosophy as biography. *The Symptom: Online Journal for Lacan.com*. From: www.lacan.com/symptom9_articles/badiou19.html.
Ball SJ (2012) Performativity, commodification and commitment: an I-spy guide to the neoliberal university. *British Journal of Educational Studies* 60(1): 17–28.
Bartlett JR (1946) The will to understand. *Pi Lambda Theta Journal* 24(4): 162–164.
Bellamy C (2011) Weapons dealer bites bullet in arms recession: Christopher Bellamy meets the man with the Commonwealth's largest private stock of weapons. From: www.independent.co.uk/news/uk/weapons-dealer-bites-bullet-arms-recession-christopher-bellamy-meets-man-commonwealth-s-largest-private-stock-weapons-1539436.html.
Bennett A (1999) *Romantic poets and the culture of posterity*. Cambridge: Cambridge University Press.
Bhattacharya S, Saleem SM & Singh A (2020) Digital eye strain in the era of COVID-19 pandemic: an emerging public health threat. *Indian Journal of Ophthalmology* 68(8): 1709–1710.
Bonger H (2004) *The life and work of Dirck Volkertszoon Coornhert*. Amsterdam: Rodopi.
Bovenkerk F (1995) *La Bella Bettien*. Amsterdam: Meulenhoff.
Bourdieu P (1986) L'illusion biographique. *Actes de la recherche en sciences sociales* 62(3): 69–72.
Brogan P & Zarca A (1983) *Deadly business: Sam Cummings, Interarms, and the Arms Trade*. New York, NY: W.W. Norton & Company.
Buchbinder E (2011) Beyond checking: experiences of the validation interview. *Qualitative Social Work* 10(1): 106–122.
Burton CS (2019) *Republican monsters: the cultural construction of American Positivist Criminology, 1767–1920 (doctoral dissertation)*. Berkeley, CA: University of California.
Cahn AH (1979) Arms sales economics: the sellers' perspectives. *Stanford, California Stanford Journal of International Studies* 14: 125–138.
Carlen P (1985) *Criminal women: autobiographical accounts*. Cambridge: Polity.
Carrabine E (2016) Picture this: criminology, image and narrative. *Crime, Media, Culture* 12(2): 253–270.
Coetzee JM (2017) *Dusklands*. New York, NY: Penguin Books.
Cohn C (1987) Sex and death in the rational world of defense intellectuals. *Signs: Journal of Women in Culture and Society* 12(4): 687–718.
Cole B (2016) Russia: jailed pilot Nadiya Savchenko swap for 'Lord of War' Viktor Bout proposed. From: www.ibtimes.co.uk/russia-jailed-pilot-nadiya-shavchenko-swap-lord-war-viktor-bout-proposed-1552036.
Collins V & Pujol M (2015) Secrets exposed?: selective state concern and the prosecution of notorious arms trafficker Viktor Bout. *Critical Criminology* 24(1): 93–109.
D'Ancona M (1991) Britain: business before disclosure. *Index on Censorship* 20(10): 16–17.

Deakin H & Wakefield K (2014) Skype interviewing: reflections of two PhD researchers. *Qualitative Research* 14(5): 603–616.
Denzin NK (1989) *Interpretive biography*. London: Sage.
Dolza D (1990) *Due donne intellettuali tra'800 e'900*. Milan: Franco Angeli.
Druckman D (2005) *Doing research: methods of inquiry for conflict analysis*. London: Sage Publication Ltd.
Farah D & Braun S (2007) *Merchant of death: money, guns, planes, and the man who makes war possible*. Hoboken, NJ: John Wiley & Sons.
Faria R & Eski Y (2018) Een wolf onder de wolven. Ethiek en ethische commissies in criminologisch onderzoek naar 'the powerful'. *Tijdschrift over Cultuur & Criminaliteit* 8(3): 43–58.
Feinstein A (2011) The shadow world: inside the global arms trade – an address at the Los Angeles World Affairs Council On November 14th, 2011. From: www.lawac.org/speech-archive/pdf/1631.pdf.
Ferrarotti F (1983) Biography and the social sciences. *Social Research* 50(1): 57–80.
Ferrell J (1997) Criminological verstehen. *Justice Quarterly* 14(1): 3–23.
Ferrell J, Hayward KJ, Morrison W & Presdee M (2004) *Cultural criminology unleashed*. Cavendish: Routledge.
Ferrell J, Hayward KJ & Young J (2008) *Cultural criminology: an invitation*. London: Sage.
Fijnaut C (2010) De voorlopers van de moderne criminologie in België en Nederland. *Justitiële Verkenningen* 36(2): 10–29.
Filmer P (1978) New directions in sociology (book review). *British Journal of Sociology* 29(1): 136–139.
Fleetwood J (2016) Narrative habitus: thinking through structure/agency in the narratives of offenders. *Crime, Media, Culture* 12(2): 173–192.
Foucault M (1977) Nietzsche, genealogy, history. In Bouchard DF (ed) *Language, counter-memory, practice: selected essays and interviews*. Ithaca: Cornell University Press, pp. 139–164.
Frankfort-Nachmias C & Nachmias D (1996) *Research methods in the social sciences*. New York, NY: St Martin's Press.
Gaakeer J (2005) "The art to find the mind's construction in the face". Lombroso's criminal anthropology and literature: the example of Zola, Dostoevsky, and Tolstoy. *Cardozo Law Review* 26(6): 2345–2377.
Garcia AC, Standlee AI, Bechkoff J & Cui Y (2009) Ethnographic approaches to the internet and computer-mediated communication. *Journal of Contemporary Ethnography* 38(1): 52–84.
Garraty JA (1957) The nature of biography. *The Centennial Review of Arts & Science* 1(2): 123–141.
Gelderman C (1996) Ghostly doubles: biographer and biographee. *The Antioch Review* 54(3): 328–335.
Goodey J (2000) Biographical lessons for criminology. *Theoretical Criminology* 4(4): 473–498.
Greene MT (2007) Writing scientific biography. *Journal of the History of Biology* 40(4): 727–759.
Groombridge N (2006) A cultured criminology: who are the zookeepers?. From: www.criminology.speedy.uk.net/A%20cultured%20criminology.pdf.
Gun Digest (2021) Interarms/high standard. From: https://gunvalues.gundigest.com/interarms-high-standard/.

Haggerty KD (2004) Ethics creep: governing social science research in the name of ethics. *Qualitative Sociology* 27(4): 391–414.
Hand M (2014) From cyberspace to the dataverse: trajectories in digital social research', big data?. In *Qualitative approaches to digital research (studies in qualitative methodology, volume 13)*. Emerald Group Publishing Limited, pp. 1–27. From www.emerald.com/insight/content/doi/10.1108/S1042-319220140000013002/full/pdf?title=from-cyberspace-to-the-dataverse-trajectories-in-digital-social-research.
Hanna P (2012) Using internet technologies (such as Skype) as a research medium: a research note. *Qualitative Research* 12(2): 239–242.
Head S (2016) Survival of the most memorable: Darwin's textual afterlife through rhetoric in On the Origin of Species. *Antae Journal* 3(2): 196–215.
Hedgecoe A (2014) A deviation from standard design? Clinical trials, research RECs, and the regulatory co-construction of organizational deviance. *Social Studies of Science* 44(1): 59–81.
Isikoff M (1986) Samuel Cummings. From: www.washingtonpost.com/archive/business/1986/12/22/samuel-cummings/1fc70837-3b0e-42d2-afb0-2f07c69a4dd3/.
James N & Busher H (2016) Online interviewing. In Silverman D (ed) *Qualitative research*. Thousand Oaks, CA: Sage, pp. 245–260.
Janghorban R, Roudsari RL & Taghipour A (2014) Skype interviewing: the new generation of online synchronous interview in qualitative research. *International Journal of Qualitative Studies on Health and Well-Being* 9(1): 1–3.
Kadar M (2014) Resisting holocaust memory: recuperating a compromised life. In Kadar M & Perreault J (eds) *Working memory: women and work in World War II*. Waterloo: Wilfrid Laurier UP, pp. 111–128.
Karskens A & Smits HW (2018) *Operatie laat niets in leven Het bizarre leven van oorlogsmisdadiger Guus Kouwenhoven*. Amsterdam: Volt.
Kessler R (2017) *The richest man in the world: the story of Adnan Khashoggi*. New York, NY: Hachette Book Group.
Klikushin M (2016) Freed Ukrainian pilot curses at Putin and walks in public fountain. From: http://observer.com/2016/05/freed-ukrainian-pilot-curses-at-putin-and-walks-in-public-fountain/.
Klockars CB (1974) *The professional fence*. New York, NY: Free Press.
Koelsch LE (2013) Reconceptualizing the member check interview. *International Journal of Qualitative Methods* 12(1): 168–179.
Kruse K (2016) What I learned from an international arms dealer. Available from: www.forbes.com/sites/kevinkruse/2016/09/12/what-i-learned-from-an-international-arms-dealer/?sh=1b929aeb54a0.
Lahiri I (2020) Community resilience is the way forward: critically reflective academic commentary. *Journal of Mental Health Education (Special Edition: COVID-19 and Mental Health)*: 1–7. From: https://jmhedu.org/wp-content/uploads/2020/06/6.pdf.
Litovkin N (2016) Moscow swaps Nadiya Savchenko for Russians captured in Ukraine. From: http://rbth.com/politics_and_society/2016/05/25/moscow-swaps-nadiya-savchenko-for-russians-captured-in-ukraine_597353.
Lombroso C, Gibson MS & Rafter NH (2006) *Criminal man: Cesare Lombroso translated and with a new introduction*. Durham: Duke University Press.
Lottin J (1912) *Quetelet; Statisticien et Sociologue*. Louvain: Institut Supérieur de Philosophie.
Mac Cormick D (1965) *Peddler of death. The life and times of Sir Basil Zaharoff*. New York, NY: Holt, Rinehart and Winston.

Marks H (1997) *Mr Nice*. New York, NY: Random House.
Marsh N (2002) Two sides of the same coin-the legal and illegal trade in small arms. *Brown Journal of World Affairs* 9: 217–228.
Martin M (2000) *Verstehen: the uses of understanding in the social sciences*. London: Transaction Publishers.
Maruna S & Matravers A (2007) N = 1: criminology and the person. *Theoretical Criminology* 11(4): 427–442.
McGarry R & Alker Z (2018) Using biography and autobiography in criminological (and victimological) research. In Francis P & Davies P (eds) *Doing criminological research*. London: Sage, pp. 363–384.
McGarry R & Walklate S (2015) *Victims: trauma, testimony and justice*. Oxon: Routledge.
Merrill B & West L (2009) *Using biographical methods in social research*. London: Sage.
Mills CW (2000 [1959]) *The sociological imagination*. Oxford: Oxford University Press.
Morrison A (2001) Entrepreneurs transcend time: a biographical analysis. *Management Decision* 39(9): 784–791.
Nilsen A & Brannen J (2013) Contextualising lives: the history-biography dynamic revisited. In Scott J & Nilsen A (eds) *C. Wright Mills and the sociological imagination. Contemporary perspectives*. London: Edward Elgar, pp. 88–104.
Nissenbaum H (2004) Privacy as contextual integrity. *Washington Law Review* 79(3): 101–139.
Nordstrom C (2000) Shadows and sovereigns. *Theory, Culture &* Society 17: 35–54.
O'Neill M, Robert B & Sparkes A (2015) *Advances in biographical methods: creative applications*. Abingdon: Routledge.
O'Neill M & Seal L (2012) *Transgressive imaginations: crime, deviance and culture*. Basingstoke: Palgrave Macmillan.
OCCRP (2010) Viktor Anatolyevich Bout. From: www.reportingproject.net/people ofinterest/profil.php?profil=1.
Peeters H (2002) *Gerrit de Stotteraar: biografie van een boef*. Amsterdam: De Bezige Bij.
Piacentini L (2005) Cultural talk and other intimate acquaintances with Russian prisons. *Crime, Media, Culture* 1(2): 189–208.
Potter M (2012) *Outlaws Inc*. London: Pan Books.
Presdee M (2004) The story of crime: biography and the excavation of transgression. In Ferrell J, Hayward K, Morrison W & Presdee M (eds) *Cultural criminology unleashed*. London: Greenhouse Press, pp. 41–48.
Presser L & Sandberg S (2019) Narrative criminology as critical criminology. *Critical Criminology* 27(1): 131–143.
Punzo VA & Meara NM (1993) The virtues of a psychology of personal morality. *Journal of Theoretical and Philosophical Psychology* 13(1): 25–39.
Quinn A (2016) Russia will release pilot Nadiya Savchenko if US releases world number one arms dealer Viktor Bout. From: www.telegraph.co.uk/news/2016/03/30/russia-will-release-pilot-nadiya-savchenko-if-us-releases-world/.
Raab J & Milward HB (2003) Dark networks as problems. *Journal of Public Administration Research and Theory: J-PART* 13(4): 413–439.
Ragnedda M (2018) Conceptualizing digital capital. *Telematics and Informatics* 35(8): 2366–2375.
Reiner R (2007) Neophilia or back to basics?: policing research and the seductions of crime control. *Policing and Society* 17(1): 89–101.
Roberts B (2002) *Biographical research*. Buckingham: Open University Press.

Rock P (2005) Chronocentrism and British criminology. *The British Journal of Sociology* 56(3): 473–491.
Rosenthal G & Fischer-Rosenthal W (2004) The analysis of narrative-biographical. In Flick U, Von Kardoff E & Steinke I (eds) *A companion to qualitative research.* London: Sage, pp. 259–265.
Saleh-Hanna V (2020) Colonialism, crime, and social control. In *Oxford research encyclopedia of criminology and criminal justice.* From: https://oxfordre.com/criminology/view/10.1093/acrefore/9780190264079.001.0001/acrefore-9780190264079-e-650.
Schrooten M (2012) Moving ethnography online: researching Brazilian migrants' online togetherness. *Ethnic and Racial Studies* 35(10): 1794–1809.
Scott D (2018) The politics and ethics of criminological research. In Davies P & Francis P (eds) *Doing criminological research.* London: Sage, pp. 137–160.
Shaw CR (2013 [1930]) *The jack-roller: a delinquent boy's own story*. Chicago: University of Chicago Press.
Singh JJ, Iglesias O & Batista-Foguet JM (2012) Does having an ethical brand matter? The influence of consumer perceived ethicality on trust, affect and loyalty. *Journal of Business Ethics* 111(4): 541–549.
Sklar J (2020) 'Zoom fatigue' is taxing the brain. Here's why that happens. From: www.nationalgeographic.com/science/2020/04/coronavirus-zoom-fatigue-is-taxing-the-brain-here-is-why-that-happens/.
Sluys K (2016) *Herman Bianchi en zijn levenslange strijd voor gerechtigheid.* Amsterdam: Uitgeverij Bas Lubberhuizen.
Stewart K & Williams M (2005) Researching online populations: the use of online focus groups for social research. *Qualitative Research* 5(4): 395–416.
Sutherland EH (1937) *The professional thief.* Chicago, IL: The University of Chicago Press.
Tamboukou M (2013) A Foucauldian approach to narratives. In Andrews M, Squire C & Tamboukou M (eds) *Doing narrative research.* London: Sage, pp. 88–107.
The Economist (2008) The illegal weapons trade: suited and booted. Available from: www.economist.com/node/10853742.
Thomson D, Bzdel L, Golden-Biddle K, Reay T & Estabrooks CA (2005) Central questions of anonymization: a case study of secondary use of qualitative data. *Forum Qualitative Sozialforschung/Forum: Qualitative Social Research* 6(1): 1–18.
Tierney J (2010) *Criminology: theory and context*. Harlow: Pearson Education.
Uden G (1968) *A dictionary of chivalry*. New York, NY: Crowell Company.
Van Amerongen M (1968) *De roerige wereld van Pistolen Paul.* Amsterdam: De Bezige Bij.
Van Gemert F (2011) *Van prison gang tot tbs; Biografie van een gewelddadig man.* Meppel: Just Publishers.
Van Gemert F (2015a) *Straat krediet; Biografie van Said Bensellam.* Meppel: Just Publishers.
Van Gemert F (2015b) Life history and biographies in criminology. In Copes H & Miller MJ (eds) *The Routledge handbook of qualitative criminology*. London: Routledge, pp. 74–87.
Van Gemert F (2015c) Biografie en Levensverhaal. In Decorte T & Zaitch D (eds) *Kwalitatieve methoden en technieken in de criminologie*. Leuven: Uitgeverij Acco, pp. 349–378.

Van Gemert F & Van Swaaningen R (2012) Boevenbiografie; Inleiding op dit themanummer. *Tijdschrift over Cultuur en Criminaliteit* 2(3): 3–16.

Warren Everett C (1966) *Jeremy Bentham*. New York, NY: Dell Publishing Company.

Weber M (1980[1922]) *Wirtschaft und Gesellschaft: Grundriß der Verstehenden Soziologie*. Tübingen: Mohr Siebeck.

Weil JR (2011 [1948]) *"Yellow Kid'" Weil: the autobiography of America's Master Swindler*. Edinburgh: AK Press.

Weinberg S (1992) *Telling the untold story: how investigative reporters are changing the craft of biography*. Columbia, MO: University of Missouri Press.

Weiner T (1998) Samuel Cummings, 71, trader in weapons on a grand scale. From: www.nytimes.com/1998/05/05/world/samuel-cummings-71-trader-in-weapons-on-a-grand-scale.html.

Weiser B & Moynihan C (2012) Conduit to arms sting, a star witness apologizes for his crimes. From: www.nytimes.com/2012/05/24/nyregion/andrew-smulian-star-witness-against-viktor-bout-gets-5-years-in-prison.html?_r=0.

Wiederhold BK (2020) Connecting through technology during the coronavirus disease 2019 pandemic: avoiding "Zoom Fatigue". *Cyberpsychology, Behaviour, and Social Networking* 23(7): 437–438.

Winlow S & Measham F (2017) Doing the right thing: some notes on the control of research in British criminology. In Cowburn M, Gelsthorpe L & Wahidin A (eds) *Research ethics in criminology. Dilemmas, issues and solutions*. London: Routledge, pp. 204–219.

Young J (2016) Voodoo criminology and the numbers game. In Ferrell J, Hayward K, Morrison W & Presdee M (eds) *Cultural criminology unleashed*. London: Routledge, pp. 27–42.

Zaitch D (2002) *Trafficking cocaine: Colombian drug entrepreneurs in the Netherlands*. The Hague: Kluwer Law International.

3 A troubled childhood

His parents, siblings and lack of friends

> Okay, you go on. "Child and teenage years". [...] I don't know how relevant that is to the arms industry [...] I guess what you're trying to get to is: how can a normal person go into the arms trade?
>
> (Constantine)

Telling someone's life story starts by delving into the past, beginning at the very first memories. At first, Constantine did not understand why it would matter but then soon started to realise why it is biographically crucial to share his very early past with the public. In the quote above, it becomes clear that by talking about his childhood and the role of his parents and siblings in it, he assumed I wanted to know about the 'normal life' he was born into and raised from, ipso facto, declaring arms dealing is abnormal. What becomes clear from it as well is that regarding childhood, it is considered the most 'normal' and 'neutral' time of our lives. This chapter will cover Constantine's most vivid memory, looking at how he was as a child and in what kind of environment he grew up in. Also, the chapter shall focus on his parents and siblings, and relatives (even pets are included!). Moreover, the chapter will discuss school, interaction with peers and teachers, who his role models were when he was a child, and things like what his favourite spot was to 'hang out'. On top of that, the chapter will go into his dreams and goals before he started to work, and what differences he thinks there are in growing up today from when he was growing up. In answering questions relating to his childhood and teenage years, the chapter will aim to retrieve an understanding of how his younger years have shaped him.

3.1 His father, Richard

> My father was Catholic, my mother was Protestant. Well [...] the both of them, are of XXXX descent. At that time Catholics and Protestants intermingling, was certainly something not looked on in favour. [...] It was not done, but they did it. [Did it influence] my religious experiences as a child? [...] My mother, alright, she was christened from a Protestant

DOI: 10.4324/9781315148236-4

family. My father was Catholic from a Catholic family, but neither of them had any deep religious beliefs. My mother is an atheist, or so, she claims, my father doesn't. I think he is agnostic. He never says. If I see them now, or you know when I go over and see them sometimes it's [...] We'd already made the arrangements to meet each other or they'd come and pick me up at the airport in XXXX. They'd always be: "Oh, hello! How are you?". Very, very distant. [...] Shake hands. Not a hug! "Men don't hug", haha! Except, men only hug women. Men don't hug men [according to my father]. My mother is very much still, shall we say, not so much now. She used to be under his thumb. [...] I can remember, as a child, I remember now, terrible, terrible fights between the both them in the kitchen. The table and the chair flew around the place, haha! This is funny, because I actually mentioned this to my mother who couldn't remember anything about it. I was in one of the primary schools. I don't really remember who told me and I don't remember. All I remember is somebody had mentioned the words "tits" to me at school, as in women's breasts. Tits yeah? It's normally used every day, and in an everyday world today. At that time, MY GOD, it was a terrible word. So I got home and I got off the school bus, and inside. So incredibly HAPPY to be able to give my new knowledge to my mother, and I pointed at her breasts. She was standing by the fire, warming her arse against the fire probably, because it was cold. I pointed at her breasts and said: "I know what these are" [my mother replied]: "Oh what?", I said: "Tits!". And she hit me SO hard I flew from the kitchen and beat my head on the stairs going up. It was like maybe 5, or 6 meters. I cut my head open. I remember there was blood all over the place. And she was screaming "Don't you ever say words like that! Don't ever say words like that again! Who told you that?". I said: "Kids at school". [She replied]: "That's a bad word". I'm like come on, you know? What?? Many, many years afterwards, I said to her: "Do you remember?" [She replied]: "No I don't remember that", and I thought: well, how fucking convenient.

When we started to talk about his childhood, Constantine made clear it was bringing back 'really bad memories', as the one in the above. Although he emphasised that he was happy just having a roof over his head and food to eat, he said then he did not have a very happy childhood. In the 1950s, Constantine was born into a catholic family, with highly gendered male and female roles associated with from the 1950s to the 1970s (cf. Black & Pemberton 2017; Hague & Wilson 1996; Honch 2012; Young 1999). Richard, his father, was away mostly, while his mother was bringing up him and at the time, his two other brothers, with the youngest being still very young. At the time, bringing children up was tough, he imagined, and he also explained that his parents never really had any experience, otherwise he would not have turned out the way he is now, and the same goes for his younger brother, the youngest of the family. With conviction he believes he 'was the experiment on how to bring a child up. It wasn't "Do what I do", but "Do as I say, or else"'. Especially his father kept a tight rein on the family, especially on Constantine.

It is not strange that therefore his first, most vivid memory was of his father: 'There are many VIVID memories. Pffff, my father never being at home [...] because he was always at work [...] He got shaped by his job, yeah, for sure, for sure'. As a family, they lived on an army base. Right after the Second World War, his father was conscripted into the air force. When he was demobilised and his national service was over, he worked on a pig farm, Constantine remembers, after which his father worked for the Ministry of Defence police, which was the air force police, and later on amalgamated into the Ministry of Defence police. His father was an air force policeman, 'which was the ministry of the defence. Basically he was a security guard; he was in charge of other security guards working for the ministry of defence'. The military background of his father influenced his brother, Arthur, 'following father's footsteps!', something Constantine would never have done. Several times Constantine told me the only time his father was there and thus the only moments he could remember ever seeing him was when 'he either had his slipper in his hand to beat us! Or there was a lot of shouting and fighting and arguing going on in the house', between his parents.

Only on Sundays, his father would be at home and he would take Constantine and the other children out for a walk.

> It was myself and the other four and we'd all be in line, behind my father who'd be marching like a fucking drill sergeant. We would be behind him in a row like the mother duck with her ducklings. We'd go for this walk and we'd be out an hour, and we'd come back, and he'd go on off to bed and lie down. He'd say, that was on a Sunday: "Do your homework". Those were the only words that we'd hear from him. After the meal he took us for a walk, which was [...] I mean we didn't stop anywhere, we didn't play. It was just walk march, walk march. It was very, very regimented, military.

His father disciplined him often for which Constantine disrespected him and felt like he was an experiment, to which Constantine seems to tie up his identity: an outsider within his family, a black sheep who was always beaten and took beatings for his siblings. He blamed that kind of abuse to his father being in the army.

> We had two bunkbeds in one room, for the 4 boys. Then my sister had her own room, when she was obviously older. First of all she was with my parents in their room, as a baby, and then we moved to another house on the same air force base, which was bigger, and she had her own bedroom. Anyway, we were 4 boys, in the same room, 4 young kids, obviously. You know kids? You can't keep quiet, yeah? Screaming, shouting, jumping around on the bed, one thing led to another. There was a [...] whenever my father was at home, there was always a slipper hanging next to the door.

> One slipper, hanging next to our bed room door. If […] after the "lights out" [strict voice], it was like being in the army, basically: "Lights out". If there was any noise after that, he would come out, grab the slipper, and beat the 4 of us. I mean, BEAT the 4 of us. […] Yeah, it's pretty horrific, but […] like I said […] I hold no grudges, now, because I realise that my father AND my mother had no experience bringing up children, apart from the fact the way THEY were brought up, which was, well, I am assuming this, yeah? Having talked with my mother […] my father won't talk about it, anything, he is old […] Very closed, no feelings, very cold. But I had some talks with my mother and she has often said: "Well, you know, this is how we were brought up". I said: "Didn't ever think that it was wrong?" [my mother said]: "Oh no, look at us, we turned out alright". I'm like: "DID YOU??" haha, yeah? So, I mean like […] and she said: "Yeah we got 6 children and 5 of them turned out alright". That was me being the one that didn't turn out alright, yeah? Because I was the experiment. They learned from their mistakes with me how to bring the others up. Like I said, if you look at my youngest brother [Paul], he is […] I would imagine […] one of the […] he is the best of the experimentations haha. As each child came along they differed their way, they saw their experiences that they ruined with me, and they said: "We got to change that if we're going to have another child". So they would gradually change their way of bringing up children. Obviously, they were obviously set in their ways from the way THEY were brought up as children. So obviously when they saw the road I took in my life as a young child, and the way I reacted to certain things, which they didn't like, they realised: "Well we can't do that with the other one because he'll go down that road as well, so that wouldn't be good". With each child they would change their way of bringing up that child . So you know, they learned, which is what life is about. I just wished I hadn't been born the first one haha. I was the one who was supposed to set an example to the others: "You're the oldest, you have to set an example!", I will never forget those words [of my father] "You're the oldest, YOU'RE THE OLDEST!" **BAM!** [being hit]. Oh God, yeah, we got the hell beaten out of us with a slipper, with a belt, with whatever he could get hold of.

The beating and extreme disciplining of Constantine by his father made him feel as if he was never loved.

> When he was there, there was never any relationship between myself and my father. There were never any feelings of love, as far as I am concerned. And as far as I am concerned there was never any [love] towards me! There was never any shown. […] Because it was all […] Everything was REGIMENTED. It was like: "Do this! Do that! Have you done this, yes? Okay do that". "Don't argue". Very, very few words that ever came out

> of his mouth. When they did come out they were mostly negative, and aggressive.

Despite the abuse by his father and how he experienced that as a child, Constantine has tried and still tries to understand his father.

> I can understand [...] NOW [...] with [...] my brain [...] I can understand the reasons why. Doesn't mean to say I can understand the reasons here inside [my father's heart]. [...] I can understand why the situation was as it was. I can understand that obviously my father had a lot of stress with kids, bringing up the kids. He'd obviously had a rough life as a child himself, otherwise he wouldn't have brought us up the way he did. [...] I know that his father served in the War and lost one leg. I can still remember him. I know that his mother wasn't there. I never met her, my grandmother, from his side. I know that his sister had a bastard child from an American soldier. this was never talked about [...] so I can imagine that he had some rough times as a child as well, which is the only reasonable explanation that I have [...] is why he brought us up the way he did, and why he WAS and still is the way he is. You can't get close to the man. It is just not possible. I've never seen any emotional reaction from him, whatsoever, apart from anger. I can talk about this now, it doesn't [...] I've gone past the "why did you do this"-stage. I've gone passed it. I don't blame them. [...] Because there is no point in thinking about it. Doesn't change anything. Doesn't change the fact that they brought me up the way they did or the way they brought my brothers and sister up the way they did. It doesn't change anything. It doesn't do anything to go back and try and dwell on the past, because you can't change it! You can understand it, and that's all you can do. I can't change the situations or the feeling that I had at that time. It's just not possible, so I have to say: "Okay that's the past, it happened as it did". I just put all the bad memories in [...] I got lots of little boxes in my head, yeah? And all the bad memories, I have put them in a little box, close them up and throw the key away, so. That's the way I am, that's my self-protection unit.

Next to trying to understand his upbringing from his father's point of view and life experiences, he also thinks that not only the beating but also that he was allowed to own a gun in his younger years – a pivotal moment for Constantine – turned him at a very early age already into a grown-up. In fact, Constantine thinks his father wanted to try and make an adult man out of him *because* of letting him have an air pistol.

> I guess he was trying to make a man out of me [...] you know? [...] I don't remember how old I was at the time. I think 10, possibly 11. [...] I was very young and I had an air-pistol. I was like "I got an air-pistol, yeah!" I was

> really, really over the moon! In fact, I got it as a Christmas present. Yep! I think I got it for Christmas. I remember my brother saying: "I want one, I want one!" and I said: "No you can't have it". My mother saying: "You can take turns with Constantine's. It's Constantine's but he will let you shoot with it". So I'd take my younger brother and teach him how to shoot. I hardly knew it myself, I'd seen it on the films yes, so I knew basically how to do it. But one other thing with my mother, the other experience, that's right. My father was away, as usual, and she took myself and my brother to the local cinema, to go and see a film, it was called "Born Free". It's about Elsa the lion. I don't know, you'll have to look it up. Google "Born Free" with Elsa the lion. You can see what it's about. That was one experience, or rather one memory, that I remember at that stage in life, for me, was […] a lot of my memories became […] tumbled up, when I look back at them now. They're just basically flashes of well pictures, basically, pictures being flashed in front of my inner eye of memories, like that one with the cinema. Now, if we hadn't been talking, it probably never would've come up.

Next to giving his father credits for turning him into a man by the ritual of allowing him gun ownership, Constantine blames his father and his disciplining for making him aggressive.

> My father was very abusive and you're not wrong there, and I'm not going to correct you. When he put the kids to bed, the only thing I remember, my brother told me about this, and I certainly remember this, he was right, because obviously I've been back to the [home country] since I've been here and met up with my next brother, and the whole family in fact. […] Okay, my father's now what, 85, 87 years old? My mother's 83, 84, they're getting on. There's no point in throwing abuse at them now for what they did when we were younger. No point in it. But I remember my brother saying to me: "Do you remember when we used to go to bed and dad used to hang the slipper over the door and saying: 'I don't want to hear any noise'" […] Oh yeah […] I said: "I remember". The times I got beaten with that, that and the belt […] We had a slipper on the door. […] [I]t made me the way I am. It made me the person […] well, it contributed to the way that I am now, I'm sure of it. You don't go through something like that without it having any effect on you. […] If I get into a situation I don't like I would become aggressive, because I think that was beaten into me at a very young age, that the answer to a problem in many cases is violence. I can see now that it's wrong, but it took me many, many years of being able to make up mind that it was wrong. 10 years, 15 years […] I mean, there were times when I was younger, in the University, we would go out on a Friday night to the pub and everybody would be getting wrecked or drunk, because the next day was a Sunday, there was no school, no classes. We'd usually end up in a fight in the middle of the

> street in XXXX. Somebody would say something wrong and it wouldn't take much from to pop. Poing! [...] It hasn't completely gone. There are still occasions now if somebody says something that I don't agree with, I have to fight my inclinations to resort to beating their heads against the wall and say: "You're talking shit".

It happened that Constantine would get into a conflict with his father occasionally.

> It was basically just me until I turned around and thumped him once. I hit my father, I hit my father, because I think he was on about something with my mother, something about the food and he picked up a chair and threw it at her, so I jumped in between them and then I hit him. My mother turned around and said: "GET OUT!!!" So, I protected her and they ended up kicking me out the door for a while. [...] I was at boarding school and I was at home on holiday, I must have been around 14, 14,5. I was [...] don't look at me now. I used to have muscles haha, this is unfortunately the chemo [...] no [...] I hit him and he went down. He went down like a ton of shit. My mother screamed at me. The only thing he did, was get up and hold his jaw and turned away from me. There was so much that had probably built up inside me that it was just a release. It was just a way of getting my own back.

As a young child, he never really dealt with the violent behaviour of his father. He just felt he had to get over it and deal with it in his own way. His family or friends never told him the way he was treated was a form of abuse. At the same time, he did not complain and there were not any social workers that would come around. He was left on his own.

> I just did it my way. I would go out, I'd go to the pub, the local village pub, I'd go into the off-license and buy a bottle of beer or a pint of beer and sit down and get drunk. That was how I dealt with it. I never told anyone about it. Which was something I had to deal with myself. My brother, the next one down from me, he knew what was going on. [...] Even to this day he [...] I mean we sit and talk about things that happened a long time ago [...] he would just say "It was how it was", and I'd just say "Yeah it was how it was and I dealt with it in my way". [...] I mean, parents of that age had been brought up basically in the same way. They were brought up to be seen and not heard and that was the way that we were brought up as well. You'll be seen and not heard.

All this together, the violence, the prohibition on everything Constantine ever wanted to do and the overall memory of his father make him disrespect his father to this day.

I don't respect him now either. I never knew my father. I can't say I know who my father was. I can't say I know his character. I said to my mother once "You know I don't know dad". She said: "Well I never knew my father either". I'm like "Well, you know, that's not an answer". He's too old for me to sit down now and have a deep conversation with him because he's a little bit "dotters" and he would never […] and even if he did remember, he would NEVER admit to remembering the things that he's done when he was younger. […] I'm not going to ask. The only thing I might do is tell him I forgive him. That's about the only thing I might do. Yeah, that'll give me some sort of closure. […] It never seems to be the right moment [to ask and talk with him]. When I […] I don't see them very often and they're getting older and older and I'd certainly wouldn't want to open up a can of worms by saying "I forgive you for beating the shit out of me as a young kid", because he would turn around and say "That was the only way I could bring you up and you also did a lot of shit". You'd just open up a can of worms. I think it is just best, as far as I'm concerned, and probably for him as well, just to let it ride […] I know in my heart of hearts that I've forgiven him. That's all that counts. He couldn't do anything. He was in a rut of a life. He had kids every two years, 6 of 'm. He was in a shitty job until he got promoted, and promoted and promoted. He was hardly ever home, so, he was under a lot of stress as well. I mean I could find a thousand and one reasons for the way he acted. Doesn't mean to say I excuse him for it, but I can understand it. […] There's physical abuse and there's mental abuse. It's two kinds of abuse. […] There would always be, if my father was away, and we've done something at home, my mother would always use the threat of "Wait until you're father gets home and I will tell him what you've done!". We would be shaking in our boots for 2 weeks until he would get back and then she would not SAY anything, so to me that's mental abuse haha yeah […] So […] I don't think that I can blame my parents for anything. They did the best they could with the tools that were available to them. The fact they may have fucked up my life is neither here nor there. I think personally they are quite proud of me now, and what I've done with my life. The fact that I sell guns doesn't bother them one little bit. The only thing they said to me […] I said to my mother once "What do you want from your children?", she said: "The only thing we ever wanted for all of you is that you're happy". So, I mean, where do you begin a conversation with that? You can't. "Are you happy?", well I said "Yes, I am". I have the feeling that they are […] they feel guilty about certain things in the past, because I only have to make a telephone call and say "I need some money", and they will say "How much do you need?". I remember once, I was short a €1000 or something, and rang 'm up, "Do you have […]?", and they replied "Yes of course. we will send it to you tomorrow by Western Union or by MoneyGram". It's not the first time that's happened. So maybe they do feel in some way a certain amount of guilt. I don't know. It doesn't really worry me. [...] They're not going to 'buy it off', maybe if it makes THEM feel better, I don't know, maybe they think "The least we can do is support him now that he's older when we couldn't do it when he was younger" sort of thing. I don't know Yarin, I really have no idea. It's something that's not really worth getting into as far as I'm concerned, because you can never find a concrete answer. You can't say definitely "THAT is [...] 1 and 1 makes 2". In this case 1 and 1 makes 11.

Although he disrespects his father, and regarding his overall feelings towards his parents and how they raised him, Constantine does sense he has taken over qualities of his father he does not like, such as being emotionally distant.

> I'm cold. I've been let down in my life so many times. What's to say? I wear 1001 patches on my heart haha. You know what I mean? So, I've become which I didn't want to become and that is, basically, perhaps, a mirror image of my father in some way. [...] Bitter in the fact that he also, obviously, didn't or couldn't show his emotions. I mean, obviously I've got more emotions for people that I know, as opposed to people that I don't know.

Still, he explains it did make him stronger today and made him think about how he wants to treat people, in particular those who are close to him.

> I decided I was not going to treat people that were close to me the same way I was treated as a child. All my brothers have done the same and my sister as well. [...] I mean I let these three [stepsons of mine], that are here, basically, do what they want. They're young men now. There's nothing I can tell them. The oldest is now 34, never mind the fact that he's still studying in university haha! He's the way he is. He's a very, very intelligent clever young man, of 34 years old that is still studying fine arts in XXXX, in the university, but that's his business, not mine.

During the final interview, I asked him if it was difficult for him to bring back his childhood memories about his father.

> Yeah, the abusive father. This is something that I've pushed over my shoulder for many, many years, like [...] it's just not [...] it's just not worth even reflecting on, because the poor old guy is 86, this coming Wednesday on the XX [...] yeah, 86, yeah, it's not worth reflecting on. He will never change. He's probably forgotten now what he has done, and if he hasn't well you know, it's his problem, not mine. I wasted enough years of my life wondering why [...] and I decided a long, long time ago it's just not worth even thinking about it. [...] Like I said, I told you in one of the interviews I can say, honestly, in my heart of hearts, that I've forgiven him

> and just haven't told it to his face yet and I wouldn't anyway, because he's going to turn around and say "What's to forgive?". That would just bring everything [...] pfff [...] exploding again, so fuck it. It's just not worthwhile. [...] Not if I apologise [...] if I told him that I forgive him [...] he would say "What's to forgive?" [...] that would just blow up everything again, because I would have to explain to him what he did. He'd say [...] well [...] this is just too much! It's just too much [...] it would be a massive [...] just for me [...] would be [...] I can imagine [...] quite traumatic for him as well [...] to have that thrown back at him again because he would have probably got it not just from me [...] I'm sure that my brothers have already told him, that they remember how he used to treat us. As far as I'm concerned, the story is over. It's a chapter that's gone by and it's just not worth digging up. I buried it a long time ago. [...] Of course it's still [...] I won't say it bothers me. It still hurts me the fact that somebody could do that to their own children. Especially since I got the beatings for things that my siblings had done, yeah so [...] comes with the territory.

There was a time where Constantine confronted his father with how the Constantine was raised by him.

> When I was still a rebel haha! 30 years ago? Possibly more? [...] Because I wanted to get my own back at him [...] I wanted basically, I guess, to hurt him for what he has done to me, for the hurt he'd given me. Revenge is sweet and its best served cold, so they say. Like I said, it's just not worth it. It really is just not worth it. [...] I guess. Time mellows, not only wine, haha it mellows also human nature. I guess [...] I mellowed. Apart from that, I got other things [...] I got more important things in my head, like how to make the next buck. [...] I don't want to confront my father. Those times are over. It's like I said [...] It's just not worth the effort. I expect I may well regret in my heart of hearts, not ever saying anything. I wouldn't know how to say it without hurting the old guy. So, it's just not worth it. [...] This is it [...] you just sort of say "Fuck it, it's not worth it". It's just not worth it. It's not worth hurting somebody just for your own satisfaction or ego. What are you going to achieve? What are you going to achieve by doing it, apart from hurting somebody? Nothing. Okay, so you're going to get that little bit of weight of your heart "I said, thank God, I said it". Well, you know [...] some things are best left unsaid and left undone. You just can't do everything you want to do, especially not to members of the family. [...] You can't choose your relations. You can choose your friends but you can't choose your relations. Whether you like it or not, whether you like the way they are or are not, they're still your relations, they're still family. If you don't respect that, well then you just might not be part of the family. [...] Blood is thicker than water. [...] There's really nothing you can do about it, it's just the way it is and you

> have to take [...] sort of [...] dig a hole, put it in there, and just bury it and say "Okay, it's gone", forget about it. There's nothing you can do.

Interestingly, Constantine, in a way, protects his father from himself, whereas his father did not do so. Actually, Richard seemed to have needed Constantine to establish his strict father role. Constantine does not need retribution as a 'just punishment' for his father for being abusive; meaning, he does not need his father's suffering for his own good. Constantine realises his father does not have anybody else who would confront him with his poor parenting, and therefore Constantine said:

> He's a lonely old man. [...] Why should I injure him on purpose? Because if [...] I know myself, if I bring the subject up, it's going to injure him. [...] There was a time when I would've thrown it in his face. With pleasure I would have thrown it in his face. It's just not worth it now. Why should I hurt him now after all those years? It's just not worth it. Some things are best left unsaid and undone. [...] The old guy will die and that will be the end of it. Then there's no point in it. There's just no point in saying anything to him. He may have another heart attack and I would hate to be the one responsible for giving it to him. That would kill my mother. It would turn the rest of the family against me, so, I washed my hands of the whole affair. I'm just going to say "Okay, it hurts, it still hurts, and I don't want to think about it". End of story, basically.

3.2 His mother, Victoria

His mother Victoria, compared to his father Richard, took up a different role in his childhood.

> The tortoise's name I think was Rich, same name as my father haha! I called him Rich. [...] That's right, my mother bought [Rich] for me, that's right. [...] Oh God this is another experience now, but I will [...] She said: "This is a tortoise". I said: "Oh wow is it for me?" She said: "Yes, what are you going to call it". I said: "Rich!" She said: "Are you sure?" I said: "Yes". So my father got home and I said [to him]: "Look I've got Rich here". He said: "What??" [angry] haha. I just remember all this. Another time I [...] after Rich had been cut to a 1000 pieces by this lawn mowing machine, by this tractor with a lawn mowing machine, I remember afterwards having hamsters. I had a hamster, that's right. [...] I was upstairs having a bath and I remember my mother screaming, calling for my father. I got out of the bath and I was like, hush, into the bedroom and sent to bed, and then in the morning my mother came to me and said: "The cat ate your hamsters" haha! The cat got into the box and killed both of them. [...] Dinky the cat. Dinky, Dinky, he was a bugger, well, he was a cat. I mean,

> cats kill mice. This was a large mouse. So my mother said: "I'll buy you another one", I said: "I don't want another one" haha, not giving any more [hamsters] to this damn cat.

During the interviews, Constantine displayed more sympathy towards her parenting than his father's. Her role was one of a service hatch due to the fear she had herself of his father Richard. That role makes Constantine respect her.

> She was bringing up the kids, trying to keep these two uncontrollable brats [my brother and me] out of trouble, with my father [being] away, and I always remember the words [from my mother]: "I will tell your father when he gets home". We knew the chances of him coming home. She probably had forgotten about it by then, unless it was something really bad.

Constantine explained she was a stay-at-home mom when she was having and raising children. 'She was either pregnant or she was looking after young kids', he said. Later in life, she had a couple of part-time jobs and she studied to become a veterinarian. She enjoyed working with hunting hounds and looking after them as a kennel maid. She also worked as kennel maid at one of the army stations, meaning, she too had an occupation within the military. Constantine emphasised a difference between his father and mother in that regard. 'My mother was not *in* the [army]. […] Just a civilian who managed to find a job at one of the [army] stations looking after the dogs, police dogs. […] She was very animal friendly'. During fox hunting, she was the whipper-in, according to Constantine, a respected, higher position for person to be in charge of all the hounds. There was a sense of pride in how he said it.

> I remember going with her once [to a fox hunt]. I must have been in my early teens. Don't ask me which year because I have no idea, because this is long in the past, and like I said, it's put up here and locked away. […] I remember all these guys and ladies, gents and ladies sitting on their large horses. My mother [had] these riding breaches and boots on and she was there with the whip cracking the dogs on. It was the first time in my life. This guy came around with a silver tray, with white gloves, with sherry. And he gave one to all the riders, and then he came around to my mother and he gave her one. He looked at me and said: "Would young Sir like a sherry?" […] It must have been before I was shoved off to boarding school. […] So I said: "Yes I will have one please". And my mother looked at me with a smile on her face and said: "Go on". […] When I think about it now, it was an incredible experience. That was the one and only positive I remember from my late, or rather early pubescent years. […] Out of 12 years [of bad memories], that's a pretty good memory.

Although he has been more sympathetic and respectful towards his mother, still, most of his memories of her were that of her being passive, if not too passive, towards Richard. For example, she had to do something that went against her own love for dogs, only because Richard wanted to discipline Constantine and his brothers and sister.

> I do remember one Sunday. There was actually a roast leg of lamb that went onto the kitchen in the table. The next thing I remember was my mother screaming, my father shouting, and he was chasing the dog along the road. The dog had jumped on the table, taken the leg of lamb and disappeared, and he was WHOOP, gone. So they caught the dog in the end obviously, but we didn't have any lamb that day. The next day, it was a week day, and I heard my mother and father discussing about the dog. It was told to us the dog would be put down because it was 'sick'. My brother didn't like the idea of this at all [...] so [...] my father was leaving on the Monday, that's right, he left it to my mother to take the dog to the vet to be put down. He said: "I'm leaving when I come back I don't want to see the dog". Very nice guy [sarcasm]. So I talked with my brother: "Let's run away", like kids "Let's run away and take the dog with us. I'm not having them kill the dog". So we agreed, basically he was [...] I influenced him, I was the oldest, so I influenced him. So we got up at 2 o'clock in the morning, snuck down into the kitchen, I took my air pistol and we took some food out of the fridge, took the dog and started walking. I had no idea where we were going, I just didn't want that dog being put down. Anyway, we were walking on the road, it was like 3am, and there were cars going by, little country road, and a truck stopped: "Where are you guys going this time of night?". I said: "We're going to go and see our aunt in XXXX" some bullshit story. Anyway, he drove off, and afterwards the police came. Obviously he told the police there are two young kids walking on the road, in the middle of the night, with their dog, so the police came and picked us up. They asked us what was going on. We told them in the end. They took us back home and nobody had noticed we had gone. [Police officer instructs]: "I want you to go upstairs and wake your mother while we wait here". I said: "Now we will go in, there's no need for you to wake her". Like I didn't want [...] I could imagine the hell that would break loose if she [...] when she told my father. He said: "No, no, no, you have to wake her and tell her we are here". I said: "I'm not waking her". So he went upstairs, I showed them where her bedroom was, and he knocked on the door and she got up. When my father left he always left her a small truncheon. That's the stick that the policemen have. She came out, she opened the door with the stick in her hand, I still remember that. She asked what was going on. We got sent off to bed and obviously, the police talked with her and the next morning [she said]: "Wait until I tell your father what you've been doing!" [...] Afterwards nothing happened because of my father, so I think that, if I remember correctly, I don't

> know […] I got beaten so many times, I just don't remember. But I think that nothing happened. After that, things started to change a little bit, from what I can remember, but my mother was like a very, very quiet little mouse. She never said very much. […] The dog got put down in the end anyway, we were told that it had distemper. That it was sick from the mother, and that it was given to all the puppies, and that was the reason why it had to be put down. I didn't believe it, I believe it was the fact that it stole the Sunday [lamb] joint, and then my father didn't want it around anymore. […] I saw that, from my opinion, it was wrong for that dog to be killed just because it's stolen something. It may well have been that the dog was sick, I don't know. I was a kid, yeah? But for me that experience was like "Oh you're not going to kill my dog". I mean, the dog got killed anyway, so it didn't really make any difference what we did. I mean, afterwards we got another one, so. I don't know, whether the dog was sick or not, because we did get another dog.

Only very sporadically Victoria would speak up to Richard, sometimes trying to protect her children, Constantine thinks. Still, that protection never really was effective in his eyes. There was one memory specifically he shared, also one in which he told me about his possession of his first gun and that he felt betrayed by his mother.

> [My father] was away once and we'd gone off into the woods for a […] weekend or a holiday, I don't remember. Certainly would not have been during school times. I had an air pistol which I was told not to take out of the house. I was only allowed to shoot in the garden, because we had quite a large garden. But we went into the woods, […] that was the first pistol I ever had, it was an air pistol. A Webley .22 was a pistol with breach top, like you could put a little lead pellet in. Anyway, we went into the woods and there were big fat pigeons in the trees, so I thought: "We're gonna have those buggers to eat". So I took a shot at them and killed 2 and we took them home, and I gave them to my mother and she said: "I'm not cleaning them, you can clean them". So my brother and I cleaned them and she cooked them in the oven. My father came home and said: "Oh this is nice, where did you buy those from?". She said: "I didn't, the boys shot them". [He replied]: "What??" So we got another beating for it. I mean, FREE FOOD, and we got beating for it, so […] haha. There never seemed to be anything we could do right. My mother was […] whatever my father was […] I would say he was a ehm […] When he was in the house nobody said anything […] including my mother, yeah […] I only ever once remember […] I mean they were obviously fights that I can't remember […] between my mother and father, but I remember one time I was up in bed and I heard a big argument going on, downstairs […] so […] I went and I crawled down the stairs, and I could see the table being turned over and a chair flying through the air and I just, I just […] sat there

> in horror. Then I went back up to bed, and I thought [...] I don't know what I thought at the moment. I don't know what I thought [...] it was a pretty, pretty horrific experience. That was sort of the impressions that I have from those years, with my mother. [...] I remember when my brother and I were off on one of our walkabouts, we found a bird under a tree, we thought it was a hawk, a peregrine falcon, or something like this, a bird of prey. So we took it home, yeah? Course mother said: "Oh you have to put it back". I said: "Well you know [...]". [She replied]: "You can't bring that here. it's too late now anyway, it will probably die because you've taken it away. You should have left it there". So anyway, we put it in a box, and we fed it cat food with a straw. It turned out to be a big eagle. A big owl, sorry, not an eagle, [but] an owl. This thing grew and grew and grew and grew. And we built in the back garden, my brother and I, a long [...] I think with the help of my next brother in line, Matthew, I'm not sure [...] we built a big bird cage. Like I don't know, like maybe 4x4m with wire around it, some trees in there and put this owl in there. Well she was the one basically who stood up for us when my father said it [the owl] had to go and she said; "No" and she put her foot down, yeah? [...] I think it was [the only time], if I remember correctly. I mean there may have been other times, but like I said, it's getting on for 60 years ago now. It's difficult to remember.

As with his father, Constantine has difficulties still today talking with his mother about his childhood and his relation with her and his father back then. According to him, his mother was and remains to be 'a timid little grey mouse, who probably was in a situation that she didn't very much like'. He thinks that if they would have been in today's day and age, they probably would have even been divorced.

> But it is how it is, as I said last time. [...] What's water under the bridge is water under the bridge. I've not had the opportunity to talk with my mother about these subjects and I don't think I ever would, because if I accused my father in front of my mother or if I said to my mother "Yeah I remember the bad times that you had when I was younger", etc. etc., arguments, tables flying, chairs flying, she would probably deny it. [...] I've tried talking about certain subjects that have been close to me and so like, "Oh do you remember the time when [...]..." and like I said last time when I said, when I came home from school and I pointed out her breasts and said: "I know what these are", like the proud little son yeah? I got hit so hard I flew about 3 meters, split my head open, yeah? So, I wasn't [...] so you know I mean [...] I'd mention that to my mother once. [She replied]: "Oh I can't remember that", I said: "Yeah, you did it" and I [...] [She replied]: "Nope" you know? So it's basically blacked out and they have like [...] [They would say]: "Oh that was such a long time ago, and why dig up the bad past?" It's a waste of time, and a waste of my energy. So I just scrub over it, and move on, yeah? Only thing you can do.

3.3 His brothers Arthur, Matthew, Samuel, Paul and sister Josy

Constantine had fond memories of his siblings. Still, he admitted to have felt like a bully most of the time and less so a protector of his younger brothers and sister. He is the oldest. His first memory of one of his siblings was regarding his oldest brother Arthur, and it was military-related.

> We were [with] six children. [...] The first vivid memory was of, let me think, good God, being on some [army] base in the middle of nowhere, with my brother [Arthur], lying on the side of the runway, the grass side of the runway, and watching the planes land. That's quite the first vivid memory that I can think of. We'd lie there right next to the runway, we shouldn't have been there, but you know [...] kids. Our house was like 150m away. So we'd get out of the house after school and we'd go to the runway, and lie on the side of the runway, and watch the planes touch down.

As they were not allowed to do much as a child

> we were basically left to our own imaginations. [...] To run riot, let's put it that way. [...] I don't remember exactly where, it was another XXXX camp somewhere. [Arthur] and I had gone off on our bikes, I mean, we had gone into somebody's orchard. We'd gone off on our own pushbikes into an orchard and we'd fill up the saddlebags on the bikes with apples, and pears, and other fruit. Obviously stolen from this orchard! You know, like young kids do: "It's an orchard!" so what it's a tree with fruit on, we liked the fruit, we took it. Totally, I won't say immoral, [but] amoral! Not knowing, basically, the difference [as a kid]. We got back home and the sun had come down, and we were told to be back home before the sun goes down. So we got back, weren't too bothered, we had lights on our bikes, but there was the old man, my old man, waiting there for me [...] or us [...] and we got the slipper haha. We got the hell knocked out of us! One for being out after we were told to be out, and two for taking the fruit of the local farmers and being forced to eat it all.

Later on, in his teenage years, Arthur and he would go out on pub crawls and visit nightclubs together and get in fights. It was the brother he wanted to be with the most. Sharing sometimes violent encounters with their father makes Constantine feel closest to Arthur, which continues to be the case today.

> He used to be a police inspector. [...] He's retired now, he's got his pension. Now he is a photographer. Well that's what he wants to be. He likes to think he is haha. No, he's okay. He's actually very good. [...] My brother said to me once: "I really envy you". I said: "Why??" He said: "You lead such an exciting life. Me, I get up in the morning. I got my company. Me, I get up in the morning, I go to work, I come home, sit with my

> wife", actually, his girlfriend, he's divorced, "we go out, we go to eat, I go to sleep, I get up in the morning". He said: "You don't do anything of that!", I said: "How do you know???" I said: "Just because this is my [social media] profile, and this and this and this, it doesn't mean to say that I lead an exciting life". I said: "Sometimes I think you know, I would have preferred to have lived a somewhat more normal life", shall we say. He said: "No, no, no!! If only I could change with you", I said: "Be very careful of what you wish for" haha.

At the end of writing this biography, Constantine told me about a post Arthur shared on social media that week. Arthur posted a picture, reminiscing about how their local river used to be their swimming pool when they just hit puberty. A river that almost took his young life if it had not been for his elder brother Constantine. He warned that weirs, or sluice gates, are not the place to jump into when you cannot swim. With some nostalgia, Constantine talked about how he saved Arthur's life at that time. He completely forgot about it, but it brought back many fond memories he has of Arthur.

About his other siblings and their role in his childhood, at the time, it was not all too positive: 'I never had any relationship with ANY of my siblings. From the time I was sent off to boarding school, I was considered the black sheep of the family'. Yet that has changed in his life later on.

> Most of them I get along with quite well. There's one that we don't get along [with], we don't get on very well. Matthew, well he had as a child, which I didn't know at the time until very much later on, as a child he had meningitis […] It's a sickness of the brain, it affects the brain and he had this a child. Now why he had it? I don't know but he was the only child born at home as well, so it might have had something to do with that, or whatever. He is very black or white in his world. There's nothing grey in-between, and we had some very, very, myself and Arthur, we would taunt him as a child. He was the third one, it was his tough shit now haha. We, myself and Arthur, we would want to go out and lie by the side of the runway, and watch the planes. [Matthew] was the youngest, and he couldn't do the things we did, and he was always getting in the way, so we would taunt him until he'd go away. Now he never forgave me or my brother for these things, and I guess this wormed a way inside him. […] I remember, at one Christmas party as children, the [army] had a Christmas party for all the kids. Santa Claus was there giving presents out so he called out our names, Constantine, Arthur, Matthew, he spelled the name wrong. He didn't go up and collect his present, and afterwards, he said: "Where's mine?" He said: "Well, what's your name?". He said: "Matthew". "Oh not Maddy?" [Santa replied]. "No, Matthew", [Matthew replied]. "Well, have this anyway" [Santa replied]. It was a doll! […] He would run off crying, and when I think about it now, we were real bastards to him. He never ever, forgave us for that and it must have

> wormed away at him for so long, for years and years we never spoke. Ever! It's only recently that we've met.

For his father's 80th birthday, Constantine visited his parents, where he saw Matthew again. It led to Matthew confronting him with the bullying when they were younger. During the birthday, he told me, the following happened:

> I pulled him over to one side, I said: "Look this is stupid, tell me what is wrong?". [Matthew replied]: "You don't remember?" I said: "I don't remember what I've done to you, tell me". So then he told me. I said: "Jesus Christ, that's years and years ago, we were kids!". He said: "Yeah that's what mum told me as well". I said: "Why do you still let this eat away at you?" He said: "Because I can't forget it". I said: "Well, you know, you are going to have to. You know, I am sorry, forgive me please". My other brother said the same. […] He's now on better terms with my brother than he is with me, because we don't see each other often, well we hardly see each other at all. We'd talk a couple of times on the phone, but that's it.

Constantine had a much closer relationship with his next brothers down, Samuel and Paul. He does not have a clear explanation for why that was the case exactly. Still, he indicated the poor relationship between Matthew and him back then had something to do with the meningitis Matthew had as a child.

> [It] made him a little bit […] I wouldn't say slow, or nuts, but very, very fixed in his ways! Black! Or white, nothing grey. […] Meningitis did something to his brain. […] He's just very set in his stupid ignorant ways. So you could never have an intelligent discussion with him because even if you knew you were right, and you tried convincing him, and if you'd say "It is black" and he said it was white, you wouldn't be able to convince him that it was black. […] You have to take him as he is, or not take him at all. That's how he is. […] He works for the [military police] as well now. He carries a gun all the time. He has a Heckler & Koch MP5 which he carries at work. Before that he used to have a […] he is a dog handler. […] I don't think he feels anything to be quite honest. He's never said anything to me [about being an arms dealer].

His sister Josy, when they were younger, Constantine explained, was a daddy's girl. She was very spoilt, whereas he and the others were not.

> She was always treated, in my opinion, I don't know what the others would say, but she was always treated differently to how the boys were treated. She was always given a lot more attention. […] She as a girl got more attention than the boys did. I didn't get any attention at all. The only attention I got was when my father got home and found out we'd

> done some shit and he would beat the hell out of me. […] Basically, she was quite a Tom boy, but anyway, by the time she was old enough to. […] I was 13 and got sent off to boarding school, no 12 actually […] I was 12 years old, so she would have been 4. I don't really remember that much about it. She certainly doesn't remember much about me.

She was too young to remember how Constantine was treated by his father, whereas he was sure his father never treated his sister as violently. Still, he does not (want to) remember much about her, and only through sporadic stories from his brothers he would know about her. They got in touch when she was grown up. She came to visit him and his wife when he was living abroad. There was never any real connection between Constantine and her, but compared to the other siblings, she does have the most outspoken opinion about his work as an arms dealer.

> '[She said:] "How could you DO that?". I said: "What do you mean?". [She replied]: "How can you sell guns?". [I said]: "Like selling sweets. People come in and they buy them. They ask for them, and I sell them". […] [She replied]: "Yeah but […] Don't you realise they're going to go and kill somebody". I said: "No, not necessarily". [She replied]: "Yeah but how can you do that, you're giving someone a piece of equipment to kill somebody". I said: "Car dealers do it all the time!" […]. [I asked her]: "You got a driving licence". [She replied]: "Yes". I said: "Well you got a license to kill". She said: "That's not the same". I said: "Well, I am sorry, but you know, it is to me". Apart from that I am not selling them illegally. If I was selling them illegally, I would say: "Yes, you're absolutely right, naughty me, slap on the wrist, mustn't do it again". But I am not, I am licensed by [my] government. She said: "But that's not the same! You're still selling weapons of war. You're selling things to kill people". [I said]: "I don't tell them […] I don't put the bullet […] I don't a gun to the head and say 'Go and kill people with my guns'". […] She disagrees with the fact that anybody could do it. She is extremely, what shall we say, she is a tree hugger. Let's put it that way, give the trees some love.

3.4 No friends

Whereas there were some meaningful bonds he had with some of his siblings, Constantine never mentioned a lot about having childhood friends, besides his brother Arthur being a friend to him. He blames his father for this.

> I was 13 years old, I was shoved off to boarding school, because we were back in [my home country] at the time my father had moved again. Because between the ages of 5 and 11, I had been to about 15 or 20 different primary schools. Because [my father] was always working to get promoted and with each promotion he would be moved to another air

> force base. So we would move around. As soon as I'd get settled in in one school, I'd be taken out, we'd move somewhere else. So for me it wasn't a very stabilising time in my youth. [...] I never had any friends. I had acquaintances. I never had any friends. There was only one friend that I ever had. Well maybe two or three. I had one friend when I was quite young. One of the other kids at school, because his father also worked in the air force. On the base, and after we became friends and the family was uprooted, we moved to another area! I mean that was quite a hurtful. Not understandable. I remember [...] God this is bringing back some memories [...] I remember being extremely disappointed and upset about having to move and move away from my friend. I think the feeling hurt me that much that I never, ever got close to anybody again. Then I won't get hurt, yeah I am sure. I don't have friends now.

Being an 'army kid' did not allow him to establish strong ties with others outside of his family, which explains why he became close with his brother Arthur as a friend. He simply gave up trying to make friends.

> I must have thought to myself: "Alright, there is not much point in making friends with anybody". [...] There was nobody in my age that I was really interested in, hanging around with, I mean they were just kids. As far as I was concerned, I wanted to do something. When I was a kid, it was like: "I can't wait until I'm 11 and then I can go to the secondary school" or "I can't wait until I'm 16, and then I can go in the pub". "I can't wait until I'm 18, cause then I can go". It was that sort of thing. So I was like, you know, I wanted to be independent. "Leave me alone and let me get on with my life", sort of thing. It was just the way I was at the time. There were no other children in the area of my age. The ones in the village were all 'numtees' anyway, they were real kids. They were younger than their age.

Once he hit puberty and left the village, he tried to look for 'acquaintances' and he in particular enjoyed hanging out with older acquaintances. Also in his later life, that had an impact, because having no friends became normal to him.

> I don't let people get that close to me [...] then you'll end up getting hurt one way or another. Because up until now I have never met anybody who isn't two faced. Everybody has an agenda, everybody will, in my opinion, everybody will use whatever you say against you. In one way or another, I mean I have business acquaintances, I have business friends. I have friends, who I would call friends, but not the kind that I would go around and knock on their door three o'clock in the morning and saying: "Take me in, I need a place to sleep for tonight". No, I'd go and find myself a hotel somewhere and then cry alone in the room haha!

3.5 Conclusion

Like any of us, in his childhood, Constantine has been civilised into society (cf. Elias 2000) and (his) upbringing reveals something about larger social forces that play out in everyday upbringing of children; in fact, childhood is anything but an innocent era of someone. It is by definition political (Jenkins 1998), which became clear from Constantine's childhood, family and friends, and the problematic relationship he had with his parents, specifically his father. There was strict, military-like family governance in his house that heavily influenced his upbringing, reflecting the time of age, the 1950s and 1960s, he was born and raised in (cf. Brownfield 2010; Honch 2012). His brother Arthur was a beacon of light, may it be dimmed light, and who supported him. It altogether turned him into a closed-off person, he thinks. To end this chapter, it is interesting what Constantine had to say to me when I asked him whether he would not have wanted a different childhood. Although quite offended, he did answer.

> Yarin, that's a stupid question, I'm sorry. They do say there's no such thing as stupid questions, only stupid answers, but this is a hypothetical question, and you'll only get a hypothetical answer which is not really gonna be anything apart from words. [...] Who doesn't wish for a better childhood?! [...] Is there anybody that doesn't wish for a better childhood? Could have been more presents, could have been more loving? I could have been the only child and had love and attention smothered on me instead of it being spread about six children. It was how it was. You can't say "I wish". Go and find a fucking fairy godmother if you wanna wish for something, doesn't work otherwise. What was, is what was, you can't change the past. You can only change the now and possibly the next hour or two because you don't know when you're gonna die. You cannot change the past. There's very, very little point in reflecting on the past unless of course you want to do a psycho-analysis which I've done many times, so where's the fucking time? Because reflecting on the past, trying to make you understand how you react today, doesn't work in my opinion, maybe not all of it, certainly not the key parts of who you are. Obviously your character is developed by the time you're five, you already have a character. [...] I think that just reflecting on the past will only cloud your future. It will make you question yourself and your ideas and how you feel. [...] What's wrong with it? It stops you from moving forward if you're always thinking about the past. "Why am I like I am? That's because the way I was brought up", end of story. That's it for me. It doesn't go any further than that, Yarin, because there is no point in chasing down the rabbit into the rabbit hole, you would just lose yourself. You start thinking about the past, you'll only consider the past, you won't consider the now, you won't consider the future. I am who I am, because that's what happened to me. Be it good or be it bad, or whatever,

> that's what happened, this is who I am. A leopard cannot change its spots. My character is my character. I like to think that I'm a straight shooter, I don't mean with a gun, I mean me personally. I like to think that I don't intentionally hurt people. I like to think that I'm a good guy, that I will go out of my way trying to help somebody if I can, but if I can't, I won't hurt them. That's how I am, yeah, so.

Now, going from his childhood to teenage years, higher education and early career, he still had to come to terms with the pressures of his father's reign of family-level war doctrine. Yet the process of being formed and shaped into that straight shooter had commenced in his early childhood. Still, before having fully accepted that born-out-of-war upbringing and reaping the benefits from it by becoming the man who he became and still is today, he first needed to rebel; an all too human rebellion taking place during his coming of (r)age, as Chapter 4 will go into.

References

Black L & Pemberton H (2017) *An affluent society?: Britain's post-war 'golden age' revisited*. London: Routledge.

Brownfield C (2010) *My nuclear family: a coming-of-age in America's twenty-first century military*. New York, NY: Knopf.

Elias N (2000) *The civilizing process: sociogenetic and psychogenetic investigations*. Hoboken, NJ: Wiley-Blackwell.

Hague G & Wilson C (1996) *The silenced pain: domestic violence, 1945–1970*. Bristol: Policy Press.

Honch M (2012) The military-industrial-suburban complex: the race for nuclear arms and nuclear families in Southern California. From: www.pugetsound.edu/files/resources/2012honch_hist400thesis.pdf.

Jenkins H (1998) *The children's culture reader*. New York, NY: NYU Press.

Young J (1999) *The exclusive society: social exclusion, crime and difference in late modernity*. London: Sage.

4 A coming of age and rage

Adolescence and early career

This chapter will explore his life from his middle adolescent years to his first job and following career. It will additionally explore his life as a student and his early career as a diving instructor and dog trainer, and his jobs in healthcare, counternarcotics, counterterrorism and, rather contradictorily, in counterproliferation of arms and ammunition.

4.1 From boarding school to university life (1979–1986)

As his parents did not manage to control him, he said, they put him into boarding school.

> There was no controlling me. I did what I wanted, because my father was never there, my mother could never control me. [...] I got in with some interesting people, on the streets. [...] At the time, there was a war going on [in my city]. [...] I was out all hours of the day and night when I wasn't at home.

The closing off from others and that he, in fact, preferred that over building relations with others, continued when Constantine was

> shoved off to boarding school at the age of 13. [...] I guess [my parents] thought it would be the stabilising effect in my life. Well, if they wanted that, they shouldn't have put me in [another country], they should have left me in [my home country], where we were. Because that's where [at the boarding school abroad] my life was, I would imagine, mostly, not stable. It's a part of your life that becomes most impressionable.

At boarding school, he felt like an outsider due to his nationality being different from the other teenagers there. Constantine explained it formed him, mostly because of the fact he felt the need to protect himself.

> I had the fun taken out of me a lot. The only way to stop that, obviously, was with my fists, which is what I did. I was always getting into trouble at

DOI: 10.4324/9781315148236-5

school, always beating other people up, or getting beaten up! […] I didn't stay there very long, I left […] Fuck, I ran away! […] I didn't like being there [at the boarding school]. […] EVERYTHING forms a child when they're growing up. I mean the sum of what we are today is the sum of our experiences. I wasn't always a nice guy. Many times I was a real bastard, yeah? I'm being quite serious. I used to be […] What did my father say once? "Too fast with my fists". […] I think I must have been about 15, 14, 15. […] That was when I was at boarding school. I remember being picked on by two kids at school. At the boarding school, there would be a lot of tables and then we would take turns. One on the table would be the server for everybody else. When it was my turn, I would get picked on. [The other kids would say]: "Go on get this, go on get that", and I never had time to sit down, and eat my own food, because I was running around for the others. In the end, I said: "No, go on get it yourself". When we went outside from the dining room, one guy grabbed me from behind and held me with my arms behind me. One guy started hitting me. So, I said: "You're real men, two against one". The guy that was hitting me, said: "Let him go", so he let me go, and the next thing I knew, without even realising it, I hit this guy in the face. His bottom teeth had gone through his top lip and his top teeth had gone through his bottom lip, his nose was broken. I only hit him once. He is lying on the ground, crying his eyes out. So I just walked to him and said: "Don't fuck with me, yeah?". That was the time I realised, that you can get somewhere by using violence. […] That was how I protected myself at that time.

He got disciplined for his behaviour and several other violent outbreaks.

I got put on detention for the weekend, cause you couldn't go home at weekends, you were only allowed like once a month to go home for weekends. I got put on detention which meant I couldn't go out, I couldn't do anything, and I remember I had to cut a football field with a pair of nail scissors. […] After that, that was the Saturday, on the Sunday, I had to paint the coal that was used to heat the school furnaces, I had to paint it white. Just what they called 'jankers' [military punishment] at the time. That was my experience at boarding school.

And that experience is one of, once more, military discipline, punishment and harshness, just the way it was during his early childhood. Having been sent off, led him to never return to his parents' house again.

After being in a boarding school, I was never, I never lived back at home. As such. I would be there for visits, very short visits. Because I couldn't stand my father, and he didn't particularly like me either. There was always an argument. When I went there, there was always an argument. Whether it be my choice of music, be it my choice of clothes, be it my

> choice of hairstyle, whatever I did was wrong. So in the end I just didn't go visiting. We drifted apart, I went my way, and they went theirs.

Right after boarding school, and before going to university, he lived on his own, but back in his home country's capital, nearby where he was raised, he

> didn't really know what I wanted to do, I just knew what I didn't want to do. Like a lot of people at that time, yeah, growing up in post-war [times] with post-war parents. I just knew what I didn't want to do. [I was] 18 years old, 17,5, 18 years old. I took my O-levels, my A-levels, and managed to scrape through on them. And then I was basically a bit of a bum around the town. I just didn't want to […] I didn't know what I wanted to do. So I'd go out, have a few beers, and generally, raise hell on the streets. […] At the time I wasn't living at home. […] I must have been 16 when I left home. 16, 16,5 because I left boarding school and I went straight to, well, I didn't go straight into university. I did a couple of small jobs round and round.

Boarding school for him was also the time when he experienced something so impactful for him, a life-turning event.

> I had an accident. This on the top [teeth] aren't mine, I was in a car when it got blown up. […] I was in the back of car, no […] I was in the front of a car actually in the passenger's seat when the car got blown up. It was in [my home country], silly games. Silly games at the time. […] Somebody kindly blew up our car when we were in it. […] Obviously someone who didn't like us. It's going back to the 70ies. […] I still have a piece of bullet in my leg. Not only did they blow the car up, well they did, apparently, they put a magnesium strip into the petrol tank. Then with two wires, they wired it up to the break-lights, so as soon as you'd put your foot on the breaks when the ignition was on, BOOM. So the car blew up like that, tipped over, I crawled out and someone shot at me.

I asked him whether and how being blown up and similar events influenced him.

> Yeah, for sure they did. […] It's pretty obvious, yeah, of course. Of course they did, I can't say they didn't. But I mean, I can't say […] If you said to me, "What exactly, what effects did it have on you?" I don't know. I would certainly think that at that age [19] it made an impression on me. It made an impression on me and two of my friends getting killed, and the other one losing one of his legs. I was very, very lucky. […] It gives you a totally different perspective on life, because one minute you sit, and talking to them, and the next minute you're covered in blood and guts. […] It makes me enjoy every second as best as I can, but it certainly doesn't give me any

> positive thoughts toward my fellow men, let's put it that way. Especially in situations like that.

It made him think about what he wanted to do with his life and thought about doing a university degree, but he did not know in what exactly. His father did know, however, as he eventually convinced Constantine to go to university to do a degree in IT.

> I got sick and tired of him NAGGING me. So in the end he wore me down, and I said: "Alright, for FUCK's sake", yeah? I did 5 years of it and I took a year out.

Despite that he rebelled against his father, he listened to him and followed his orders.

> My father said: "Okay, it's time you decided. You're going to go to school for computers. That's the industry of the future". I said: "I don't want to do that". I didn't really want to do anything. [His father said:] "You're gonna go and study computer science, in [my home country]".

It was at the end of the 1970s when he was pushed into doing an IT course.

> I wasn't really interested. I mean, I did it […] I went through uni, and I got my bachelors, and I remember […] haha, another vivid memory. The day of the award giving. Everybody was there in their black capes, and square hats, the mortar hats. We were given our certificates, and shook hands, "Thank you very much", etc., etc. So after we've thrown all of our hats up in the air, I said: "Okay, that's the end of that". […] I walked over to where [my parents] were, and there's my father with a big smile on his face. I said: "Are you happy now?" [My father said]: "Oh yes, I am so very proud of you, congratulations son!" It was always "son", I hate it. So I said: "Well here, you take this, and you shove it where the sun doesn't shine"[…] "Now I'm going to do what I want to do" haha. […] I could not, I could NOT, imagine myself EVER sitting in an office, from 9–5, and just doing boring things. To me, everything was boring at that time. Like "normality" […] to me, normality was boring.

He was not sure what he wanted, but he knew what he did not want.

> I didn't want to live a normal, routine life. […] and then going home to the white picket fence, a wife, and 1.5 children. That was never for me. So I decided to do the things that people don't do, become a little bit of an outsider. I've always been an outsider, always.

Like in boarding school, he felt like an outsider as a student. He never really liked his studies at university, although he thinks going to university in the time he did it still meant something compared to studying nowadays.

> I mean I remember when I took my MA, the first one, no, the first BSc I took. I was old, not just me, the university [as well]. […] That was the computer sciences. […] I mean, we were proud to have the BSc. It was something that you, something that […] it was not normal to accomplish. I did five years, because I took a year out. But, nowadays, every idiot has got an MA. It's true! I mean the garbage collectors, they'll be requesting from the garbage collectors "You got to have at least a bachelors or a masters to…" […] Come on, it's getting worse and worse. "You got to be technically minded to press this button and now about what's going to happen when you press it". I mean, for Christ's sake, you're emptying garbage cans, for God's sake.

Constantine never did anything with his degree in IT though, at least, not the way his father expected from him.

> I never worked in the computer industry, studied it, and afterwards I said: "Fuck I don't want to do this". So if somebody says: "Oh you got an MSc in Computer Science", yeah right. When I was at school, at college, at university, we had banks of computers about as big as your kitchen where we would feed them printed cards. That's the sort of thing, and if somebody would said to me now: "Can you programme?", [I would reply:] "Yeah, tell me how many holes you want in this piece of paper", then yeah I can probably do it. If somebody came to me and offered me a job in the computer industry, I'd say: "There's just no way". There's no way. In fact, sometimes I wonder why I even have those letters after my name because, you know, it's basically, the MSc and the BSc. I got the certificates and diplomas, but as for working with them, would be impossible.

For his master's degree, he specialised himself in security- and terrorism-related themes, which was in his early 20s.

> That was fulltime. I was in the army at the time but it was a, what shall we call it, a stage jump in the hierarchy so that I could go to another department that they wanted me to work in. I can't say too much about the time that I was in the army. I'm still covered under [a certain act that forbids sharing any military-related information]. So I can't really say much there. But one of the stipulations, and one of the prerequisites for me being able to work in that department was the fact that I had [a master's degree in

> security, terrorism and counter-terrorism] to which I took the course at [another university]. [...] During the [masters] [...] I was very much at that time interested in where these [paramilitary groups] got all their arms from, what made them radical, what made normal people want to go and shoot someone's knee-cap off. How they actually got into [...] Okay, one man's freedom fighter is another man's terrorist, or the other way around, you can call it. I can certainly see why they wanted to do what they wanted to do. I agree with what they did, but certainly not with the methods that they used.

Although he felt obliged to study security and (counter)terrorism in order to make a career, he shows here a deeper interest in humanity and violence. Still, despite having such an interest in human nature, university was not the ideal place for Constantine either, just like boarding school.

> I was in the university, I was studying, and I dropped out of the university for a year because I didn't want to work in this computer industry. Because you'd go out in the evening with other students, friends, from the university, and the only thing you talk about is bits, bytes and megabits, and gigabits, and the rest of the crap and I didn't want to do that because I could see [...] it was just like a one way road. Then it was all they had in their heads. To me, life should be, well that's what I thought at the time, and I still do, life should be varied. You know what they say? Variety is the spice of life. So I didn't want to do this [computing]. So I dropped out of university for a year and I decided to become a deep-sea diver, I wanted to do something out of the ordinary. I never wanted to do anything ORDINARY. I didn't want to do what other people did.

It was also during that time in university, he started to use drugs and his drinking increased enormously. He drank and used drugs almost on a daily basis.

> The alcohol, drugs, I mean who didn't experiment with drugs when they were in the university. Do you know anybody who didn't? No. I mean, you live in one of the countries in Europe that sells shit on every street corner, the Netherlands, go to Rotterdam, go to Holland, go to Amsterdam. [...] I smoked joints, dropped acid, I've done coke, but those were back in my days as a student. I think everybody in the university at the time. I was there smoking [weed], and acid as well, that was our weekends. We didn't go out partying in the pub yeah, we'd go tripping. It was the time, it was the eighties. End of the seventies, beginning of the eighties.

Due to experimenting with drugs, he became more interested in spirituality and different religions but different from how it was introduced to him during his childhood. It was an interest born out of a more drug-infused spirituality, as happens all too often at universities (cf. Stewart 2001). In a way, the manner in which he considered religion at university formed a type of resistance to how religion was enforced by his parents.

> I would imagine late teens when I was in university, experimenting with the various psychotropic substances that float around universities haha [...] LSD and hash, cannabis, the usual sort of stuff that floats around universities especially at that time and I think that especially the LSD put me into touch with a search for a cosmic world for want of a better word [...] I found myself reading the bible. [...] I found myself reading the bible after I've come down from a trip. [...] It was out of the wish for knowledge. The big question I always found myself asking when I was on a trip was "Why? Why are we here?", it's like having a conversation with yourself, yeah? "Why? Why what? Why are we here? Well I don't fucking know, well let's find out". Then you go into your head, it's difficult to explain unless somebody's actually doing a trip, I can imagine. You sort of go into your head and then you start to explore "There must be a bigger reason that we're put on this planet, on this world, on this earth, in this cosmos. Why?". This is what basically gave the kick to start [...] I won't say research, that's too dry, to start looking. I looked into all sorts of religions from Buddhism, Sikhism, Hinduism [...] the only one I haven't looked at and I'm certainly not going to, is Islam. Catholic church, okay, I went to church as a child. In fact, I was one of the bell ringers in the church. One of the choir boys as well. It didn't really interest me until I started experimenting with the psychotropic substances at university.

If anything, and regarding his studies at the university, doing drugs and getting genuinely interested in religion seems to be his true (academic) achievement, because he has never been proud of his university career. He did not consider the degrees he retrieved from it as big achievements, except for the MA.

> I mean there [are] achievements and [there are] achievements. There's professional achievements and then there's life's achievements. I prefer to think of my life as not just being a part of doing business. I prefer to think of my life as learning things. Interaction with other people, advancing my character defects, or rather getting rid of my character defects haha, not advancing them! But you know, that was the busiest and the best time for me [at university] as far as my professional life is concerned. [...] [My] biggest professional achievement [was] getting certified by a [prestigious board on counterterrorism abroad] as a [certified specialist in counterterrorism].

The reason why Constantine is critical of academia is because of the 'lifelessness' and 'fakeness' of it, he explained.

> I've seen so many academics that are only academics and they don't have a life. They haven't done anything. They haven't ever gone on a ship, or worked in a steel yard, or worked on a […] you know, something about they can say: "Ah! Yeah I did this! I made this! This for me is a life experience!"

Yet, when I told him I actually made something, that is to say that I wrote a book based on my PhD research (Eski 2016), he replied quite enthusiastically.

> You just finished a book?? You're […] really? Which one? Send me the title over in Skype and also the ISBN number. Is it in English?

Overall though, he finds that academics lack a sense of reality.

> You have to excuse me here. Unfortunately a lot of these people at these conferences are only liberal academics. They have no idea of the real world. A lot of them live in Lalaland where everybody is sitting around the campfire singing kumbaya. […] They only know the academic side of things. I told you about the argument I had with [a university professor]. I did an online course with them, terrorism. [A professor] was in charge of that course. He was a real idiot, you can't think like this academically. I said to him: "Unfortunately academics only know the academic side of things before anybody is allowed to write a book on an academic subject, especially in the field of terrorism. They should go and work in the field and THEN write the book", because otherwise they don't know jack shit about what they're writing. He didn't particularly like that haha […] I said to him: "I'm sorry but academics are not the be all end all to any subject, they only know the theory of things. They don't know jack shit about the practical side, unless you've done COIN operations, counter-insurgency operations, then you don't know what the fuck you're talking about". I said this in a live teleconference between myself and 350 other students who're doing the same course, and to the professor. He got quite upset haha but some of the students on the course, and a lot of them were, I won't call them my peers, but they also worked in the same areas that I have. I got some emails from them afterwards "At long last somebody who speaks their mind that is not only a loud mouth but also can back-up the words that he says". Finally somebody has got the balls to say how it is. I said to him: "How many books have you written?", he said: "I don't remember, 10, 15". I said: "All about terrorism?". I said, well, you know, "I'm sorry, they're a waste of space in the library. You don't know jack shit. […] You're only theory. Theory is not practice. If you want to talk to me about practice, then we can talk as much you like, you may be a doctor and have a PhD, but I also have a masters [specialised in (counter) terrorism and security], so don't tell me I don't know anything about the academic world of terrorism, because I've already fucking proved it.

> I also happen to have the practical knowledge as well which you don't. As far as I'm concerned, however, many books you may have written on the subject, you don't have the faintest fucking idea of what you're talking about, because it's only theory".

All in all, he is academically well trained, specialised through several master degrees and certificates, and he enjoys abstract thinking as well as empirical fact-finding, which is important for arms dealing. Still, he has always preferred applying knowledge and hands-on work more than academic work, as his career path after university clearly testifies to.

4.2 Training people and dogs (1986–1988)

> People ask me: "How many jobs have you done?". I say: "Well, you know you want me to start with the alphabet?"

Before he became an arms dealer, Constantine did several jobs, several of which he told about with fond memories. While looking for jobs during and after university, he

> was looking for excitement! Of course I was looking for excitement. Like I said, I want to do something that other people didn't do. I didn't wanna be just the kid next door. [...] I don't know [why] [...] I really don't know. I REALLY don't know. I've asked myself this question hundreds of times. Why was I like [...] Why was I the way I [...] Why WAS I the way I was? What brought [...] Why did I do this? And why [...] I'd ask myself these questions [...] A LOT of times [...] and I'll be quite honest, I don't know. And I'm just too lazy I think to possibly dig and find out. [...] I'm certainly not going to waste my time [doing that], I've got other things to do. I've got bills to pay, I've got a wife and family to look after. I got deals to make! [...] I'm not dumb. If I was dumb I wouldn't be doing what I was doing. [...] You have to understand, there are two types of people in this world, I think I told you this before. Those that live to work and those that work to live. [...] I work to LIVE!

It was during his first semester at university when he decided to quit and start as a deep-sea diver.

> "I can't do this anymore, fuck it", I said to the dean. I said: "Look, I want to take a year off. I got to get my head together. I don't know whether I want to continue doing this course". He was actually quite supportive of me, doing what I wanted to do, because, he said: "You're a bright student, you've got the capabilities to do this, but do you really want to?". He was basically [...] I thought he was very good actually. He was basically the one that gave me [...] I won't say the incentive [...] but he was very understanding of

> my need to be able to do this […] what I wanted to do. […] After a year my father got onto me about: "Not doing this, not doing that!"

Here, Constantine got understanding and support from an authority figure, something he never received from his father who did not agree with Constantine's career choice when he found out about it. Regarding deep sea diving and other future career plans, Constantine decided to continue to do what he wanted to do.

> I wanted to do something out of the ordinary. […] I became a deep sea diver and I worked on the oil rigs for a year. […] It's not so much heavy work. I was diving once. I did a three-day dive, that was the thing. When you're working on the platforms, we would be doing dives of three days, at the time at 180 meters because at the time there was no depth limits to the divers could go to. The Health and Safety Executive wasn't too worried about the diver or the threat to the health of the diver. These things weren't so much known at the time, because it was still very young days for the diving community. […] I was making good money as a diver! But it was something that you couldn't do for a long time. There was no future in it […] because your body is under pressure. We would do a dive for 3 days to 180 meters living in a diving bell. […] So you'd be underwater at 180 meters for 3 days. And you'd been working with Trimix, which was helium oxygen and nitrogen, or Heliox, which is helium and oxygen. 75–25 mix. It was something that you couldn't do for a long time because I'd seen older divers who had gotten bent basically from it. The recompression or decompression rates weren't held. It's called Caissons disease, which they call the bends. I'd seen older divers that had accidents, and I saw some of them would […] they weren't quite right in their head anymore. […] Looking back, I think it was a good experience. I enjoyed it very much but I'm glad I didn't continue. Because at the time there were no safety measures in place. Let me put it this way: there were safety measures in place that just weren't rigid enough.

He stopped his work as a deep-sea diver for a while to then become a social worker, on which more will be said in Section 4.3. Later on in his career, he picked the diving instructor job again, but only for a short while. This time it was from 2000 until 2002. He explained that you have to be a specific type of person to do dive and instruct diving. I was told I

> probably never would make a very good diver, a scuba diver, because intelligent people they don't have this touch to nature. I had this one guy, he was a college professor living in XXXX when I was teaching him how to dive, and he couldn't get over the fact that it was possible to breathe underwater. He couldn't get it in his head even though I explained to him exactly about the bottle of air and the regulator, and all the other stuff,

how deep you go which depends on how much air you've got in the tank. He could not get it into his head that it was possible to breathe underwater. For his first dive I put him in like a meter and a half, to two meters of water, so that he could stand up. The guy was about 2 meters 20. He got his head underwater and immediately started splattering, I mean he got the regulator in his mouth. I said to him: "You know your problem is you think too much! Think too much". He said: "But it's not normal to be able to breathe underwater". I said: "You're an idiot. You were swimming around in your mother's womb for 9 months".

The skill set he had was perfect for the job; nevertheless, he disliked diving instructing.

The only time I've ever felt like [I was not enjoying my job anymore] was when I was a diving instructor and I got pissed off with teaching people. [...] You can become a diving instructor, you don't have to work fulltime to become a diving instructor. I taught so many people, I used to really love diving, but now if I go for a dive, I go alone, because I don't want to have the responsibility having to look after people all the time when I'm underwater trying to enjoy myself. If I go to a dive centre on a holiday, they always ask me "Do you have your diving cards with you?" and I give a book with all my certificate cards in there. I say: "Yeah, take your pick". "Oh, can we use you as dive master on this dive and have the dive for nothing?", [I'd reply:] "No! I'm here on holiday. I don't WANT to look after your students". Which is for me always the same, whether I'm in the water with students or divers that are experienced, I still react as if I have to look out for them, which is to me stressful because it means I can't enjoy my own free time. And that's when I said: "God no, I don't want to educate anymore any of these people". [...] I'm not a teacher, I'm an educator. You get burnt out after a while, doing the same thing again and again and again and again.

What bothered him the most about the diving instructing was how he had to look after people, which was too demanding for him at the time. Another element of being a diving instructor and he could not deal with was management being too demanding. He truly detests being micromanaged.

This is not good, micromanagement is not good, because you're not left with any freedom to choose the way you want to educate people, which is not good. [...] Micromanagement is never any good, never, because it means you don't have control. You're the educator not the person doing the micromanaging. [....] I turned around and told [management] to fuck off. Had a couple of contracts that I had: "You have to do this and you have to do that, this has to be done this way, this has to be done that way", and I'm like: "You know, I got certifications in this shit, I know what I'm

> doing". "Yeah, but I'm your boss" [management would say]. I said: "That doesn't give you the right to tell me how to organise what I'm doing. It's the end result that counts. If you don't like that, do it your fucking self", and I walked out.

According to him, he never micromanaged people himself.

> No, I would never do that to somebody; it's cruelty in the first degree, because it means you don't have any trust in the person. It means to me that you're looking at his qualifications, and saying "You might have these qualifications but I don't recognise them" and that to me is cruel! You can't do it. It's like having a dog and giving them always the command 'sit', 'stand', 'sit', 'stand'. After a while the dog is going to turn around, and either bite you or just turn around and walk away.

Next to his diving instructing, for a long while, he trained dogs himself, much like what his mother used to do. It is something he still likes to do once and a while, but was never his core business though.

> I used to be dog trainer as well, but that's a while ago. I used to train dogs. You know, I have had loads of jobs. I've always been a dog trainer, I still do it now occasionally. If somebody comes to me and says: "I got a Doberman or a Rottweiler, or a German shepherd and I need training, can you do it?", "Yeah sure I can do it, I can come on the weekend". Book like 4 or 5 weekends one after another and fit the time in with my schedule. I'm a versatile diverse person. […] [I trained] in XXXX […] when I had my own Rottweiler, it was during the time I was working as a social worker. […] If people ask me to train their dogs, I will train them. […] I love dogs, I hate cats haha […] but people want me to train their dogs for protection, as protection dogs, which is what I do very well, I learnt from one of the best […] a German guy. […] He was a world renowned dog trainer, he still is. He spent 6 months in Germany training show dogs and then the other 6 months of the year he's either in Australia or Asia training people's guard dogs.

As with being a diving instructor, he stopped training dogs for a living at a certain point as the market was not fruitful enough, he discovered. It remained a hobby for him though.

> There's not enough dogs! Too many dog trainers. I use the word dog trainers in a very, very wide broad sense haha because as far as I'm concerned they're not dog trainers. They're idiots that put an electric collar around the dog. […] It's cruelty. I have had some of these dogs that have been trained by XXXX, come to me, and they're in a real mess. It takes months to get the mistakes out of them. It's very easy to make a

mistake with a dog, and after, it takes months, if ever you can get rid of it. [...] It's trust building and if the dog doesn't react to the trust, then unfortunately you have to use a somewhat harder route. The dog is a group animal and has to be treated when it's still in its natural environment where you have the hierarchy. You have the dogs altogether, and you are the boss. That's it, but that was the dog trainer. Like I said, I still do it if they want me to [...] I get paid for it, don't get me wrong, I don't do it for nothing. There's not much I do for nothing. If people want advice, I sell them my time, it's a bit like you, right, educator.

4.3 Taking care of people (1988–1996)

Keeping his dog training as a hobby on the side for extra income, he moved onto becoming a paramedic for a short while and after that, a social worker. We talked about why he thinks he wanted to work in a sector where he was made responsible for people's (mental) health and overall well-being, which is something he did not like about the diving instructing. Also, taking care of people is not quite in line with what arms dealers are usually associated with (cf. Edwards & Gill 2002). And that is exactly what he enjoyed about telling me about it: to be an outsider, also as an arms dealer who, in this case, takes care of people.

> I always have been an extreme person haha [...] You know that I'm also a qualified male nurse? [...] I am a qualified paramedic as well. There are so many pieces of my life, so many facets, that if we talked about all of them, we'd only be talking and you would never finish that fucking book. I can tell you that now. [...] I worked as a male nurse, I studied for 5 years, I passed my state exam in XXXX [...] This was before [the social work]. Started off working in old people's home, helping old people and then I decided, this was without any qualifications. I was just a helper. Then I decided I want to learn more, so we moved from XXXX to XXXX. This all can't go in the book [...] I got an allowance of the state of XXXX and went to train in [a clinic]. [...] I like helping people! I like helping people as much as possible. I can't stand to see people hurt. I don't like seeing people hurt. I like to see people healthy. I'm a natural born helper. Here again, you're going to say "How the fuck can an arms dealer say that?" [...] At that time it was what I wanted to do, at that time it was how I felt. At that time it was something that I had a NEED [...] to help people. I couldn't do it for life, because that fucked me up as well. Working in the ambulance is going out Friday nights, on the crash cruise, going out Friday night, Saturday night, picking up the dead bodies from the [highway] in between [two cities]. Yeah that's fucking great: "Which part was body bagged, which plastic bag does this head belong to?", "Oh I don't know, put it with that part of the guts over there". That will fuck you up more than selling arms. [...] You know, you get anaesthetised to

> it after a while, but it's like [...] I didn't want to become anaesthetised to it, because it took away [...] I feel that it made me [...] less human. To not feel disgusted by seeing guts of somebody pouring out of their stomach on the highway, wrapped around the safety bars, with the head lying over on the other side. This, I did every fucking weekend. Fridays and Saturday nights. Sometimes we'd go out and then we got somebody who got a busted leg or cut-up face, and [we] would transport them to the hospital. Most of the times though, it was after critical accidents. Well, we had to come and pick up the pieces. Then the fire brigade would be there and hose off the blood, and the guts, and the brain matter. That will fuck you up. That will fuck you up more than thinking about arms and bullets. That will really fuck you up. That would give you nightmares at night.

Still, he remained in healthcare and became a social worker

> because the opportunity was there, and it was also a well-paid job. Very well paid, because the state had said that for social workers, at the time, they were paying between 35 and 75 XXXX an hour.

I asked him whether he also became a social worker to help the helpless, as he was slightly helpless himself when he was younger, as he explained.

> No, I don't think you could even say that. There was nobody at school that would look into things like there is today. The infrastructure at the time for social nets just wasn't there. I don't know if it would have done any good. Even if there were, I certainly don't think that's the reason why I became a social worker. Social worker was just, well, maybe! Maybe, being honest, I can't say. I've never thought of it that way, perhaps subconsciously. Perhaps, I can't say now "Yeah that was the reason why I became a social worker", but that would be a lie. I don't know.

During his time as a social worker, he lived abroad. It was not his best part of his life and was actually 'a very stressful time for me and that's why I didn't do it for very long'. The combination of being an arms dealer and having been a social worker may have appeared rather contradictory to me, Constantine thought.

> I was a social worker for the XXXX courts in XXXX, which fits very well with arms dealing yeah haha. [...] It doesn't fit at all, it's the exact opposite. Helping people on the one hand. But these people were helpless. They were psychologically, physically or mentally not able to take care of their own affairs, so they were classed as wards of the court, psychologically or physically not able to take care of their own affairs. At the time, I was a professional social worker. I don't have qualifications as a social worker. [...] Normally this job was given to lawyers but then there was a

> change in the law that said they wanted people to have a more personal touch and not just be, what's the word in English anyway, in XXXX it would be "managed". So they choose people. I went for an interview to the social services. I met some people there, had a chat with them, and we spoke about what I had done in the past, what I thought about this job [and they asked me]: "Why do you want to do it?" and I said: "I think it'd be nice and interesting to work with crazies yeah". [...] I have very black humour Yarin, I have very black humour. [...] The guys that were in charge of that department in the social services department in XXXX, they thought I was obviously very good for the job, so [...] they said: "Okay". So I opened up a business with two others, with two other social workers, we opened an office. Every one of us had 40 clients, so I did that.

For the clients – 'I won't call them "customers", or "patients"', as he explained – under his supervision, he had to make sure that they could live as normal of a life as possible while living under governmental control.

> I had people that were gambling addicts, violence towards their family members because they'd spent all of their money and they wanted money from their parents. I had people that were psychotic. I had people that were old and decrepit, where the family had wanted to try and push the person out of the house to be able to have the house sold and put [that person] in an old people's home. [...] In some cases even family members are put as "supervisors", what is called the legal aspect, but the families were mostly, well, they had hidden agendas. So, it wasn't put to a family member, it was mostly put to people like us. [...] Obviously you don't come and see them every day. There's mostly paper work in going to see them. Sometimes [you] make sure that their health was okay. Make sure that if they're in an old people's home, for example, they weren't tied down to the bed. That the medication was proper. As far as medication was concerned, [we were] making sure that the doctor wasn't just giving them haloperidol, psychopharmaca, to keep them in a zombie state, talking to them, finding out what they wanted, whether they were lucid, whether the psychologists or the psychiatrist was correct at their diagnosis, it being Alzheimer's, or whether the person in question just being totally dehydrated that they were totally disorientated and couldn't make themselves understood. [Checking whether] they were lucid, because psychopharmaca will do that to a person, especially older people.

There was one client about whom he was professionally and, to an extent personally, more concerned about than others. It became clear he pitied her and it made him reflect on his social worker role as it being an extension of the state.

> I also had a case of one young woman who was psychologically fucked up yeah. I mean, she could run her life, but she was always having sex, and always getting pregnant. She was given to me. I know the reason afterwards why she was given to me. […] I arranged for her to have a 3 monthly injection, a contraceptive injection so that she couldn't get pregnant. She'd already had 3 children, who were adopted out. It was all by different men. She'd go out and would get drunk or stoned, end up getting screwed by the next person that was sitting next to her and she'd end up pregnant. Anyway, so I arranged for her to move out of her apartment, and she went into a home, basically, for people like her. Young people that couldn't look after themselves and all went well for quite some time. Then she stopped going to the doctor's to get her quarterly injection and I asked her why. She said: "I like having kids". I said: "You can't look after them. Apart from that, it's not good for your health. You're getting older, the risks are there. You're not mentally stable, the child could be born with mental instabilities. Could be born deformed, etc. etc.". So, in the end, I was forced into the position of asking the court to allow her to be sterilised. Against her will. This is why they gave it to a foreigner, because if they'd given it to a XXXX […] You know what [they] did in XXXX? They sterilised them all. So they didn't want to have to make the decision themselves. In fact, they waited, I waited, because I found out afterwards, that I could see where this was leading up to, and I thought: "Now I know why they gave her to me". I waited until there was no other way out. Then I made the application to the [court dealing with guardianship].

The situation with this particular patient made him feel horrible about himself.

> [I felt] pretty sick! You mean, how did it make me feel that I had to apply for sterilisation against this person's will? Or how did it make me feel that they'd given me this person, knowing full well that I would have to do in the end? […] I felt betrayed, for one thing. The fact that they done it without informing me in the beginning of where this would probably end up. I had a rough idea when I saw the case file. I was of two minds whether to take it or not. But I took it. For better or for worse, and I had to make the decision in the end whether to apply for it or not. In the end, I believed, and I still believe, that I made the right decision by applying for this, even against the wishes of the person themselves. It was obviously granted by the courts. It was granted. There was a whole psychological evaluation, psychiatrist evaluation, medical evaluation, drug history evaluation, pfff […] Morally I think I made the right decision, because it would not have been in the interest of this person to have more children. She was being used and abused by men. The child would not have been wanted by anybody. It would just have been another person that grew up inside the system. May well have been psychologically impacted by the fact, later on obviously, that he was a child of […] They may well have even been born

> psychologically disabled. These were all factors I had to evaluate. When the evaluation came back from the psychiatrists and the psychologists, and the doctors, and the courts, and the social security services, it was still my decision. I had to make the decision to apply. It was on me. I had to do it. There was nothing else I could do. So, as far as whether I thought I acted morally [...] I don't think I had any choice. I held it off as long as I possibly could. It was getting to the point [where] she was escaping from this home at night and going out and getting drunk, just going through this whole behaviour once again, which she really, really regretted afterwards, that she couldn't help herself. I said: "Look, if you don't take these monthly shots, then you don't leave me any option". I said: "You won't take the pill, you're too unreliable, which is why I arranged for you", because she was on the pill in the beginning, well, when she took it. If she didn't take it regularly, she didn't take it at the time she was supposed to, which is why it was arranged for the monthly shots for her. The doctor called me and said: "Mr Constantine, Ms So and So hasn't been in for her monthly shot". [I replied:] "Alright, thank you very much indeed". [The doctor:] "How long has she been out of the cycle sort of speak?". I said: "Three weeks", which would have meant that the whole cycle of treatment would had to start again. So, you know, for me morally there was nothing else that I could do. She had her tubes tied [sterilised] and that was the end of the story. [...] It was the hardest thing I ever had to do. Ever. It was the hardest thing I ever had to do. I had to [...] Pfooh [...] I had to decide over somebody's life, basically.

As much as he had internal struggles by being a social worker, it was a job he enjoyed. Nevertheless, due to extreme situations as the above, in the end, the job was taking its toll too much as he noticed his own mental health started to be affected by it.

> After a while it got a bit too much, psychologically. I remember I was taking people up to the psychiatric hospital, practically every day. These people were haha totally crazy, I mean, they were people that had not taken their medication for schizophrenia. There was another guy there, he was very, very famous, he was a client of mine. He was a very, very famous programmer for [an IT company]. He was completely flipped in his head and I had to take him up to the funny farm, yeah, which is the psychiatric hospital. I remember the head doctor there saying to me: "Oh Mr Constantine, we've always got a bed for you whenever you need one". [I replied]: "You're not getting me in here, don't worry about that", haha. Every time I heard that, I think: "This is getting too much, this is getting too close to me and see these human disasters every day, and getting right up close to it yeah, having to deal with these people, and basically see inside their heads and the problems that they got, and trying to help them with it. [...] It was too much in the end, so I just said: "Fuck it" and

> I said: "Okay, what I'm going to do now?" [...] I finished with that [social work], and I said: "No, that's enough for me".

His own mental health was affected owing to the high levels of stress he experienced at his work, which he had not experienced before, nor after.

> There was never the amount of stress and pressure that I had in that job, as opposed to anything else I had ever done. [...] That was the hardest job I've ever had. I'm not just talking from [...] I mean, there were some funny points as well obviously. There were things that I can laugh about now with different people. For me, she [the patient who had to take contraceptives] was [...] one of the hardest decisions that I ever had to make, and that was to apply for sterilisation against her will. Because she wouldn't have it voluntarily. I talked to her and talked to her and talked to her. I sat down with psychiatrists, sat down with the doctors, and sat down with other social workers to try to explain to each other [...] She just said: "No, I don't want it, I won't have it", and I was left with no other option.

I asked him if he realised how it sounds (to me) when he said he helped people from destroying themselves, given how arms dealers monetise on people using arms to willingly harm and destroy people, whether it is offensively or defensively.

> But they don't destroy themselves. [...] You seem to forget, I sell arms to legal governments. These arms for defence purposes, this is within the law. Of course, it's also within the law, written down in the Human Rights Declaration, yeah, the UN Declaration on Human Rights. Self-defence is an inherent right.

Overall, he looks back on his social work career with satisfaction, despite it did mentally break him. He is proud of the fact that unlike the people he helped as a social worker, he himself did not (let it) destroy himself.

> The mind-set was to get the job done. [...] I'm proud that I managed to help so many people. Obviously I didn't help them to get back into a normal life but I helped many from destroying themselves. [...] You have to know how to deal with these people. You have to be a little crazy yourself. [...] I was there for [...] how long did I do this job? I think 5 years altogether [...] no, less than 5 years. It may have been 3, 4 years. I was so fucked up in my head in the end I just couldn't do it anymore. Talking with crazies all day, every day, you know [...] and seeing the kind of social destruction that goes on in their minds and the way that certain problems [...] Because [...] most of them were crazy, apart from the old people.

4.4 Government consultancy (1998–2000)

After the social worker job, between 1996 and 1998, he 'did some private company consultancy involving SALW', after which he had several professions in semi-governmental service from 1998 until 2000. It was in 1996 he also had the pancreatic attack and eventually cancer, as section 8.4 of this book will look into more elaborately. The work comprised being a private consultant for various foreign governmental services and a security consultant to two different governments on illegal proliferation of arms, narcotics, human trafficking and terrorism. The exact role was consulting for counterproliferation of narcotics, human trafficking and arms, in an unofficial capability. He did that for 2.5 years in total and did so because of his keen interest in making money.

> I wasn't making enough money, I wanted bigger things out of my life. [...] I was offered a job there on a loan from a government agency. [...] It means I was a sort of a semi-government official, semi [...] I wasn't attached to the government but I was semi-attached. [...] It means I was working with another government on behalf of the government that I was a member of, or a citizen of, sorry, XXXX. [...] I spent most of the time in XXXX because that's where all the coke and all the whores come from going into Europe. [...] From Venezuela they come through into Curacao, from Curacao they go to Bonaire, from Bonaire. [...] I was working for, basically, a government agency. [...] You'll always find that when there's a lot of money involved, you will always find that [corruption] [...] also in XXXX yeah. I've seen some things a lot of people would not believe, like on mega-yachts.

The consultancy work was for him also a way to walk the straight and narrow.

> This was something I liked doing. It was exciting, adventurous, and so I did it. Obviously the money was quite good as well. [...] I could have become a total wreck, I'd probably ended up doing something stupid. Getting involved in either with drugs, or black arms, or well, anything. Because at that point in time I didn't give a shit about myself, I didn't give a shit about life. I just took things as they came. I said: "This has come to my way and if it's an opportunity to make the same money then I'm gonna do it". It was at that time that I said: "You can't do this, you will end up in a lot of shit if you get caught, it's not worth it". [...] It was the whole kaleidoscope of thoughts about what will happen if you do this and if it doesn't work out. You get caught, or if you don't get caught, and you keep doing it, sooner or later, you're gonna get caught, and you've ruined your life for what? So, I said: "I'm gonna do it, but I'm going to do things in a different way".

For certain actions that were undertaken, there was and still remains plausible deniability from everyone involved, also from him. Constantine could only talk further about his undercover consultancy work if I made sure specific details would be kept out of his story about a yacht. For him, it was a situation he will never forget.

> The one [most memorable case], the only one I can talk about there, but it's going to have to be [redacted] 'cause otherwise it's going to be a shit storm. No names, obviously, but there's details that can never come to light, that's the problem. One of the most interesting cases there was [...] I was working undercover for the counter-trafficking of narcotics in XXXX. There were boats that were taken-over, pirated, the owners had been killed and dumped overboard. There were also drug barons coming in from XXXX. Drugs had come in from XXXX and they had been loaded onto boats. I got in with some people who were well-connected with that circle. One of the funniest occasions that I had, well, not funny, but it was amusing to me. There was [...] a mega yacht, big, big, very expensive yacht. It's a yacht where there were mountains of cocaine. 100s of bottles of very expensive champagne, Don Perrion 1969, 1972, very, very good champagne. Nymphs, or nymphets, or whatever you want to call them, good-looking chicks running around half-naked, and you couldn't get a glass of water. If you wanted to drink, there was champagne and that was it. Champagne and coke [...] This was long after my social work. This was in the middle of the 1990ies, 1997, 1998. Yeah, it was one year I was there. 9 months, nearly 9 months. That was one of the things that stuck out in my memory, which was being on-board this vessel where there was [...] You couldn't get a glass of water. If you wanted to drink something, you drank champagne. [...] It was just a totally crazy situation. People running around stoned all over the place. I mean [...] Have you ever seen the film *Scarface* with Al Pacino? Well, you can remember him sitting in his office at the end [making a sniffing sound] snorting from this big mount of coke. That's basically what it was like. There were mirrors everywhere like with this much coke on it [indicated by his hands above the desk]. Champagne everywhere, women everywhere, but no FUCKING water. You could have been in a desert and you'd have died of thirst. It was just the fact that it was on-board this luxurious yacht and there was no cold water! You'd have died of thirst if it had been in the desert. That was one of the most impressionable things that stuck out in my mind. The fact that that yacht disappeared the next morning, when I say "disappeared", I mean, it sunk with everything that was on-board, in the middle of XXXX.

According to him, those sudden disappearances happen often in the world he was consulting for at the time. The events go unnoticed by the majority of people and the people that do notice them will tend to forget about them very quickly because they do not want to get involved. As long as it is done by a legal authority, Constantine does not have any ethical dilemmas, as the following makes clear:

> A funny story that got stuck in my head and that was a banka, which was basically a dug-out canoe with a very big engine on it. You know these outriders, they have the bamboo outriders, and you have a cabin put on top, and this marine plywood on the side. We had one of the fastest ones in XXXX, in XXXX, which was the area I was in at the time. The coastguard came out with us a lot of times. We went out to XXXX, which was the island where all the animals are, where a lot of them were disappearing. As we were sailing there, we heard some large explosions from behind an island. So, on the front of the boat was a 50 calibre machine gun. We went around the island and saw two XXXX fishing boats with nets in-between both of them, and they were just scooping up the dead fish that they killed with dynamite. The captain of the coast guard said: "Open fire!". He took a look through the binoculars, saw the names of the ships, and they just killed everybody and blew the vessels to pieces. I said to him: "Why did you that??". He said: "They've been arrested 3 times and every time their boss, who happened to be XXXX, paid to have them getting out of jail". The boats were impounded, they have enough money, so they used to doing it again, and again, and again. This time he said: "They're not going anywhere, they will feed the fishes". [...] I can still remember the screams from the people in the water, with the sharks swimming around and eating them. [....] After they have been arrested three times and have gone to the court three times, and they didn't learn their lesson, and the owner of the vessels were only interested in the money. [...] I mean, I can understand the coast guard commander's actions. Whether I condone them or not, is neither here nor there. He was in charge, he did it, and it's his responsibility. They shot the boat to pieces because those boats were just marine plywood. There was nothing left. The engine was so heavy that when the plywood on the side was shot to pieces, the engine just dragged the whole boat down. [...] The world is a cruel place, Yarin. The world is a cruel place and you can't always find a safe space and cover yourself with your little blanket, saying "Please oh please don't show me this or tell it to me", because it's not going to go away. [...] The only thing you can say as far as the episode in XXXX is concerned, that justice was done and was seen to be done. [...] It is a lawful body that is doing it. [...] If I see something wrong, I want to stop it. Whether this is lawful, what the person is doing is not lawful, and there is no law enforcement agency around them, well then it should be up to me or anybody else for that matter to do their job and stop this person from doing something illegal. [...] I'm not saying "Kill them", I'm saying [...] I mean, if you can arrest them and turn them over to the authorities, okay, great. If you can gather enough evidence to put them behind bars, then great. If they've done it once, and they got away with it, they done it

> twice and got away with it, three times and got away with it, fourth time, if I see them, they won't get away with it. [...] If I had known what that coast guard captain had known, I would have probably shot them as well, as cruel as that sounds. [...] It was a pretty hard thing to watch, but afterwards, in retrospect, I can understand why they did it and I think it was the correct thing to do.

Not only did his first professional ethical considerations pop up, but the consultancy work also allowed him to discover he was good at understanding the arms dealing domain. In fact, it triggered his interest in the legal side of the arms trade.

> I was there a year that was long enough for me. You can go, on an island, crazy afterwards. Then they asked me if I'd like to go to XXXX and work down there for the local or rather, not work for them but with them, the local customs and coastguard agencies. That was then started out as counterterrorism, counter-proliferation of small arms and light weapons, narcotics, but it turned into smuggling of animals [...] wildlife smuggling, being slaughtered and sold onto XXXX and XXXX paying off XXXX terrorists with XXXX arms. I won't say XXXX government, I cannot say that, but certain XXXX businessmen were supplying large amounts of T56s, which is a Norinco knock-off of the AK47. That's Norinco T56. They were supplying these and other equipment to a [...] XXXX [terrorist] group which was down in XXXX in XXXX where I spent the last 6 months of my 14 months there. Yeah when I finished that I said: "Yeah that's enough, I don't want to do this anymore, I want to make some real money". That's when I thought to myself: "Now how can I do that?". [...] I was very much interested in: "Okay, where do the guys get their weapons? How do they finance them, break-ins, bank robberies". [...] And they go off to XXXX for their terrorist training, learn how to make bombs etc. etc. I wanted to basically to be able to follow that chain and find out where these things were coming from and be able to stop them. Or I wanted to learn ENOUGH so that I could learn HOW to understand how it was all done, which I did. You don't make much money of being in the army though. So I decided: "Okay there must be legal ways to sell these things" and that's when I put my nose into the books and started digging and finding out, you know: "How does one become an arms dealer?"

In a similar way to his social worker job, going from counterproliferation of illegal arms into legal arms dealing appears contradictive. For him though it makes perfect sense.

> Why, what's to explain? [...] Counter... yeah but proliferation is illegal! Arms dealing, what I do, is legal. [...] I don't like illegal fire arms being sold around the world. I much prefer that legal ones are sold around the

> world. [...] I am not and I never was a left-wing tree-hugger, okay? As far as I am concerned, war will always go on. It's mankind's cross that he has to carry. [...] It's never going to end, [illegal] arms dealing will never end. The only way you can stop it is to make it legal or at least supply the legal entities in the world. [...] As far as the illegal side of arms trading is concerned, it's a dirty despicable business, okay? As far as the legal arms trade is concerned, it's also a dirty despicable business, but it's legal. It's still legal. This is the thing. Does it mean it's moral? I don't know. I'll be quite honest, I don't really care.

In sum, his work in counterproliferation of arms introduced him to the arms dealing domain and made him see and decide he would be better at it. These and other motivations that made him enter and make money in the international legal arms trade, will be discussed right after this chapter.

4.5 Conclusion

After his abusive childhood, Constantine was sent off to boarding school, where he was once more confronted with violent treatment, this time by bullies. He explained how it turned him into a rebel, making him feel ever since like an outsider. That feeling is not that different though from how he felt as 'an experiment' during his early childhood years when he still lived with his parents and brothers and sisters. However, at boarding school, he resisted more than he did in his younger years at home. In this chapter, we learnt about a young teenager's first development of a resistant attitude to 'oppressors' and authority, which was not much different while studying IT at university. Although he did not want to study IT, his father somewhat compelled him to do so. This was one of the last times he would listen to his father. Once he graduated from university, he did several, rather diverse jobs: a diving instructor, dog trainer, a social worker and a government consultant. The build-up of those jobs resulted in him being introduced to arms dealing. Moreover, the work experience he retrieved as a 'slave to the wage', while embracing and strengthening his anti-authoritarian attitude, motivated and assisted him later on in his arms dealing career, as will become clear in Chapter 5, which is the first out of the three chapters on the arms dealer Constantine.

References

Edwards A & Gill P (2002) The politics of 'transnational organized crime': discourse, reflexivity and the narration of 'threat'. *British Journal of Politics and International Relations* 4(2): 245–270.

Eski Y (2016) *Policing, port security and crime control: an ethnography of the port securityscape*. London: Routledge.

Stewart C (2001) The influence of spirituality on substance use of college students. *Journal of Drug Education* 31(4): 343–351.

5 From arms to amenities

His motivation, companies and offer

When he was asked 'What do you sell?', he made very clear that *that* is the wrong question. Constantine does not ever have possession of the weapons he offers. He deals in them.

> See, I don't sell guns, I broker and trade in them. There's a big difference. I don't buy before I've sold. That's the difference. I sell them before I buy them. People come to me and say "We want, how much?". That's the difference. I don't have a garage full of AK47.

Having explored his troubled childhood and his coming of (r)age, we have arrived at the point of Constantine's life as an arms dealer. Next to considering what it is he sells before buying, this chapter will consider when and where his career started. What is it that he exactly does when dealing in arms and why does he do it? How does he experience all of it? Answers to these and more questions regarding his profession will follow here and in Chapters 6 and 7.

5.1 The will to firepower

The thrill of doing arms deals and feeling a sense of freedom that amplify his will to do arms dealing are enriched by several motivators. But the most important thing for Constantine is to do what he likes in arms dealing, for several reasons.

> You do your job because you want to make a buck. Everybody does their job because they wanna make money out of it. Everybody! I don't care if it's the road sweeper or a politician. Everybody that works, does it [...] I'd say 99.9% of the people that work are in a job where they do it ONLY to make money. They get very little job satisfaction out of it. They certainly don't do it to change the world. [...] "Why am I doing it?", yeah? You know, this is the thing. There are so many people in the world that do not have the luck to be able to work in a job or a profession that they actually like. There are so many people out there that are so pissed off with

DOI: 10.4324/9781315148236-6

their 9–5 routines. They don't like what they're doing. They do it because they HAVE to. They HAVE to do it to pay for the two days of piss-ups, drug smoking or whatever. On Saturday and Sunday, and on Monday it's back to normal again. That's all they LIVE for. They become [...] or we have become, "we", as in the general population [...] I'm not a fucking robot, yeah? But the populations, the general populations, especially in the Western world have become robots. They don't see what's going on around them. They watch their TV's, they watch their sport shows, they watch the reality shows, and you know [...] to me that's just fucking stupid. So much more to life than TV and sport shows. People are SO dumb. [...] It's true man! This my [...] This is [...] You know? I mean. Wouldn't it be nice if you get up at 11 o'clock in the morning, and think: "What am I gonna do today? Oh! I know. I will sit on my balcony and I will watch the birds". Wouldn't that be nice? It should be 2 on, and 5 off. Two days of work, and five days off. It should be a five day weekend. It would certainly get rid of the unemployment. [...] They would be able [...] Perhaps, unless they get bored, ehm [...] They probably wouldn't know what to do with themselves, because it's like [...] the general population. Like, when you meet somebody new, at a party or something, first thing [...] they introduce themselves and they say: "I'm a teacher", or "I'm a bus driver", or "I'm train driver", and they identify themselves with their JOB. I don't do that. Me, I'm me! [...] "I'm Constantine", and if they ask "What do you do?", [I will say:] "I make money", which is what EVERYBODY does! I make money, I make money to live, I make money to buy things. I make money for my wife and my kids. [...] I just don't like boring life. Like I said, for me a day has to have something in it. I gotta have that feeling that I got something from that day. From the time I get up until the time I sleep at night, there's gotta be something that I've done in that day that I feel self-rewarded with. If it's not, for me it's a wasted day. It's wasted breath, waste of air that I breathe. That's just boring otherwise. [...] I have to have something of excitement happening in my life, YES. [...] You know, making somebody laugh or smile, that for me is a reward. There has to be some rewarding factor during the time that I am awake. Be that giving somebody some good advice. I've got many friends at the moment who joined the French foreign legion, they're always pumping me for information. One guy wrote to me last night saying: "Oh I've got a 30km, a 30 clicks forced march coming up next week, any advice from an old soldier?". Yeah, so I chatted with him for half an hour, giving him tips. That was rewarding for me. That's something positive that I've taken from that 24hrs order [...] for the waking hours that I've been alive. That's what it's all about for me. [...] You have to look at this life with a pfff [...] It's a big cosmic joke anyway [...] because we're only on this earth for like a small amount of time. [...] It's a cosmic joke, everybody is rushing around like little ants, building houses, making this, doing that, planning for the future! People just seem to forget that life [*snaps fingers*] is over in a

> split second. Live for today, live for the moment. […] This is the problem, this is the rat trap that the human race is in. […] Like, how do you want to live? Do you want to live in a world that's just considered to be work, work, work? At least you have a job or a profession that you enjoy! But the thing is to be able to separate that from your private life as well. It's difficult. Here, you go to the gym, you rush back here, and get on […] The first thing you do is get on Skype with me! Instead of sending me a text, saying: "Hey Constantine I just got back from the gym, give me 10 minutes, I'll go and take a shower". You know, big fucking deal? I'm still here hahaha […] You need to have the respective realities in a row. What do you want from life? That's me. That's me. I know what I want. I don't want stress. I obviously have stress sometimes when I'm working, that's normal! But I know how to deal with it. I go to the range every Friday and shoot 300 rounds of bullets at an imaginary person! […] I am of the opinion that everybody should have a gun if they want one and if they can supply the papers for it. Because it's what I like doing, it interests me, I've always been. Let me put it this way, it interests me to find the loopholes in the law that allow me to still do it LEGALLY and sell to the people I want to sell to.

The intrinsic motivation of dealing arms, comes from the fact, he told me, he has always been 'interested in arms, always, always. Going back to my childhood'. It is an interest that started when he was a young boy and got stimulated further during his time at boarding school. One day, his brother Arthur and he wanted to go out and go hunting for rabbits. As they were not able to hit any rabbits with the air-gun his father had given him as well, he took his father's shotgun that was locked in a case. It was a proper shotgun, a double-barrelled shotgun, he told me.

> I was like, 9, or 10 years old. I mean this thing was bigger than I was so we went out and I had seen my father open it, so I knew how to open it, and I put two shells in there. The next thing I knew, before I knew what was going on, I had blown a hole in the ground between myself and my brother. I could have damn killed him, yeah? I closed up the barrel and I pulled the trigger at the same time, just blew a hole in the dirt between us. So, we put that back, haha! And we never spoke about it, I don't think he knew. I have no idea. And from that day onward I always thought: "If you're going to have a gun, you got to know how to use it". So that was basically it. […] You would never forget an experience like that. Especially when I think: "God I could have killed my brother at the same time" and that would have been horrific. […] I got a great satisfaction of being able to hit something with a gun. I was very good. Yeah, I was very good. I was in an air-gun club afterwards. I used to be a very good shot. […] That was in boarding school, night classes, because when you live-in [the boarding school], there's nothing to do at night so they have to do some

> kind of recreational for you. There was a chess club, I was a member of the chess club. There was air-gun club, so I was a member of the air-gun club. […] It was just something to do in the evenings and not sit down and do homework all the time. The best thing I liked was the shooting, and at chess I was quite good. I enjoyed chess.

Explored in Chapter 4 already, it was during his government consultancy work at the end of 1999, he got introduced to the arms dealing business. It was also the moment he had enough of his consultancy work, and for the first time, he seriously considered a career as a business man by dealing in arms in the legal international arms trade.

> I remember sitting there. I don't remember exactly where I was but I remember there sitting and thinking: "I got to find something to do, I want do something interesting with my life. I don't want this 9 till 5 shit that is draining me every night when I go home just to crash in the chair and switch on the TV and pop the top of a beer". That's not me, I want something more out of my life. Then I thought to myself: "What CAN I do?". It was like a conversation 1-to-1, yeah: "What CAN you do? What do I know? I know guns. Okay, you know guns? Then sell guns". […] I remember once, I had a conversation with a [man]. […] I remember him saying to me: "Doesn't matter what you do in life, just make sure you're the best at it. If you want to be a road sweeper, make sure you're the best at it". So, I thought to myself, okay, if I'm going to sell guns and I'm going to be the best there is, that's it. And since then I've done my best to be the best at what I do.

When he said that, I told him it made me think of Heath Ledger's performance of the Joker in the Batman movie *The Dark Knight*, who at a certain point said 'If you're good at something, never do it for free' (Nolan 2008). Constantine completely agreed: 'Make sure whatever you wanna do in life, make sure you're the best at it. Pick something that you know and make sure you're the BEST at it'. Also, arms dealing, '[b]asically […] was the only thing I knew! It was the ONE job where I got job satisfaction out of it'. His motivation and being self-aware of his own potential and interest finally made him decide

> I'm just gonna do arms. Arms and military equipment. Bullets, guns, tanks, planes, helicopters, submarines, what anybody wants. […] I didn't have a company. I was freelance. Somebody approached me, it was the very first deal that we'd done.

According to Constantine, to become an arms dealer, you do not need a degree in anything. He did not feel the need to obtain any specific diploma or to even know anything especially significant to do the job.

> What I'm doing at the moment, the only thing I need to know is, as I taught myself; you don't get an exam for being an arms dealer. [...] Nobody can teach you to be an arms dealer. There's no college degree on how to export arms, yeah? [...] There isn't, believe me.

This made me wonder: how could one study the craft of arms dealing and it led me to the question about whether one needs to have seen war in order to deal in arms.

> Do you need to see war to do the business? No, not necessarily. Not necessarily, but you should know what you're dealing with. You should know the equipment, or the machine guns, or the weapons that you're selling what capabilities that they have, and what damage they can inflict. [...] Have you ever been to a warzone? No. Well, I hope you don't ever have to go. It's a horrific experience, especially in the midst of war when you realise that people that are getting killed have possibly a wife and children, and they're working because they can't get another job. They're working for an extremely low wage to pay to live. I'm talking about Third World countries now, forget about modern, civilised world. [...] I've seen enough.

How he rolled into the business was somewhat coincidental. There was someone who had a client for him who was looking for a certain amount of 'items', vis-à-vis arms and ammunition, he could supply them after having retrieved more details, because 'I never say no until I got the details. Who is it for, where is it going?' This way he can determine his strategy already before having agreed to broker a deal. As it was the first deal he referred to, I was wondering what his first-time experience was with an arms deal. His first deal was the selling of thousands of AK47s at a wholesale rate across the world. Jokingly he told me around that time that an AK47 would cost less than a set of Victoria's Secret matching underwear or a carton of Pall Mall Cigarettes.

> It's ecstatic, you know "Yeah! I made my first deal, yeah! I got so much money now!" [...] I'm going to quote you a line from the film *Lord of War*: "[Your] first deal is a little bit like having sex. You don't really know what you're doing, it's exciting and it's finished very quickly". Haha! It's a little bit like that. It's not quite, but it's a little bit like that. It's exciting, I must admit. You never meet the client. [...] The film is a piece of crap. You never meet the clients and you never see the weapons either because you're just a facilitator. [...] The fact that you've done it! The fact that you've sold them! Without even having them in your hands, you sold the damn things and you got money in your account! That's what is exciting about it. So basically, you're just using what you got between your ears to make MONEY. [...] [The first deal] still makes an impression on me when I think about it. That was like the turning point in my life. From not

> knowing what I was doing with myself, I mean, everything to me, you see Yarin, life is very short. For me, to sit and work 9–5 somewhere is my idea of torture, that is hell, so for me to be able to do something that I really enjoy […] I don't even have to make a lot of money out of it. It's the enjoyment I like. It's the adrenaline, it's the feeling of "These [arms] now are going there because of you". Not because of somebody else, but because of YOU. Because of your brains, your knowledge, your ways to circumvent legally […] certain restrictions and still be able to supply [arms].

The intellectual challenge is what drove him from the beginning onward and still drives him. In a way, his arms dealing is much like his evenings spent at boarding school, namely shooting and playing chess. However, arms dealing is then like playing chess with its pieces being 'guns and powder'. You have to be strategic and must enjoy the logistical chess game that goes behind arms dealing, importing and exporting arms and ammunition.

> I get a rush from it, I got to admit. I have at the moment from a Middle Eastern country a request for XX.XXX Glocks [handguns]. This is gonna be exciting, because, well, to find that amount of Glocks without going to the factory is gonna be extremely difficult. […] That is a very large amount of pistols. Normally these kind of orders would go to through the factory, which means the factory would be selling them. The factories don't work with distributors like me, yeah? So that means I have to find XX.XXX Glocks from somewhere without letting the factory know that they're being sold, which means ordering them from various contacts around the world, putting them altogether and then sending them on to my client. This is interesting, logistical challenges! […] It's like [a piece of art], it is most definitely! It's like trying to put a jigsaw puzzle together when you're blindfolded. […] You don't have the same logistical challenges with other things.

He could not do it with any other product, as it would not be exciting enough. For him it has never been something else than guns, 'because', he said 'it's my life. I'm a gun nerd. You show me a gun I can tell you exactly what it is, I can probably tell you when it was made approximately'. He asked me to take a look at his merchandise, consisting of assault rifles and machine guns. There was joy to hear in his voice. I asked him whether arms logistics are different because of the nature of arms (dealing).

> Oh shit yeah! Especially when you know it's your arms that are helping somebody win a war! […] You have a logistical challenge of how to get these products from A to B without annoying countries C, D E, F and G. This is where the fun starts. Or you have to find them from somewhere else. It's the whole finding of the products that you've been asked to find. It's the whole thing. The money is just a cherry on top of the cake. […]

> Alright, the money is the bread and the butter, the other stuff is just the cherry on the cake.

He truly enjoys doing his job, especially because he gets satisfaction out of making a deal work, but he also gets a decent pay out of it. Money-wise it usually takes five to six deals per year to make a decent living as an arms dealer.

> If there's a dry time then I maybe have one or two [deals]. [...] It depends on the quantity and how much money is involved. [...] That's [five, six deals] more than enough for me to live on for a whole year and live very comfortably.

Still, and although paid well, it remains most important for him that he is passionate about what he does. For him 'it is exciting to sell guns, it is interesting and exciting for me to know that my product has gone where it's supposed to [be]'. The excitement is increased when he is logistically succeeding, especially given the legal restraints of arms dealing, because he is and remains a *legal* arms dealer. It is a logistical and legal puzzle of 'how to transfer [arms and ammunition] from A to B, without breaking anybody's laws. There's always ways around many, many things. There are many ways to skin a cat, and still remain legal'. He continued:

> I don't think I could work for somebody else anyway. I'm too set in my ways. I'd probably tell the boss to fuck off in about the first week. I'd see that they are not making the money they could be making. That's the thing when you're working for somebody else, you work usually for a pittance, and when you see and when you know what the boss of the company is making from those arms deals, you'd be thinking to yourself: "Why the hell is he making so much? I could be making that!".

It is a type of freedom, maybe just an illusion of freedom, which he associates with the arms dealing life. Not unexpectedly and rather quickly after his first deal, it was therefore only a matter of time and 'just a question of opening up a company', he told me.

5.2 Going solo: The glory days

Setting up your own arms dealing business is almost as easy as buying a gun at Walmart, he made clear.

> It is very simple, you just register a company and register for the applicable licenses from the XXXX government, that's it. [...] I was the one and only person so to speak. I was a sole proprietorship and after a while they started to give me a hard time about taxes and VAT, and from one thing

> to another, and I said: "It's just not worth it anymore" and I closed. So I closed and I opened up a limited company in XXXX within 4 hours. Yeah, over the internet, it cost me €320 [which was] end of XXXX. [...] That company has been closed now since 7 years. Then I had another one, changed the name, rebranded it, that's still going. I'm in the process of selling that one, so if someone wants to buy it, okay. Then I opened up another one and that's the other one that's running at the moment, but they're both still active. Plus one company in XXXX [...] it's [a] security [company].

From when he started until now, Constantine founded four companies, of which the last one is still running at the time of writing this book. It is not just arms dealing as such, but also the related professional skills he has that make him good at what he sells: arms, vehicles, training, security services and software. As long as he sees a potential business opportunity, he adapts. His offered services, products and specific types of arms and ammunition are wide-ranging: armaments, sensors, specialised training, weapons systems, defence consultancy and platforms, security specialism and tools, and risk assessments. The brokering licenses and other specialisms he has are diverse too, including consultancy and training in diving in polluted waters, hazmat and bio-chemical environments and other war-related areas.

Although the coming and going of his companies have been volatile, up to 2012 his business was thriving. His enthusiasm to do what he does was much higher up till then as well. There definitely have been 'glory days' he sometimes reminisced about, which were mostly glorious because of the fast life involved alongside the arms dealing itself.

> Those were pretty good times. I wouldn't call them golden years because it was a fucking mess out there, but people were buying. They were buying like crazy. They would buy anything that they could get a hold of. From antipersonnel mines up to anything. Obviously only being sold to legal entities. [...] 2010, 2011, everybody wanted guns! There's all the private maritime companies that wanted guns. Then [there was] war. Practically EVERY African nation that wanted guns, it was the end of the embargo for Rwanda. It was a busy time, 2010, 2011, 2012. It was a very busy time. Sudan, Rwanda, they were all taken off the embargoed [countries] list.

I asked how he managed to get through such busy times as sole proprietor of his companies.

> It's very simple, 18hrs a day on the computer. 6 months of the year running around in Africa, knocking on doors, meeting generals, ministers of defence. [...] It's very tiring, very tiring, jetlag, dehydration. If you're not careful you get dehydrated very quickly from all the flights. "Today is Tuesday, must be Mombasa" haha or "Today's Tuesday, must be Cape

> Town", yeah? That's how it works or "What have I got to do today?" Well you can't go out of the hotel because you got six or seven different business appointments. [...] I never was just in front of the computer, but the majority now is in front of the computer. [...] More business, more excitement, one deal after another. This was also the time when piracy from Somalia was hitting the Indian Ocean. It was the very beginning of [specialist security companies] and not one of them had any idea how to acquire legal weapons. So I helped them. They bought through me, it was a brilliant time. I made a lot of money, I won't say how much but I made quite a lot of money in that time.

He in particular enjoyed that time as well because of the fast life involved when having to travel around for his arms dealing affairs in

> the Africas. Every time I go and see anybody down there, it's always good. It's always nice. The people are always friendly, nice hotels, nice people to talk to, go out for meals. Interesting places to see, you get the grand tour, they take you out to all the nice places. Casino's, clubs, wined and dined. It's just another world, it's nothing a normal person would even dream off. [...] One occasion that comes up in mind. I was in XXXX on business and we had gone out for a meal. Maybe I even told you this. We went out for a meal, and the restaurant we went to, it was a bit like a big carvery, where there's a lot of meat. Big long tables, there you're in a group of four, or there's a group of six, a group of whatever, I don't know, two or three. They'd all sit at a long table and there was a table that was basically full with these black guys, with all these women around them. They were black guys, dripping with gold chains, and gold rings on every finger, the women as well. The guys we're XXXX. We sat down and said: "Guys do you mind if we join you, because there's no other place?". [They said:] "Yeah sit down". We sat down and we got talking and they said: "What kind of business are you in?". I didn't want to say "I'm an arms dealer". You don't talk about sort of thing, so [I said:] "I'm in [security]". They laughed! These were some of the warlords of XXXX that were basically funding the pirate attacks, in XXXX, which was quite funny.

The large sums of money and the easy access to exclusive social environments where extravaganza parties were organised; it was all very much seductive to him.

> I tell you, easy money goes very fast. [...] Easy money goes very fast. It's easy come, easy go. Fine clothes, fine cars, fine women, casino's, restaurants. [...] It was then, it was "Oh yeah, great, let's burn it [money]" [...] [It did not last] too long, you can't keep up with it after a while, it's just too much. It was interesting and enjoyable at the time, but looking back on it now, I was like, God, up 24hrs a day, telephone calls, wheeling,

dealing. It's too much. The older you get, the harder it is. It's like partying when you're 18 and then trying to do the same when you're 40.

Although exceptionally, the fast life of Constantine's past included dangerous encounters.

> The other time was when I was in XXXX. I was working there on business and this was about some arms. I was invited there by a person who was later murdered, his name was XXXX. You can google his name. He was murdered in a drive-by shooting. His bodyguard XXXX who was a XXXX guy, he was shot in the lung and ended up in the hospital and they found out later on that his real name [wasn't the one he went by]. It was somebody else who was wanted in XXXX for the murder of XXXX.

On one occasion, he met people who he thought were involved in organised crime. Possibly even war crimes and human rights violations, he indicated. With some sensationalism, he explained what happened – it was clear to me he enjoyed telling about it. Yet it turned out it was mostly his suspicions of others to be in the business of illegal arms dealing, that sensationalised it.

> I was there in the hotel. He called me up one night and told me "Oh I'm in XXXX, you want to go out for a drink?". "XXXX, it's late, I'm tired". He said: "Come on, we won't go very far. I promise I will get you back in one piece". I'm like, okay. I didn't know who this guy was. I didn't know that he was an underworld boss. To me he was just a business man. He picked me up in the front of the hotel. No, in fact, I told the reception to call me when he would arrive. I didn't want sit down at the reception. So they called me and said: "Mr Constantine, Mr XXXX is here to see you". I said: "Okay, I will be down in a minute". The way that they said it was like they were afraid. Only in hindsight I realised why. Anyway, cutting a long story short, we went down and met his driver who had been shot in the leg in XXXX. We got into his jeep and we drove down to a club and before we even got to the front, we're driving down the street and there's all these nice cars. Very expensive cars parked on the left hand side just before the entrance of the club. As we drove down, all these bodyguards came out of the club and just cleared the last parking space away so that we could park in there. They waved us in, and opened the doors, and bowed. They were employees of XXXX, and that was another way he made his money, by renting out security to nightclubs, restaurants, etc. etc. bouncers, which I didn't know at the time. Anyway, we went into the club. There were three of us: me, [person 1] and [person 2]. The manager came, the owner came, greeted us. He was basically licking the floor in front of us. I thought: "There must be somebody important and it's certainly not me, and I don't think it's the driver". So it must have been this other guy [person 1]. "We want a table" [person 1 said]. "Yeah sure" [the manager said, then asking:] "How

> many people?". [Person 1 said:] "20". I'm like: "20? Where's the others?". He showed us his table, snapped his fingers and waiters and waitresses appeared from nowhere and laid this table for 20 people in a matter of seconds. So, you can see [person 1] was sitting there with a drink, I was sitting there with a drink in front me, and [person 2] was sitting in the corner. [Person 1] was on his phone and in about 10 minutes 20 people arrived. And from these 20 people, one of them was [a famous person]. [...] Tall guy, blond hair. Met him and his 3 girlfriends. A lot of other women in there as well, obviously. Then there was a guy sitting across from me, sitting there eating steaks. When I say steaks, I mean STEAKS like this big [*using both hands*]. Really big steaks. Don't know what kind of bull they got it from but it was REALLY big. They were massive. The plates were wooden boards. The steak was falling over the edges of the sides of the plate. So this guy is sitting opposite from me. How can I describe him [...]? He was also a black guy. He'd got short curly Rasta hair. He got linked chains, they must have been an inch thick, gold chains. Not just one. When he walked, he would have walked with his head down because of the weight of the gold around his neck. Covered in tattoos. I mean I've got a few tattoos, I certainly have nothing against them. I looked at him and he was in there with a t-shirt, old pair of jeans. Looked at him, we just smiled at him, trying to make a conversation. I said: "What kind of business are you in?", and he said: "I'm in scrap metal. What do you do?". I said: "I'm working with [person 1] together on [an] arms deal". He said: "Yeah that's what I mean, scrap metal". This guy was also in the arms business. Obviously not on the same [...] what shall we say [...] not same level as me. He was probably dealing under the table, hence his somewhat flamboyant attitude. These are all like flashing experiences. Other places that I've been to in the Africa's are XXXX in XXXX, where I've been taken out, wined and dined [as well].

As much as he enjoyed that life, Constantine thinks he is now different compared to others who are merely in it (illicitly) for the money. He considers himself more of an intelligent, legal arms dealer and entrepreneurial businessman who has the possibility and the capability to be able to distinguish between something that is only momentarily enjoyable and something that lasts.

> I do enjoy [the fast life], I do enjoy it, only for a certain time. Like I said, if I had to live like that every day, I'd go crazy, I'd probably become just as crazy as they are. Because once you've seen that, it's like a drug. Once you've seen it, and experienced it a little bit, then you'll always go back to it, you'll always want to go and see it again. [...] It's just nice to put your foot in the pool occasionally. I certainly like the finer things in life that money can buy, don't get me wrong. The only way you can make that kind of money is by making big deals. [...] That kind of life is not for

> everyday life. That kind of life, those kind of occasions. For me, I couldn't live every day like that. It would drive me up the wall. I'd go crazy after a while, because it's very superficial. People have no, what shall we say [...] They have no real outlook on life. They have no sense of purpose, as far as I'm concerned, apart from making money. They're only interested in what they can grab around them. "Let's find another beautiful chick to fuck" or "Let's make another million dollars", or "Let's do this deal and make a lot of money", or "Let's move into this club that has no security and put guys in there", that sort of thing. This to me is very superficial.

He would 'go nuts' if he had to live the fast arms dealing life every day, which is something of the past for him, also because he got severely ill by getting pancreatic cancer in the 1990s.

> It's the good life that I used to live. Not much of that going on at the moment, but there was a time [...] Before I started having this shit with the cancer, yeah?! That was the good life. Travelling all the time, visiting exotic places, meeting lots of exotic people, doing good business. Since I got sick, it's all just basically [...] I'm not going to say "gone to pot", because that's not right. Obviously, the travelling I did before is no longer involved. I can't travel, because I'm not allowed to. I have to be at the hospital every bloody two or three weeks. Travelling is out of the question. I used to be away like two, three months at the time. It was great, my wife and I never HAD any time to argue. Hahahahaha!

Chapter 8 will delve more in-depth into his current family life and also how he has been living with pancreatic cancer. For now, they should be considered as key aspects for his motivation to let go some of the flashier phases of his arms dealing trajectory; parts of a profession he misses. Because when I asked him if he could live without the fast life of it all, he responded:

> No, life would become too boring! You need to put [...] you need to [...] what shall we say. The grass is always greener on the other side, so to speak, but I wouldn't want to live there. It's nice to visit once and a while, but I have to have my base where I can be me. This is me, where I am. This is stability where I am now, the other world is not stable. It's constantly changing. You never know who you're gonna meet, you never know under what circumstances you're gonna meet them, you never know if they're crazy and pull a gun or knife on you, because a lot of people that I meet there, they are [...] They are so wrapped up in their own tiny little world that they don't give a shit about anything or anybody else. You might say the wrong word and they might freak out. [...] Let me put it this way, it's the world that I work in. That is the world I work in. These are the kind of people that I work with.

5.3 Going online: The deskbound years

Times have changed. Most of his days, he sits at his desk at home. Constantine barely, if ever, meets any of his clients or in-between contacts in person anymore, let alone that he is living the fast arms dealing life of excitement.

> The best part of it was making good deals, selling the equipment, that's the best part of it. [Now], it's not the same. There's not that personal contact that was there before. I enjoyed that, being able to talk to the people that are in need of the items, and also being able to see exactly what they want. To be able to go and do the various assessments, to be there and see the installations that they have. That's the best part of it, because it's the part that I enjoy. I can't sit in an office and look at pictures and say: "They need a camera there, or this needs an antitank gun there, or an antiaircraft gun there or this regiment should have RPGs". It just doesn't do it for me. I like to be there and see what they've got. See what they need. It gives me a different feeling. Call it job satisfaction.

Instead of seeing his clients or products, he is now in front of his computer, having to be available to his (potential) clients all the time. It is not exactly the image people, including myself, may have of arms dealers who are imagined instead to be travelling around the world, living the fast life and brokering exciting deals.

> I've been here all day [at home]. I've been in front of the computer. [...] I was up until 3am this morning, fixing the one hard-drive, and swearing and praying like hell that it would work, because otherwise I would have lost a lot, a lot of information! Yeah, a lot of information. I have a back-up on the other hard-drive, which it didn't want to take. Then I managed to find a back-up of 2016 which I used. [...] The information that I receive from clients and things, that's all digital. [...] [My IT security is] VERY important! I don't want anybody crawling into my computer and seeing who I'm selling to, or who I am sending my emails to, which is why I use XXXX mail which is an encrypted server in XXXX. For really secure stuff, I have a fax. [...] That's how a lot of people operate in the arms trade, be it legal or illegal. Fax can't be hacked.

It means he relies on having most of his arms and ammunition stored safely; of which all is kept somewhere abroad.

> A lot of what I've sold is in stock. Some of it, not all, obviously, because sometimes you want new weapons. Now, [a] stock [of arms] is something that's been made maybe in the 80s, 90s, and they've been stored, because [an] army [of] the country of the manufacturer had no use for them at that certain time. For example, XXXX in XXXX, they had for sale [...]

> 2 million FN FALs, you know the FN FAL? It's the rifle that was mostly used by the British Army in the 80s and 90s up to the Falkland Wars. These weapons were stock. [...] We bought 1 million of them and these are sold in Africa. [...] Mozambique, a lot of African countries. [...] Of course legally. [...] They go to regimes that are not necessarily, shall we say, human rights-friendly.

Constantine shared different company websites he has and he sent me several documents comprising lists with details and pricing of all sorts of small arms and light weapons (SALWs) and other equipment, as well as overviews of his consultancy work, training specialism and other types of services. In this context, it is interesting to mention that nowhere on his websites, nor on his CV, are mentioned the words 'arms dealer'. Next to arms and ammunition, he explained he sells

> electronic devices, we sell in fact everything that a country or a client, be it government or non-government, or security agencies related to different countries [...] we sell EVERYTHING and we DO everything. [...] I am [a] one-stop shop haha! [...] I don't just sell guns. It's the biggest part of my work [...] was up until a year ago, up until a year ago, yeah [2015], it was selling arms, yeah? I offer packages that allow me to sell arms as well, as well as helicopters, tanks.

Online, he presents his products and services with a certain language that emphasises the quality and length of experience he has, as well as the wide range of countries he has done business with. He does this to get a party interested in buying from him. Also the range of arms and ammunition is presented to impress, from SALWs to larger complex systems. He is in particular keen to emphasise the difference in his offer compared to larger arms manufacturers that are 'trying to sell you their "latest toys" that you may not necessarily require'. It is the quality of being a small 'player' in the arms dealing business that enables him (to believe) to provide customer-specific requirements which should make him stand out. Also, he remains small because he knows his humble place in the massive global market as a small player and, as he said, still manages to get 'the crumbs off the table as well!'

> Let's take shoes; we're living in a world of where you can order something on the internet and it will be delivered to you in 3 to 4 days. It will come from China or from India maybe, or from wherever. There's nothing you can't be supplied with today if you have the necessary papers. Now when a country, like America, has flooded its own market with shoes, everybody has bought their shoes. They wanna sell it outside because the owner of the company wants to make more money. The more they have, the more they want. This is the old story, money is the root of all evil.

> So what happens then is that they push their product into the rest of the world. It's economics, but in this case we're talking about arms, military equipment, electronics, that are being sold, yeah? For them to be sold to somebody, you have to be a member of the club.

Still, despite being but a small player to get arms from that mysterious 'club' of sellers, he innovates and has to keep innovating in his offer which is more than just arms. He engages in contracts with parties to also deliver specialist training, security courses, critical infrastructure risk-assessments and geopolitical analyses, other types of military and security equipment, and vehicles, such as (off-)road automobiles, tanks, (underwater) vessels and aircrafts. It is about delivering total packages of protection to clients, ensuring 'that they got the right equipment to defend the border of the country. If they don't have it, they need to buy it. [...] That's what we do'.

5.4 Guns and powder

The current licenses he holds are predominantly enabling him to broker in category A military goods, software and technology. The core business used to be SALWs, including handguns, like Glocks, and (semi)-automatic rifles such as AK47s, M4s. MP5s, G3s, as well as ammunition and grenades.

> There's a difference between selling arms and mortar-grenades and the launchers. [...] This would [require] an extra license that I would have to apply for. These are manpads [man-portable air-defense system], this Strella and the Igla, that the YPG and the PKK, and many others [used]. [...] I could sell to a State actor, with a special license, I can sell ANYTHING that I want, apart from WMDs [Weapons of Mass Destruction]. Now, my licenses at the moment cover small arms and light weapons up to 40mm. That's the size of a mortar round. So that's any pistol, any rifle and any armament system up to and including 40mm. Then you've got tanks, planes, submarines, these are all military equipment. These I can sell [...] but I would need [...] for example, I have a submarine in XXXX at the moment that's up for sale. [...] Go down to XXXX docks, you'll see it in XXXX dock. [...] It's an old diesel submarine, should be in the museum, but there's people that I'm trying to find [for them] to buy it. [...] You see, if anything falls outside of the classification of small arms of light weapons, what we do there is, we apply for a special single individual open trade control license, naming the country that it's going to, and we get an individual export control license, or an individual export license, just for that one shipping. That's how it works. [...] Those are the items that we sell. It's not just small arms and light weapons. It's military equipment. The list of countries that we sell to is on there as well, that we sell to and have sold to. [...] But we don't only sell. We also do risk assessments, so it's not just the fact that we've sold materials to those countries. We also do risk

> assessments, risk management, risk mitigation, anti-terrorism. [...] We do everything, because that actually is my specialty, antiterrorism, counter-proliferation of small arms and light weapons. It's what I try and do. [...] I don't always sell when there's a war on. Obviously, when there are wars on, it is not necessarily rifles that are sold. It's a lot of other things that are sold as well. I mean, it goes from radio equipment to ammunitions, spare parts. It's not just guns. Obviously that's my main business, but you can only sell a gun once.

For him, it does not matter who he sells to or in what way, as long as it is legal and there is a stable war, he sells to make money out of arms dealing.

> [I'd sell to] any market, I'll be quite honest. Doesn't make any difference to me as long as I am selling. [...] At the moment there's nothing going, it's very, very slow. I've had some requests for ammunition, which is what normally happens all the time. Ammo is always a good thing to sell yeah, because it means that everybody got enough rifles. What I'm after at the moment [to sell] is training possibilities and geopolitical risk assessments for countries, which is what we're pushing for at the moment. [...] We don't do just arms trading. You cannot live alone from arms trading, it's not possible. Unless you're dealing only black. [...] If there's enough wars going around in the world, you can live off it [legal arms dealing]. What happens is, before there's a war [...] it's not like a country decides to go to war tomorrow and then go to war immediately. [...] Alright, we'll say that Mr X comes to me and says: "I want X amount of these to country Y". Alright, now I need to find out where the arms are coming from, so I look at the country they're brought from. In most cases it's left up to me anyway. [Clients] are not interested, they just say: "We want this this this and this sent to this country, can you get it, yes or no?" I never said no. For the deal in XXXX we have had to source as far as XXXX. There are certain things there that other countries don't have. A lot of countries from that shopping list are sourced from ex-Russian, ex-East Bloc countries. You then look at the quantity, what kind of armour there's going. You can then say with 98%, you can see what kind of geopolitical movement is gonna happen. Then you know approximately from which country person X is representing before they come to me. Then you start digging, find the information you need, which sometimes takes quite a while. At the same time, you're shuffling things around, so that you gradually are getting this shopping list together. Then you start gathering information as to who is doing it, and why? Now if it is a straight legal deal, there's no problems. When it is so many layers of bullshit, smoke and mirrors between whoever has the original contract down to the person who is doing the deal, then you know that there's so much involved and this person at the top doesn't want anybody knowing who he or they are. So you have to go through these shadows, these layers to find out which country is more

> interested in a political shift in this country. Then you have a rough idea of who the original client is, and then you look for other bits and pieces.

One of the most popular and cheapest rifles in the legal and illegal arms trade worldwide is the AK47 (cf. Hodges 2008; Sprague & Griffiths 2006); therefore, it is not entirely surprising that Constantine has a large bulk of AK47s and knows how to get them cheaply.

> AK47 and AK74, AKMs. I buy them for a 100 dollars apiece. They sell for […] depending on how many I order […] I don't sell anything less than 5000, if I can get away with it. If somebody wants to buy a 1000, I'll think about it. But if I sell maybe 5000, they'll go for approximately 300 to 400 dollars each. These are all new. They've never been fired. It's all surplus war stock. […] It's 200 dollars on every rifle [I make].

Next to arms, the main product he brokers in is ammunition.

> I prefer if my guns are shot, that they come to me and buy bullets, yeah? You can only sell a gun once. After that, you sell them the bullets, yeah? So, you know? I mean […] It's just […] I don't feel anything […] People wanna buy guns. If they don't buy them from me, they'll buy them from somebody else. […] As long as the weapons are being fired, that's all I'm worried about, because then they have to buy more bullets. As far as I'm concerned they can shoot them in the air. Sooner or later they will come back and say: "We need 26 million rounds". "Okay, no problem, I got them here". […] It's the ammunition that makes you the money, it's the repeat buyers that come back for the 9mm [bullets], that come back for the 7.62x39 for the AKs, for 7.62x51 NATO rounds. This way you make your money. […] [T]o sell ammunitions, the guns have to be fired. So, even if it's on your training exercises, it's good for me, because then they come to me and say: "We need some ammunition, we need some spare parts". I don't really want people kill with my guns. […] That's just it, it's like a car accident. They happen. As long as they're being fired. […] Just because someone's firing a rifle doesn't mean they're killing somebody. I fire a rifle, and I fire my pistol every week. I go to the shooting range.

There is one type of weaponry Constantine will never broker deals for, which is for weapons of mass destruction (WMD).

> I don't sell nuclear weapons, no. But very, very quickly, I can sell some sticks and stones for the fourth world war though, because that's what it would be fought with, if there's anybody left from humanity [after a nuclear war]. I don't sell nuclear weapons. I wouldn't know where to buy one anyway. […] For one thing, it's illegal. Secondly you'd kill too many

> people at once! You destroy the whole world [...] I would never even think about it. Chemical, biological, nuclear, no way, NO WAY! A country representative came to me, where was I? At the XXXX in XXXX, [one of] the biggest arms exposition[s] in the world. One client came to me, I was sitting somewhere, and I got into a conversation. I was at the XXXX, which is the XXXX AK producer. XXXX concern from XXXX in XXXX. I was at their booth, and I got into a conversation with my contact there with them, and another contact from XXXX export, and we were talking some small details, and this guy had obviously picked up I was a dealer. He was from another country, he was black. Obviously from Africa, by the way that he spoke English and he gave me his card, he was a representative of an African nation. He said: "What do you supply?". I said: "I supply everything". [The man replied]: "What really?" I said: "Apart from WMDs", and with that, his smile disappeared, because I didn't supply WMDs. I'm not crazy man, no way. [...] What if it was legal? Haha! No, still no. You see, the thing is, I like repeat customers. When you start selling WMDs, you don't have repeat customers. [...] I mean, come on, you sell one bomb and you kill the whole world. There's no repeat customers. [...] Wars are good for business, as long as it's not nuclear, because in a nuclear war: nobody wins. Everybody loses. I don't sell nuclear weapons, I can't make any money out of it anyway. [...] There are no nuclear arms dealers. That's government to government. That's for example Pakistan to Saudi Arabia. That's how Saudi-Arabia got their nukes, it was through Pakistan. [...] There may well be some people that are not part of the government that do these deals and go make the connections, but in the end it's government to government. Because you can't just go onto the market. I can't put an advert in the newspaper and say: "I'm your local friendly arms dealer, you can buy whatever you want from me, including nuclear weapons". I'd be locked up straight away. You just can't do that.

What we can see is how Constantine does not necessarily require war and conflict to offer his produce. He also does not want to sell equipment that could potentially wipe out all of his clientele. Actually, he rather favours providing arms and ammunition structurally, for example, for the purpose of training military or police personnel. Such arms dealing is good for his business continuation, which he also achieves by providing training and other kinds of services to make a living out of.

5.5 Security services, consultancy and technology

There are several other services he delivers, as well as technology, especially cybersecurity-related items. For example, it is possible to purchase a wide range of courses Constantine has that are focused on all kinds of security trainings and professionalisation, as well as doing risk assessments.

> These are the training courses that we've got out. [A certain course] is basically 5 modules, where there's the physical security, maritime security, cybersecurity, values and ethics, [and] one other. I don't remember exactly what off the top of my head, I'd have to look at it. That's what we're doing now. I already got some people interested. We're offering it to veterans, women, and people in UN-listed countries with economical poor conditions. As long as it is on the UN list.

The 'Values and ethics' course triggered me and I asked him to elaborate on it, to which he replied rather concisely: 'Yeah of course, you can't do anything without values and ethics. You can't even be an arms dealer, haha!'

His training courses also involve training people to become fighters and know how to use arms.

> I've got some friends, some XXXX friends who actually live in XXXX, in XXXX who are pretty much up-to-date with things going on there [a conflict area] plus I also have volunteers of a group which is called the XXXX.

For him, friends, I had to understand, were the only ones that he would train in counterterrorism if they were to be part of rebel groups. He would definitely not be involved in supplying arms to rebel fighters to combat terrorist groups, as he and other small arms dealers agreed that they 'don't supply fighters. That's not what we do. I know people that have gone to join [a rebel group] and also females that have gone to join [a rebel group]'.

Next to courses and training, Constantine sets up risk assessments of buildings and also conflict areas. These assessments can be part of some of the security (training) packages he offers.

> It depends on what they want doing. If somebody comes and says: "We need a risk assessment of the government buildings", then I do a risk assessment of the buildings, the physical security, the infrastructure, the computer systems, etc. etc. etc. Now, if somebody comes to me and says: "Okay, we would like to buy new military equipment for the integrity and protection of our borders. Can you please come over and do an assessment?". Sure, but each one [of those risk assessments] is individual. There's no such thing as a check list. [...] No, it doesn't work like that. [...] It's not negotiated. They say to me: "We need a risk assessment of our borders". I go and look at the borders, look what they've got, whether it's outdated, whether they haven't covered things that they should have covered. [...] There's simple things like barbwire, minefields, and the rest of the shit that they put down. [...] They know what they want analysed, but they don't know what they want to buy for it. This is the thing. A lot of places think they got [...] that their systems that they have in place are adequate [saying]: "We bought these 5 years ago!". [I'd reply:] "Well you

> know, 5 years ago you didn't have these problems with your neighbours". [...] I don't have to sell the products, I just say: "Here's the possibility we have...". [...] I was asked to do a risk assessment between XXXX and XXXX. It's 240 miles of desert border. You can't put 240 miles of barb-wire fence up and expect nobody to come through. So what do you do? They had tracked vehicles, control post outlooks and they thought that was sufficient. I went there and said: "No guys, you need for example 1 command base, you need quad bikes, you need UAVs [unmanned aerial vehicles], you need drones, you need pressure points on your borders", which is an electronic system that you bury under the sand and it goes off when a human being or heavier goes on there. It won't go off if some camel crosses over, yeah? So they don't have the guys running out to check for camels coming across the border. We went with that, and in the end they were happy. I can't tell you where it went. [...] They said: "We don't want to put command posts all the way along". I said: "Okay, no problem. We put a remote-controlled machine gun there". They have a sensor, they have a thermal camera, could recognise a human being. There are signs put up at the border [stating:] "Do not approach. If you come within 50 yards you'll be shot". These things are set up just after the border. If they cross the border, they get shot. They're all automatic, very expensive. [...] It depends on the order. If it's a robot machine gun, you can pay anything up to $250.000 each. You got thermal-camera's, you got night vision, you got forward-looking infrared. [...] It can move so many degrees. It doesn't just fire straight, it will track whatever it is approaching.

The risk assessments he provides, in particular those of conflict areas, require geopolitical information he must gather to estimate what and where he can sell his products. He does so by figuring out in which region in the world the arms may be used. He started talking about a war in Libya that was going on at the time of interviewing.

> There's a war going on against ISIS in Libya. The Americans are involved, the Brits are there, the Russians are there. [...] You have to have your finger on the pulse otherwise you lose money! [...] If somebody comes to me with an order and a genuine EUC [end-user certificate] and says: "We need this, this and this", a big shopping list, I'm going to take a look at it and say: "Hmm, now that's interesting, let's go and have a look what's going on in this country". Then you can roughly see if it's going to be a war or if there's an uprising, human rights violations, possible human rights violations.

So, for him geopolitical analyses are business intelligence that is based on various sources. For his business intelligence to remain up-to-date, he carries out open-source analyses of conflict area.

> There's quite a lot of information, for example, in the CIA World Fact Book. You pick a country, and you find out if there are any border disputes. We would then look at the risks involved with your neighbour and what his aspirations, if any, to your countries border, or your country's mineral deposits, oil, or whatever. If they're close to the border, [finding out] whether they would be stupid enough to try and invade to get those deposits. The other thing is obviously the terrorism factor. If there are terrorists in the country next door [...] We'll take Nigeria and Boko Haram for example. Boko Haram is spread out throughout the Sahel. Every country is at risk in Africa, more so Nigeria, because they started in the Northern part of Nigeria, which is 95% Muslim, and this is what they decided that they were going to do. But they use the [most] porous borders to go back and forth. If your borders are porous, and you have a country next door to you that has an international terrorist organisation, a Jihadist, or whatever terrorist organisation that is interested in somehow, "liberating" the people of your country, then obviously they are going to try and come in. It's your job then to protect your people and the integrity of your borders by putting in Claymore mines, border sensors, automatic rifles, robot rifles, etc. etc. etc. If you [as a client] don't do that and you get invaded, well, then my risk assessment you paid a lot of money for, means you didn't take any notice of it.

In addition, by having his eyes and ears on the ground in conflict zones, using 'operatives' as he referred to, he retrieves the most recent information about a situation as well.

> I have people basically from all over the world that are contacts of mine either through [social media] or other various methods, friends and friends of friends or colleagues that have been in the intelligence business, who are willing to supply information. Obviously against a sum of money. [...] Human intelligence, OSINT, which is Open Source Intelligence, SIGINT, which is Signals Intelligence, all that comes into play. [...] SIGINT is where radio broadcasts, as signals are being sent from one government agency to another, within a country, that are intercepted. [...] It depends how much of a risk-assessment that [client] want. If they're not sure what their aspirations of their neighbours are, well, they're a pretty piss poor government in my opinion. Everybody should know what their neighbours are after. They should know whether they got good relationships or not. Let's take for example South and North Sudan. There was a general arms embargo in Sudan. All of Sudan, North and South and then the Americans said: "Okay, we're going to lift the embargo on South Sudan" and I thought: "This is great" [...] because I could then sell to them.

He also has to keep close track of what is going in the world by doing daily, if not hourly, check-ups of media.

> Did you hear about the guy they caught coming from Ukraine? 100 tonnes of explosive and a whole bunch of AKs? […] This was a French guy, they caught him going between […] Ukraine to Poland. […] The Ukrainians and Polish caught somebody coming over from Ukraine, he got a 100 kilos of explosives, and I don't know how many AKs in the back of his car. He was a French guy, so ehm […] He'd obviously […] They are not buying things up now from Syria or going back with them. They're taking them from the Ukraine and bringing them into Europe […] to Paris, Brussels. Brussels is a sieve. It's got more holes than Swiss cheese, as far as law enforcement agencies are concerned. You got three languages spoken there, that means three police forces and none of them would really communicate with the others. This is the problem in that country [Belgium]. […] It's just […] for my work it's just a piece of information. Means that somebody is moving things from there to there or trying to move things up front, from theatres of war into areas of "peace", in apostrophes, to certainly not sell them to the hunters. These are weapons of war.

Not only does he use geopolitical analyses to look for selling opportunities and willing clients. As part of his consultancy work, he also sells such information itself to interested parties.

> I deal with geopolitical [information]. That's how I know what's gonna happen, wherever it's gonna happen. […] It's always good to have a finger on the pulse about what's going on in the world, so that you know if somebody's gonna need weapons. Then you can always be, shall we say, "available". […] Like I said, I have people that ask me for geopolitical assessments. I'm not just a gun runner hahaha! I've got a client in XXXX that wants to talk with me tomorrow, just an hour on the phone, it's gonna cost him like €500, yeah? That's what I charge. […] I charge over a $1000 a day for consultancy. […] If it's just a day or two, then I will charge $1500 a day. […] My geopolitical analysis are mostly always spot on! Always. […] It's what I do, it's how I make my money, which is at the moment in short supply. […] I had a couple of videos sent to me from a certain organisation about ISIS training camps in XXXX. They wanted me to do an analysis, which was quite interesting. […] They sent me the links [to videos with explicit material]. […] A XXXX company wanting to know how they can export vehicles to XXXX. I often get requests like this for information. So obviously if it's a military vehicle they need to get an export license, they need to get an import license, etc., etc. So the guy said, you know: "Can you help us out on that?". [Constantine replying:] "Yeah sure, my consultancy rate is actually very reasonable". He said: "Well […] I'll get back to you". Because everybody wants something for nothing, unfortunately.

'Not just a gun runner', he said, revealing he prides himself with the fact he provides that kind of consultancy regarding risk assessment and geopolitical analyses, next to just SALWs.

> I don't have these consulting contracts all the time. God no. I wish I did. Would be so nice to just sit here and talk on the phone for an hour, and listen to my bank account, KACHINGGG!! [...] I have companies that call me and say: "We need a 3 month consultancy contract. What is it gonna cost us?" and I will ask them: "What do you WANT? What do you NEED? What do you want me to CONSULT on?" If it's like infrastructure, anti-terror, then my rates are obviously [lower] because I'm selling my knowledge. So then I take a look at how many days [are necessary] exactly, what work is involved, and instead of charging a thousand a day, I will charge maybe $800. So I have a security company that has just opened up in XXXX and they want somebody to go over for 6 months to write SOPs, the Standard Operating Procedures, to help them set up the business, as far as the infrastructure is concerned of their building, and other buildings. Teach the people how to protect themselves when driving money around, money transporters [...] security solutions. They said: "How much you want a day?" I said: "I want $850 a day, plus all my expenses, plus the hotel, plus the tickets and my food costs". They said: "Sounds interesting, we'll get back to you". That's a good deal for them.

Cybersecurity is another area of expertise he offers services and products for. In fact, 'hardware' arms and ammunition have become far less important than cybersecurity in 21st century hybrid warfare, Constantine explained.

> Let me put it this way, it's never been only arms, never. At one point in time, arms was the biggest part of the business. Now it's become the second biggest part of the business, the first being the security industry. [...] We offer everything, like I said. We'll even do transfer-technology if it's so amenable, which is basically what cybersecurity and cyber-consulting is about. We do that as well. [...] There's always going to be the wish for small arms, yeah? They are the weapons of mass destruction, let's be quite honest about it. Small Arms and Light Weapons are the real weapons of mass destruction. The nuclear bombs and hydrogen bombs, and the rest of it that sits in their bunkers and are guarded. They're guarded. They don't get moved except when they're told to move. There will always be arms, but cybersecurity is coming. [...] The thing is, if you have guys who are working on these [digital] systems, they're going to be [...] the human factor has always been the weak link. If you do away with the human factor, then what are you left with? You have to take in AI, but you still have to have the human factor, who programs the AI? So, if the human factor is weak, then you got a weak link in the chain. It's always going to be there.

> [...] The transfer of technology is also on my licenses. It's not just SALW. [...] I can't sell Microsoft Windows to China, for example. That's illegal. That's transfer of technology and software. I have to make sure it's on the list. [...] It wouldn't be classified as a weapon. It could be used for, I'm just taking Microsoft as an example, 1000s of other programmes and bits and bobs. For example, it could be reversed engineered, bypassing Microsoft copyright on it. It's transfer of technology. [...] It still comes into the legal and illegal areas of defence equipment. [...] [Cybersecurity] won't change [the arms trade] as such for many, many, many years. What will happen is, the arms will get smarter, you'll have pistols that can automatically target a subject, and you'll have bullets that can be directed. You got them now. The only thing that you can think about there, if you really want to go in science fiction, would be somebody hacking into an arms control system that rerouted an ICBM [intercontinental ballistic missile] or something. This is science fiction at the moment, doesn't necessarily mean it wouldn't happen. [...] I think you'll find that they [North Korea] may well be working on that [rerouting ICBMs tech] now. [...] You would have to find somebody that has the right technological competence to be able to sell his services or broker his services, or to get him to write a specific programme for a certain system, which could then be transferred to a country that would like to buy it. [...] I think it will be[come] a diversified market. They'll never be able to stop selling bullets. It's impossible. Maybe in 500 years, or whatever, there will be no bullets anymore. It will be laser guns. As far as the market is concerned, it will be a much diversified market with a lot more things being asked for. Weapons are being produced and coming on the market every day. There was a new one released at DSEI [Defence and Security Equipment International] in London from FN. [...] It's still on. All of the arms dealers in the world go there. Just me, I didn't go there this year. All of the arms dealers, the dealers, the arms, lot of stuff is bought and sold there. Little bit like walking through a bazaar.

As we saw in Chapter 3 about his coming of age, he did an IT bachelor degree which he did not like to do because his father demanded it. I asked him in relation to the above citation whether that degree may have come in handy, although he despised having to do it. Rather annoyed, he responded that he hated that as it took too many years of his life and it did not bring him very much at all, he explained. Moreover, he does not necessarily do the cybersecurity work himself. Only if it is an easy job, he would consider it.

> If it's not, I have 100s of people around the world that work for me on a contract basis. 100s if not 1000s. If somebody calls me and says: "I need somebody in Panama that can do this and the other", and if I don't have somebody in Panama, I will have somebody near them who would do it.

Next to cybersecurity products and services, he is becoming more active on the market for humanitarian aid goods and the wider disaster relief industry, in which particularly 'disaster drones' are the most popular product (cf. McKiernan 2019; Sandvik & Lohne 2014). Constantine is approached for these by governments quite often.

> They've even asked me for humanitarian goods, which are drones so that they could make artillery corrections and make sure that there's no civilians being hit. […] If they want drones I will sell them, they'll be under humanitarian aid. They're not big enough to have a pay load on them. Although I must admit they did ask me if they could have [weaponised drones] as well. I said: "You won't get a license to have those". I said: "It'd be much easier to just take the drones and what you do with them afterwards is entirely up to you. I don't want to know". They have artillery corrections. They can fly them over the target area and make sure there are no civilians being hit. That's what they're being sold as, as humanitarian aid. If they drop mortars from them afterwards, then I don't want to know about it.

As long as he sells disaster drones that may be altered to the extent they are weaponised into arms, of which he would remain ignorant, he is alright with it. Also legally. So, see no evil, hear no evil, speak no evil? Not all the time, he clarified, because in times when his arms dealing business would not remain that lucrative anymore, Constantine has to diversify his offer of products and services even further, and he may (have to) abandon the arms trade altogether.

> There's hardly any business going on, having to diversify so much, it's unbelievable. I think I will start selling nappies after a while haha, I'll become a pampers representative! […] Diversification is always good because you should never sell the same things all the time, you should always have a broad package of what you want to sell. As you can see from the website, we are diversified.

It was right before Christmas 2020 that we messaged via Skype about the COVID-19 pandemic, and what it was doing in the Netherlands, where I live. Constantine was rather eager to know about the 'PPE situation' in the Netherlands, especially because there was a worldwide shortage of face masks and hospital breathing equipment at the time. He sent me the following chat messages:

> Do you have contacts to [the Dutch ministry] of health? […] Get a hold of your [university] chancellor and tell him to open channels. I have everything that's needed from ventilators to masks and testing kits. […] I have 100K testing kits now available in XXXX. […] Brochure available in 2 hrs of all our products available worldwide. Get onto your university

> chancellor, bro, he has the connections. […] Someone you know must be [connected to the Dutch ministry of health]. This is life and death!! […] They do not need to know my real name, Yarin. It can all run through you. And at this point in time, I really couldn't give a shit about anonymity (well not so much).

It was clear to me he wanted to do business, as they were not going very well for him at that point. Rather irritated, I explained to him that I am not that close with my university chancellor. I did offer to ask around, but in that case, we needed to agree that I shared his identity with those people. Moreover, I would not be directly involved but only be passing his name on. After I said that I actually felt uncomfortable in doing so though and that I also do not really know anyone relevant, Constantine gave up and replied: 'OK whatever, forget it'.

Regarding his products, services and pressures of having to diversify them, he also occasionally thinks about the future of his arms dealing business and its development. He has a couple of ideas about high-tech equipment that will become more popular in the future, he thinks.

> You got thermal-camera's, you got night vision, you got forward-looking infrared. […] It can move so many degrees. It doesn't just fire straight, it will track whatever it is approaching. […] Before long they will have robot soldiers. […] They do [exist] but they haven't been placed on borders. They're still in the testing phase, basically. […] They can't distinguish between friend and foe at the moment, that's the problem. […] If somebody came to me and said to me: "Okay we want an army of robots", then I'd say: "You're nuts, way too expensive. Use your own army, you've got millions of poor black people running around, train them, and give them a gun, yeah? It's a lot cheaper, and if they get killed, just get them replaced". […] I mean, come on? This is purely business, it's a business model. You destroy a robot, I don't know how much a robot is going to cost you, maybe a million, maybe more? What's the price of human life? Human flesh is the cheapest there is, come on, let's be honest. […] It's the cheapest meat around, believe you me.

5.6 Conclusion

Being motivated by a certain will to firepower, Constantine still enjoys his work but it used to be better. Now, he takes comfort in doing the logistical puzzles while remaining desk-bound, whereas before he had to go out and about, all over the world, enjoying the fast life of arms dealing as well. Nowadays, he sits long days behind his computer, maintaining online visibility, having to offer more than just arms and ammunition; in fact, he is pressured into having to diversify his offer, which he does not necessarily like. In tailoring and crafting his consultancy and other services for his clients, he strives to offer a unique customer experience, if only because he has to compete with multinational arms manufacturers. What is most important to take from this chapter is how he wants to stand out as a craft arms dealer. It matters for his business continuation, otherwise he risks losing his clientele to those global arms dealing conglomerates, as Chapter 6 will elaborate on.

References

Hodges M (2008) *AK47: the story of the people's gun*. London: Sceptre.

McKiernan J (2019) How drones are changing the disaster relief industry. From: https://caringmagazine.org/drones-disaster-relief/.

Nolan C (2008) *The dark knight*. Burbank, California: Warner Bros. Pictures and Burbank, California: DC Comics.

Sandvik KB & Lohne K (2014) The rise of the humanitarian drone: giving content to an emerging concept. *Millennium Journal of International Studies* 43(1): 145–164.

Sprague O & Griffiths H (2006) *The AK47: the world's favourite killing machine*. London: Oxfam International.

6 Trust and distrust

Clients, competition and colleagues

Constantine's arms dealing requires him to be a businessman that is like many other corporate professions and as such entails doing business and being confronted with clients, competition and colleagues. No 'surreptitious deals, exotic locales, [or] high stakes negotiations with evil warlords' like in the movie Lord of War (Kruse 2016 – online source). Instead, it is about trust and distrust in a strategy of keeping your clients satisfied and keeping an eye on large players to compete with – sometimes by finding solidarity in working together with other legal, small craft arms dealers.

6.1 Customer care and cynicism

> At the moment I'm getting approached more and more directly by clients, which is good for me. It speaks for my business. I can't say I'm unhappy at the moment, it could be more. It could be better, it could be worse. Yeah, that's it.

And that is his daily work reality – as much as he wants to rebel as a craft arms dealer as we saw in Chapter 5, he has to broker deals for an income to live from for which he needs clients. At the beginning of one interview, Constantine was excited about something. Before we started the interview, he explained he got a very nice order sent to him the other day by a potential client. These orders come in via phone calls, emails and text messages from his clients, I had to understand.

> I'm just getting some prices for them. 9.5 million rounds of ammunition, various calibres. [...] I got this WhatsApp [message] today, and since then everybody has been sending me messages. So I'm going to put on there "Unavailable, important calls only DO NOT DISTURB, fuck off or I'll delete it" haha. Cause all of my contacts can see that I'm there now, saying "Oh, you're on WhatsApp". Oh God, come on guys, give me a break!

DOI: 10.4324/9781315148236-7

In setting up, negotiate and close a deal, there are many parties involved: clients, other arms dealers, arms manufacturers, governmental bodies (e.g. embassies) and representatives, and the transport domain. Still, it is pretty straightforward, he explained. Direct clients and in-between parties, such as embassies, approach him mostly via sending faxes. They have a tender for an x-amount of rifles they want, for example. Those rifles have to have special specifications that give Constantine the right instructions to go through his own stock or to approach another party with the requested rifles. Either that, or he finds a company that makes these weapons new with the specifications that his clients are asking for. Then he calculates a price for them with the party of manufacturer, or he makes a non-disclosure agreement, which is usually the case. After that, he tells them who the deal is for and then he wants a quote. Usually, he makes the quote and the clients put his commission on top of the bill. Meaning, the client then pays the money that the other company subsequently pays him and the client pays Constantine for finding the goods as well. This way he is paid by both the client and the other party. He is

> letting them work out all the logistical challenges. "I need this and this" [a potential client would say]. I'd say: "I know someone who can arrange that for you". [...] [A potential client would say:] "How much would it cost me". I'd say: "It would cost you this much". Then I call the other person [and tell him:] "By the way I got somebody who wants this and this". [The other person would say:] "That's good". I would say: "It'll cost you for the further details for me to do the connection". [The other would say:] "How much?" [I'd say:] "This much". [The other would say:] "Okay". [...] I got paid from one person [the client] and from the other person. [...] There were fixed prices for doing a connection [back in 1997/8]. Now it's commissions. [...] If I bought, for example, 100.000 AKs from XXXX, at the moment it would cost me $100 apiece. They'd be sold approximately $210 [apiece], and that's without the transport. So, that's buying and selling. Well actually, it would be selling before I buy them, because otherwise I would have a whole bunch of shit that I couldn't sell. That's how it works. If it goes to a war zone then I get paid 100% upfront [...] because tomorrow there might not be a war! It has happened before. I had an order from XXXX, XXXX, from XXXX. They wanted some items. I said okay. They asked me: "How much?". I said: "50% upfront and the rest when they get there". The rest only when showing the export certificate. [They:] "Okay, okay". By the time I got [the requested items], and I got the deposit [...] the situation had changed there and they didn't want them anymore. So I had to give them back to the manufacturer and say: "Guys I am sorry, keep them on the side for me and I'll try moving them somewhere else". But to the [client] I said: "Sorry guys that's it, you're not getting your deposit back". [It was at] the beginning of the Syrian affair when ISIS marched into Syria and Iraq [...] 5, 6, 7 years ago? 5 years at least, 2011, 2010.

As there is there no credit involved in deals and as a client you want your arms, they must pay up front for it. It is too risky otherwise, unless there is a 'stable' warzone that will definitely continue. In many cases though 'today there's a war, tomorrow there's not one. What am I supposed to do with all the guns, put them in my garage?', as Constantine explained. It is not the case that wars or any type of conflict are required for him to do his business. They simply have to remain stable and last. In fact, peacetime can still be (as) profitable for Constantine as well.

> Just because somebody buys or orders, arms or ammunition, doesn't necessarily mean to say there's a conflict. There are countries that come to me, they say: "Okay we're upgrading our military or our police armament system for example. We need new Glock pistols, or we need new riffles, or we need new pistols, not just Glock. We need new pistols, what can you do? What can you source for us?"

Therefore, stability is what really makes it interesting for Constantine to invest his resources in and to make money out of a client; stability coming forward from both perpetual peace and permanent war.

He has a diverse range of clients that will come to him either directly or indirectly. These are predominantly non-embargoed governments, especially police forces, that contact him.

> To make a good deal you have to run around a lot and take a lot of time, look at who you're selling to, make sure they have the right papers. I had one guy who tried to give me an EUC [End-User Certificate] from the government of XXXX. [...] I have a copy [of the EUC] on the computer. I will send it to you if you want. It was quite funny when I got it. I just showed it to friends of mine who work with the State Department of XXXX. It [was] a no-go! I mean if they told me: "Okay go ahead and sell it", then I would have done it.

As becomes clear, one of the essential elements of setting up a deal for a client is to do your homework and get as much intelligence gathered about your client.

> If I am approached by a government or if I'm approached by an individual [...] the individual will be working for the government. The government won't directly [contact me]. [...] There are scenarios where a government official will approach me through a contact and the contact will say: "We would like you to arrange this this this and this", and there are other occasions when government officials would approach me, [I'm] talking about military government officials, and that would be a governmental contract. The other is a quasi-governmental contract. [...] There are no trails leading back to the responsible person, well, parties. [...]

> The more layers there are, the more layers of protection for whoever is ordering or whoever who wants these items to be found and traded. [...] Not only it's a question of knowing who is behind which deals. So if that goes wrong you know who to talk to, if the shit hits the fan. [...] You always find out who is doing the deals so you have the dirt on them. [...] Then you start digging, find the information you need, which sometimes takes quite a while, while at the same time you're shuffling things around, so that you gradually are getting this shopping list together. Then you start gathering information as to who is doing it, and why? Now if it is a straight legal deal, there's no problems. When it is so many layers of bullshit, smoke and mirrors between whoever has the original contract down to the person who is doing the deal, then you know that there's so much involved and this person at the top doesn't want anybody knowing who he or they are. So you have to go through these shadows, these layers, to find out which country is more interested in a political shift in this country. Then you have a rough idea of who the original client is and then you look for other bits and pieces. Political situation in this country, who stands to win if the political situation in this country changes? Then you put a brief together, an envelope, or in my case, dossiers, which I have on them. [...] Dirty deeds, done dirt cheap. So if that something does go wrong in the end, you'd know who to point the finger at.

That information, together with his geopolitical analyses to give an estimation of where the client's requested arms may go to, is used to respond to the client.

> With the security and arms industry, well basically, the security industry, which covers arms, we'll call it that. The old adage in the security industry is: "Scare them, scare the client, and then sell the product to them". [...] We point out the realistic possibilities of infringements into the integrity of their borders, and how they would need to protect, SHOULD the need arise. That's what we do. We don't scare them. [...] If they draw on the information that we've given them and become afraid, well, this is their interpretation of what we've given to them.

I asked him whether he used a specific salesperson rhetoric or 'massage' his geopolitical analyses to convince clients and get them on board.

> No, because if I did, and nothing happened, then they wouldn't come back to me again. [...] The product will get delivered, there's no two ways about it, but if the client or whoever it may be [...] has bought stuff through me or from me on the basis of a risk assessment, or a geopolitical assessment, that mentions weak points in its border security, and where there could be possible breaches [...] Well obviously those breaches are there, because otherwise I wouldn't mention them. Whether people

> come in THROUGH those breaches is a different matter. If I'd turn around and said for example: "People WILL come through these areas", I would never say that. I would say: "There's always the possibility that these and these areas, which are not correctly protected, could be used to enter your country, causing terrorist attacks", etc. etc. etc. There's a difference.

Whereas fear-mongering has been attributed to the security industry in order to sell security products (cf. Loader 1999; Zedner 2006), Constantine shows such fear-mongering is actually in and of itself a danger. If you promise a threat and there is none, your promise is broken. So, when you are mongering your clients into fear and there is no actual security threat, they will not become a return customer. Your business continuity will not be established then. So I wondered whether he did not have to provide more certainty to his clients about the geopolitical analyses, otherwise he would lose them, as I understood.

> Okay, then what I would have to do […] I'd have to go next door to the country, or draw on intelligence from operatives I have in that country, or from people that are working in that country, which obviously we have, and find out what the geopolitical situation is THERE.

With these geopolitical analyses and having all the most up-to-date, adequate information about his clientele, he achieves business continuation: customer care matters to Constantine, because it provides stable income.

> Obviously I'm really happy when my customer's happy because it means he's going to come back to buy more! He's going to ask me again. […] Listen, whoever I do business with […] see the thing is Yarin, I am a perfectionist which is sometimes bad and sometimes good. I am a perfectionist. […] I'm happy when my customer is happy, and I'm happy because I have done a good job. I get satisfaction out of my job. I get self-satisfaction of knowing that something that I've sold is that which is required and something that they want. Not some piece of junk that is not going to do the work that they wanted to do.

What comes along with genuine customer care for his clients, he explained, is being honest about their needs and the arms he can provide will fulfil those needs. Or as he said: 'I uphold my own corporate ethics, or business ethics which is to be straight and on the line with as many people as possible and not trying to rip them off'. Then again if he finds out that a client

> lied to us, it will be the last time they would ever do business with us. Which means that when people approach us to buy things, they have to be extremely honest, and tell us who it's REALLY going to, otherwise they don't GET anything!

A large part of gaining trust from his clients through a quality-guaranteed way of working is then to get the right arms and ammunition, other equipment, and possible relevant services. Given that he only has a certain stock of produce to broker contracts on, he often relies on other parties, including large arms manufacturers and smaller arms companies. He does not have positive experiences with these in-between parties who sell their guns via him.

> The problem is XXXX wanted too much money for [certain helicopters]. So I told them to go and screw themselves. They wanted X,X million euros. No way. There's 7 of them and 4 of them are pieces of junk, so basically it's spare parts, and you don't know how good they are. To be able to even see them and inspect them you have to put a 50.000 euro down payment on them. Just to see them. So I said: "I'm not interested, come on". That's the ex-communist bloc countries where they will all [...] The 50.000 euros, they call it a bond, just to show that you're serious. If you say: "I will give you so and so much", it's a bid, but the bids run out. They were to be auctioned off, they went over their time, and they can't sell them. So I got a hold of them, and said: "I heard you got some [certain helicopters] that you want to sell". [The other would reply:] "Yes, we'll send you the details". They sent me the details. In amongst the details was [stated that] "to prove that you are serious, we require 50.000 euro bond, bidding bond", which is quite normal when you're in a bid. I knew the bid was over. Of course, the lowest price for this was 1.5 million. So I managed to get some photographs of them. Don't ask where from, but I did manage to get some photographs of them, and the condition that they're in. I turned around and said: "I'm sorry, I'm not interested in buying a bunch of junk". If I want to buy junk, there's enough out there.

Clearly, quality control matters to Constantine, because he wants to be known as an arms dealer, a craftsman, who delivers a high standard quality to his clients. Therefore, it matters from whom you want to buy and then sell to.

> I'm certainly won't be buying it from the XXXX or from XXXX. Last deal we did with XXXX, they screwed us. Well a company, they screwed us. They took the money and didn't order any ammunition, now we're having to fight to get the money back. [...] The thing is in this business, there's a lot of trust, because we gave the deal to a person that was in XXXX, a person of repute. He took the money and he just messed us around, and said: "They didn't give us the export permit", and this and that. Anyway, it cost us $XXX.XXX. So that's quite a bit of money, it's no small change. That was what we were paying for it. It wasn't what we were selling it for. It costs us a lot more than that actually. It costs us maybe nearly $XXX.XXX.

When a client requires completely new arms, it gets even more complicated. Then Constantine has to retrieve arms and ammunition via in-between parties who themselves need to approach others, mostly the arms manufacturers themselves. There was one such client he was doing his research on, because new arms were requested.

> They want factory-new materials. It's got to be made in the year the contract was signed. So, the contract is signed this year, it's going to be made this year. Which is not normal, but if that's what the customer wants then obviously we try to make sure they get what they want. [...] Normally, if it's stock I mean, if somebody comes in and says, for example, with the XXXX that came and they wanted 3 million. That [weaponry] was made in 1992. I mean, I got [...] we've got lots of ammunition but none of it is factory-new. There's no reason for it to be factory-new, unless the people that are buying it intend on storing it for more than 20 years. Basically, that's it. [...] If we'd approached the factory ourselves, we could have probably done it, but we had somebody on the ground that said: "No, I can do that for you and I can get a better price from them than you can", which was possibly correct. He ended up turning around though that he screwed us for €XXX.XXXX. [...] Someone in XXXX will go and pay him a visit and make sure we get our money back. [...] Our lawyer for example. I certainly wasn't implying any threats of violence. That would be illegal. [...] Then we get the money back [via the lawyer], and we pay it back to the client, because the client has been screaming for his money for a long time. We paid the client back and they either order from us again, or he says: "No, I don't want to order through you guys again", so it's bad business for us, because we lose a client, and in this business, like I said, most of it works on trust.

However, as much as he is straightforward with his clients, and as much as he wants to gain trust, it does not always goes the other way around.

> You get people ordering what the hell they want and what they think they want and they come back afterward saying: "This is not exactly what I want, I want a refund". Then you always have to turn around and say: "We don't do refunds", or you have to say: "Okay we will take it back", which means you got to get in touch with the manufacturer or you got to put it in stock and find somebody else to buy it. [I never do refunds] unless [arms are] defective. [...] I had a deal with XXXX when it came off the B-list, because XXXX was on the B list because of the [conflicts] there, a long time ago in XXXX. When they were taken off the B-list, which meant that it was possible to sell them arms and military equipment, I approached a person I knew there and offered him, offered them, my services. They said: "We need XX.XXX AKs". [Constantine replied:] "Okay great, AKs and ammunition, fantastic. This will do as

> an opening bid and then we can take a look and see what else you need". I said: "It's going to cost you so and so much. Pay the deposit so that I can place the order. I need an EUC, and the papers, and we can carry on, we can go ahead". So, I got all the papers and he paid me the deposit, or the government paid me the deposit. I placed the order with [a company] at the time. It is now XXXX, which is in XXXX in XXXX. Couple of weeks afterward, three weeks after that, the guy called me up and said: "Sorry, we have to cancel the deal". I'm like: "Why? I've already put your order in. I almost paid the deposit for the order". He's like: "The XXXX have approached us and have offered us a better deal". I'm like: "Yeah, like what?". [They replied:] "They're going to supply all of our military equipment and they will do training as well". I said: "I could do that for you as well. What are they offering you?". [They replied:] "All brand new 5.56x45". I said: "You guys are silly. This is less than lethal. Those bullets don't kill people, unless you shoot them in the head". It's true! The NATO 5.56 round is only designed to injure people, to take them out of the battlefield, because it costs more to look after 1 injured soldier than it does to bury them. This is unfortunately true. He said: "We will have to cancel. How about the deposit?". I said: "Sorry, you're not getting that back". That's it. That was the end of it. It ruined a very good deal for me. The XXXX went in, they knew I was involved. They went in directly. […] I kept the deposit, I cancelled the order, I made some money out of it. At the same time I felt quite annoyed that they've done that.

In his experience, actually most of his clients frustrate him as they are not always honest with him, he explained. It happened rather often during interviews that Constantine would be called or emailed by his clients to which he sometimes responded immediately. He was talking to a client during one interview, a male voice from what I could hear. The discussion they had was heated and Constantine was almost shouting. When he hung up the phone, he was swearing out loud. I asked him what was wrong.

> I got a another little job running at the moment. The guy who is the client is having some problems understanding exactly what it is he needs to do. […] I'm pissed off with stupid questions, not from you, from him! […] Out of my somewhat enclosed shell of being only in touch with clients […] I have finally come to the decision that the majority of people that I have to deal with are dumb. I know it sounds extremely arrogant, but it's true.

As much as he depends on his clients, he cannot always trust them because they simply do not know what they actually need. And that ignorance is something bigger arms dealers and arms manufacturers play into. Moreover, he also distrusts clients particularly when it comes down to potential third parties his clients may sell the arms to afterward.

> I got a request from [a government] for XX million rounds of 7.62x39 ammunition. That's Kalashnikov. So, or Kalashnikov, it's AKS, but it's Kalashnikov in this case. I know that [that government] doesn't have AK's in their army, because they had X.XXxXX [ammunition], which is a NATO round, and I knew that. Or let me put it this way, I had the suspicion that that wasn't going to stay in [that country]. It would be sold onto Syria, somewhere to or ISIS, or ISIL, or whatever you want to call them. So, I turn around and I told them: "No". Some people said to me: "Are you crazy?" I said: "No man, why should I give them weapons or ammunitions that I suspect, more than just suspect, they will be sold outside of that country to terrorists?" It's just something I won't do.

The most important for a client to provide is an end-user certificate (EUC), because he cannot just rely on fully trusting clients. They might resell arms to third parties that cannot be legally traded arms and ammunition with.

> I trust but I don't trust. This business is built on trust. If somebody comes to me and says: "I need this, this and this", [I'd say:] "Do you have an end-user certificate?". [The other says:] "Nope, but I can get one". [I'd say:] "That is good enough for me". I will then start getting things together, and this is for a war zone, where I'll say: "This is the price, 100% upfront, you will get the products within three weeks. I want an EUC". That's how it works, I trust him to get me the money, otherwise I've made bookings with people who supply the stuff, not necessarily manufacturers. If he lets me down and doesn't give me the money, I've let [suppliers] down as well, which is bad for my reputation.

Through the EUC, Constantine filters out his clientele and controls his legal arms dealing, preventing guns and bullets ending up in the 'wrong hands' and playing his part in keeping the international arms trade clean, so to speak. This way he stays on the legal side of things. Then again, he wondered

> [i]t is legal but is it moral? Well, you know, if the people in XXXX came with an EUC and ask for the same thing, I'd sell it to them as well. I will sell to both sides if they get me the papers. I don't give a shit who buys them, as long as I'm covered legally for it.

Meaning, if two belligerent parties would approach Constantine and they are not embargoed, and both can negotiate an EUC, he is morally flexible and he would sell to both sides – an arms dealing phenomenon as old as the arms trade itself (Engelbrecht 1934: 122), and still going on today (Moore 2010; Raab & Milward 2003). Overall though, he emphasised, he has to take sides in who he is going to sell to.

> How do I make decisions? [...] I take sides, you know? I take sides, if for example, I'm suspicious of an order, we'll say the one with XXXX where they asked for X million X.XXxXX ammunition. I know the XXXX don't use those riffles, so [they] could have been going to somewhere else, and in this case I was suspicious that it was going to be sent to XXXX. Obviously, it wouldn't going to XXXX. It would be going to, through XXXX, to some of the [...] Ha! I don't like the word "moderate" Muslims. On these grounds I won't sell to them, for one thing, because it's against my policy. And secondly, let them find and try to source it from somewhere else. I know damn well they can't, because we control all that. [...] Take Rwanda and the war and the genocide in Rwanda. Just go back a few years. Now, if somebody were to approach me from Rwanda asking me to supply them with 10 million sickles, you know the chopping knives, that were used for cutting, then obviously I'd say: "No, if you want to do a genocide, you can use sticks and stones. You're not getting sickles or any rifles or ammunition from me", unless it was a legitimate government. [...] This is a problem. This is where you have the [...] "Do I sell them" or rather "Do I not sell to them on moral grounds or do I close my eyes and sell them because they are the legal government?". Well you know in many cases I don't. I wouldn't sell them to the legal government. Because if I knew that cases of human rights, people being executed, murder squads etc. etc. then obviously I'm not gonna get involved in there. I'm all for a good clean war.

There is one specific country, which remains anonymous, he would find it difficult to be brokering deals for, even if their request is fully legitimate and they have an EUC.

> I wouldn't supply to XXXX, even if my life depended on it. I'm sorry, but as far as I'm concerned, they can go fuck themselves. [...] I have nothing against individual XXXX soldiers, because they're just conscripts who are being roped into doing their national service. These guys are not killers. [...] I wouldn't sell them arms, even if they were my only customer. I would rather say no and watch them lose. When I say that, I'm jumping the gun a little bit. If they came to me and say: "Here's 15 million dollars, what can you get us?", then I'd say: "Two or three crates of AKs and a couple of million rounds of ammo". I would sell to them but I would make the price so steep, they wouldn't want to come back for more. [...] Yeah, [I'd supply] but at a very extortionate price. I will take your money, I will take your money. Normally an AK would cost, wholesale, I get them for 75 dollars each for one AK. I sell them at a 100, depending on the amount that's being ordered. So, if I buy at $75, and if it was for XXXX, I would sell at $15000 per rifle. Possibly even more. [...] That's the last country I would approach. I have also made it now company policy not to sell or export to any, shall we say, Muslim countries on my list.

The fact he does not broker deals for and with everyone puts a target on his back, he told me. These are serious risks of the arms trading business that are life threatening, which is something that is a distinctive part of the job.

> I'm at risk, I'm a high risk target. The Jews don't like me selling arms onto the Arabs, the Arabs don't like me selling things to the Jews [...] pfff [...] Some African groups don't like me selling things to other African groups [...] You never know, you never know [...] When I go to XXXX, I always wear a bullet proof vest and have 6 body guards. Yeah [...] My pistol is in the safe here behind me.

When he would have to travel, and fly via certain airports in countries that he rejected to broker deals for, he would be afraid of being detained and never see the light of day again.

> There've been so many "suicides" in the toilet of XXXX, XXXX airport, of people going to XXXX to help XXXX and also to go to the other places in XXXX to help XXXX. [...] If the XXXX intelligence services know that I'm involved in helping XXXX, then the XXXX know it for sure. So I wouldn't want to take any risks on going down there. It's more than my life's worth at the moment. I wouldn't feel safe, to be quite honest.

By 'suicides', Constantine meant people just disappear at a specific airport, implying that the government would try to get rid of him. Also at home, in his own town, in his own house, he has felt unsafe and he feared for his life and that of his loved ones.

> There was a big deal for two weeks after that decision [of not selling to a party] we made, when I would go out in the morning I checked the car for bombs, make sure that nobody was following me. Things like that. Make sure that my pistol was always clean before I went out of the house, before carrying it with me. [...] That was the reason I got the license to carry it because I'm considered a target. [...] I just want to be able to live nice and quietly, and comfortably. Without having to go out of the door thinking: "Somebody's got a scope aimed at the back of my head". That's how I see myself and my future.

Not only do arms dealers make money from other people's killing; they fear for their own lives as well. Still, he is convinced he should treat his clients well despite the fact they often try to mislead or could even kill him if he rejects to broker deals for them. So, as much as he expects them to trust him, he does not truly trust them in return. In similar fashion, he does not trust the large manufacturers, as they do not care about their clients and actually hijack his, which makes them evil, Constantine would tell me often.

6.2 Fearing and loathing large arms manufacturers

When looking at the list of largest arms manufacturers in the world, one thing becomes clear: the United States stands out. According to the most recent numbers, the top five arms manufacturers in 2019 were all based in the United States, headed by Lockheed Martin, and then followed by Boeing, Northrop Grumman, Raytheon and General Dynamics. Altogether these big five arms manufacturers registered $166 billion in annual arms sales (SIPRI 2020). Next to the Americans, Constantine told me

> there are a couple of big actors. There's Russians, obviously, Ukrainians. Most of the Ukrainians I know are on the other side of the fence [illegal arms trade], so to speak. Rosenborn export, which is the Russian export department company, that's straight down the line. They won't work without correct papers, they can't afford to. Some Chinese, and some from XXXX. I was approached there as well to go on and work for […] WITH, not for, with XXXX, which is a XXXX state arms manufacturing company. Not just for small arms and light weapons, they also make larger pieces of equipment. Basically, that's it. There's a couple of South Africans. […] Basically, that's it. So, it's a very small world. If you haven't met the person, you know them by name.

Competing with large arms manufacturers such as these is tough; they have the capacity to deploy personnel to reach out, as well as to handle requests and tenders, whereas Constantine operates on his own. However, large arms manufacturers 'put on false airs. I just can't stand them. I'm a down-to-earth kind of guy, pretty simple, as far as my outlook on life is concerned', he mentioned. The way he runs his business, entirely by himself, is becoming rarer in the arms trade, and his company and small-scale arms dealing companies like his suffer from it. It is something he is confronted with frequently, especially as he is not the first in line (anymore) that clients would reach out to.

> It's not unusual to find yourself in a deal where you think that you're maybe the second or the third one in but you find out in the end. It's like 10 people before it gets up to the actual client.

Arms manufacturers have their own representatives that will try and sell to the same people that Constantine is trying to sell to and has sold to. Moreover, because clients do not only come to him but to those larger companies as well, he is worried that his clients might not get the product that is right for them.

> Then obviously I'm going to do my damn best they don't get to sell their piece of junk to my client. […] [That's in the client's interest] but also for my personal satisfaction at having beaten these idiots. This is the

> thing: every arms company, manufacturing company thinks that their product is [the] 'Be All, End All', 'Silver Bullet' solution to certain problems. This is not true! All they're interested in is selling their shit and moving on to the next sale. Their product […] No product! Unless it's been looked at. There [are] certain products in the arms industry that are for certain situations. Certain, be it for jungle warfare, asymmetrical warfare, whatever. For example, you can't take an asymmetrical warfare piece of equipment and go and fight in a city, or in the middle of a jungle. So even the McDonalds of arms manufacturers [wouldn't be able to deliver for every warfare type], unless they had EVERYTHING, EVERYTHING, and that's impossible. It wouldn't just be a Big Mac or Double Cheeseburger, yeah? They would have to have EVERYTHING! NO company has EVERYTHING, which gives me the edge on the big companies. It may well be that their company has what I want for my client, but I will try and make sure that I get the client on my side so that the client would rather go through me going to the company, then going through the arms dealer [representative] for that company [directly].

The McDonaldization of society (Ritzer 2013), as becomes clear from the above, has also managed to find its way to the arms trade and industry, in the experience of Constantine. It is something he despises, not only because they lack client-customisation of their products; they also sometimes simply fail to deliver at all, while using legal loopholes to set up large defence contracts.

> This is another thing I don't like about this dirty little business: defence contracts. For example, I have an agent in XXXX who came to me and said: "I've just been told that the government is going to buy some helicopters and they're looking at this and this helicopter", and I'm just like: "Alright, well, I can tell you now, the helicopters that they're looking at, they're going to buy some from XXXX". Well this company in XXXX has only ever made XX helicopters. They're having financial problems. They won't be able to supply you. He said: "That's very strange, because the government just back-signed a contract with them". I'm like: "It looks like you're going to be paying a lot of money to finance their factory, doesn't necessarily mean you're going to get the helicopters". This is what I don't like, where you got unscrupulous companies, that are using defence contracts to subvention their own businesses. […] That's not smart business, that's ripping people off because the person who is signing the contract on behalf the factories in XXXX knows DAMN well […] I mean they've only ever produced XX helicopters and X of those crashed in the initial stages. […] The client knows now! Haha! He's not going to buy them. I think they revoked the contract, which is another reason why I'm not very popular in some parts of the defence industry, because I tell the truth. I don't bullshit.

That is exactly what gives him the edge over large arms manufacturers, which is meaningful arms dealing for him. He does not screw clients over, but in doing business with him, clients skip a large body of representatives and mid-level management, and thus a significant amount of bureaucracy and 'bull-shit', as Constantine would say. That makes him an outsider that he prides himself with.

> They don't wanna go to the [arms manufacturers]. They don't want to use the agents, because what will happen is […] You have to understand a lot of people that are the logistics officer or the government official who actually signs off on these contracts, or these tenders. These people don't want to be bothered all day and every day by [arms manufacturing] company representatives […] because they don't know what they're ordering, for one thing. They don't really know what they want half the time. Let me give you an example. An African nation comes to me and says: "Okay, we want you to advise us on what equipment we need". So then I would say: "Okay, this is the contract, this is how much it's gonna cost, just for advising you doing a report, one thing and another. Now show me what you've got". So I take a look at what they got, [at] the different parts of their armed forces, I also do a geopolitical analysis on the country itself, what the internal threats are, what the external threats are. On the basis of that, I either say: "This needs to be upgraded, this is okay. Throw it away, get a new one" etc. etc. etc. Now if it was a [arms manufacturing] company representative, they go in and they only sell or they only offer the products that their company makes. So without realising it, the guy is bombarded with all this information [but] he doesn't really know what he wants. He doesn't know how to make the decision [thinking:] "Well what's better than this? Is it better just because it's cheaper? Or do the specifications of this outweigh this?". This is the thing: most of the logistics and ministry defence officials they don't KNOW what they need. This is why the XXXX government quite some time ago decided that the logistics procurement would be done through companies such as mine. Whereby we would take a look and they would tell us approximately what they want. […] This is how we work. Now, we won't get any money in that case from the company. We don't make any orders with the company. The minister of defence or the logistics officer or the procurement officer does that. What we do is advise them what they need. […] It may well be that they don't wanna go to the company and they will use us as a medium. They will go through us to the company. […] It's built on trust these countries, or governments, or even security related agencies, they trust us to offer them the best solution within their budget as to what they want.

As much as he may profile himself and his company as fast, reliable and crafty, it remains tough to compete with large arms manufacturers. He must remain visible. However, it is his relative anonymity in the international arms trade that gives him an appeal to clients, as well as that he risks his own life when having too much visibility.

> When you are in this business, the last thing you want is media and public attention, because there's always some nut case out there who thinks he's doing the world a favour by killing you. Whether you're legal, or illegal, [he might think:] "Oh, he's an arms dealer. Bad boy. BANG", which is why I carry a fucking pistol around with me all the time.

This causes friction and frustration, because large arms manufacturers can have much more visibility and possess far bigger public relations capacity, as well as they cannot be 'killed', but can only go bankrupt. To compete with that, Constantine is trying to remain visible, partially by being physically present at arms fares. In 2016, Eurosatory took place in Paris. Eurosatory is a renowned international arms fare, attracting private and public actors in the arms trade from all over the world (Eurosatory 2022). Constantine was planning on going there.

> I will be in Paris in May for the [...] is it May? Yeah, May, for the Eurosatory. [...] I've got like 50 invitations to go. They all cover the expenses, like [it happened before]: "Oh we'd like to see our local dealer" sort of thing. "We're in Paris, come and see us" [large manufacturers would say]. So it means I go to Paris, three days. The last time I was there, I finished business in two days, and [a Russian arms manufacturer], I asked them and ehm [...] No, they said: "What are you gonna do for the third day, what are you gonna do tomorrow?" Well, I said: "I'm gonna finish business here". [They replied:] "But what are you gonna do tomorrow?" I said: "I thought I'd take a trip around Paris with one of these double-decker busses". [They said:] "No, no, no, no, I send somebody from the embassy to pick you up". So they sent me this bodyguard and a driver, big black African, Moroccan guy and an armoured Audi, newest Audi. It was great, it didn't cost me a penny. I mean, he drove around with CD plates on [diplomatic plates], we parked. He said: "You wanna take some photos here?". I said: "This is a nice place" and he stopped the car in the middle of the road. All of these cars going around, honking and honking, and I'm just standing there by the side of the car taking photographs, yeah? That was amazing hahaha. The other thing, one police car stopped [...] he saw the CD plate and he just saluted me, and just drove off. [...] I only hang out with higher-ups [...] I'm expecting a lot of problems this year. Last time I was there, there were a lot of demonstrations outside. This year it's gonna be even worse because of the Paris attacks [on 13 and 14 November 2015]. The security will be extremely tight. [...] Last time it was very good, and this year I hear there's even more gonna be present. I heard the Iranians are gonna be presenting as well, which will be interesting for me.

Constantine sent me a link to Eurosatory (2022). He offered me to come along as his employee, so that I could experience an arms fare first hand, but I could not afford it. For Constantine, those fares are important to attend, if only to see

> the newest technology from every country in the world that produces weapons, that's why I said I think XXXX is gonna be presenting which really should be good. […] I usually get put up in a hotel anyway, so that's not a big deal. That's it. When I was working with XXXX and also with XXXX, they would pay for everything. All I had to do was get myself there. They put me up in the best hotels also. I had a car picking me up in the morning, take me to the exhibition, brought me back in, whenever I wanted, yeah? Was just for me. This year I don't know whether XXXX will do the same because I can't work for them at the moment. So I have to find, maybe [another arms manufacturer], ehm […] some of the other companies I've been invited by […] and find out what they're offering. Whether it's just a question of going and seeing them, if they're not interested in paying the hotel, then I'm not interested in talking to them.

From the above, in particular the luxury treatment by potential future clients he enjoys, we should understand that he thinks large arms manufacturers still rely on smaller arms dealers like him. Why else such a treatment? It is why he also thinks that these big global arms manufacturers cannot make him and others like him ever fully obsolete.

> There will always be a need for people like me, always. When the day comes that governments rely only on manufacturing companies, they will soon come to realise […] Government employees don't know what they want. I've heard this so many times [from clients:] "We bought this and this from company XYZ but it's not exactly what we wanted". I said: "Why the hell did you fucking buy it?". [Client:] "Because they told us it was what we needed". I said: "This is why you need me. I will tell you what you want, I won't try to sell you what I have. I would tell you what you want, and I will find a supplier that has or manufactures that which you need". Going back to McDonalds; I won't take a Cheeseburger and sell you that instead of that a Big Mac. If you want a Big Mac, I will find you a Big Mac. You see what I'm getting at? Maybe there are companies that would take larger equipment, MANPADS [Man-portable air-defense systems], guided-missiles, Javelins, Milan […] there are a lot of products that are basically all the same. Each one of them has their own plusses and minuses. You will never ever find a company that has managed to manufacture something that doesn't have only plusses and no minuses. For example, I had XXXX. They wanted to buy antitank guns, antitank rockets but they wanted them to be so clever, that the […] it was a guided-antitank gun, or rocket. So, XXXX has one, the MAAWS [M3 Multi-role

> Anti-armour Anti-tank Weapon System]. I offered that to [XXXX] and [they] said: "Yeah this is great but what happens if the tank stops? Does the rocket miss?". I said: "It's not guided". These things were only here for the stationary, think about that. They said: "No, we want something that will hit when they're moving". I said: "Okay, they will hit when it's moving but if the driver hits the breaks before that thing reaches the target, it will miss". [XXXX replied:] "Oh that's no good". I said: "No, it's no good". Companies like XXXX won't tell them this. They will go into all the details about infrared tracking etc. etc. etc.! A simple question about what if the tank driver hits the breaks [they won't answer]. [XXXX] didn't buy that from XXXX in the end, they listened to me. [...] I get EXTREME satisfaction from knowing that company XYZ did NOT manage to sell their product to my client. Why? Because they weren't good enough.

He enjoys the game of being the underdog that beats the giant. It delivers him a sense of victory for the small-scale, craft arms dealers like himself, who are able 'to stick it to the Man'.

> It's not just the money. The money obviously plays a major part, but it's not JUST the money. If it was JUST the money then I would go and work for an arms manufacturer and sell as much shit as I could. I don't want to. I don't like to work for other people. I like to be my own boss. [...] I had a couple of companies try and headhunt me. I said: "You can't afford me". [They replied:] "Why?". I said: "Because I make more in a month than you can possibly pay me in a year". [...] I like being able to say NO to certain people. I like being able to say no to these arrogant businessmen of [arms] manufacturing companies that think that they can BUY anything. Like: "How much do you want?", was the question, "How much do you want to come work for us?". I said: "You can't afford me. I make more in a month than you can afford to pay me in a year". I might not make that every month, which I did not tell them, of course, but I like my freedom.

Eventually, as became clear, Constantine remains especially confident that large manufacturers will not be able to ruin his small-scale business and that of others, because they lack the street-level experience of war.

> I've seen war. A lot of arms dealers haven't seen war. I've seen people killed, I've seen people screaming for their mothers when they're dying. So, I know what guns can do. A lot of arms dealers, most of them haven't [seen war]. [...] A lot of them would only think of the money and the things that the money can buy from the deals. They say: "Fuck it, if we don't sell it, somebody else will". To me, like I said, up until now, I've not done, in my heart of hearts, I have not done anything immoral as far as the business is concerned. Either immoral, or illegal.

There is a certain noble endeavour in doing arms deals, based on having had first-hand experience in being in warzones. If others like him have the same sense of arms dealing craftsmanship, he is willing to collaborate with them. In fact, in rising up against large arms manufacturers, he considers himself to do that for other small-scale arms dealers as well, who he sometimes works together with and who he considers colleagues.

6.3 Smaller but stronger together

Doing business with other small-scale arms dealing craftsmen creates collegiality and collaborative interactions with others, but not necessarily friendship as he clearly indicated to me. Moreover, you must be careful with picking out who to work with, especially in the age of massive online presence and social media.

> You don't have friends in this business. You have colleagues. […] I tend now to keep a low profile. I fly under the radar, so to speak. […] The word gets around, you make contact with people that you have known from previous, shall we say, areas of your life, and you say: "Oh by the way I am [arms dealing] now". It's called networking. […] I'm always getting these strange requests from people I'm not even [familiar with]. I'm on XXXX at the moment. [Requests] from people that are not […] even in the same areas of work that I'm in. So I guess that XXXX is plugging my profile and is saying: "Join up with this one, he's got lots of connections". […] What I usually do is, I check who their friends are, and if I have any friends that are with them, or connections that are with them, then I'll choose one that I know quite well and I will write to them and say: "Do you know who this guy is or this woman is? What they do, is she straight [legal arms dealing]?" and one thing and another. Because, you know, I don't allow everybody into my circle, so to speak. Most people that I have in my circle are all in the counterterrorism, counterintelligence and counterinsurgency divisions.

Although remaining under the radar and sceptical of who he lets into his professional inner circle, he works closely together with only a few other small-scale arms dealers who have their own company and are not part of large arm manufacturers.

> There aren't a lot doing what I do, small arms and light weapons. […] I think there may be 5 or 6 in XXXX that do the small arms and light weapons, on an individual basis, now, I am talking about. There are obviously a lot that aren't licensed, that live in other countries, but they are XXXX, they have XXXX passports but they still do it, and that makes it illegal, for them anyway. […] As far as I know, there are only maybe

> a handful, maybe 8 or 10 people doing this. A lot have tried, a lot of fallen by the wayside. […] There are not many arms dealers in the world that deal legally. We as a group are basically outsiders of that group, because most people, other arms dealers I know, they would sell their own mothers if they could do it legally and make a fortune out of them. […] There are not many people that have licenses to sell arms. I'm talking about broker and dealer licenses. There's myself and one other guy, that I know of in XXXX. But he doesn't do very much business. In fact, he's a bit of an idiot, but that is his problem. There's only two that I know of, myself and one other guy with XXXX licenses.

On occasion, he requires help from such small-scale arms dealers to get specific arms or ammunition from countries where he does not have a strong network. For example, he told me about how he got approached by a government entity, a NATO ally, regarding the supply of quite a large amount of weaponry and ammunition that was going into a conflict zone.

> There's a lot of shit that they want in there [of which] the quantities don't make for good pricing. There's certain countries that I can't get the products from. One of the countries is XXXX. Now why XXXX? I thought: "This can't be right", because normally they would ban like Pakistan, China, Russia, Belarus, Ukraine. They would ban those countries, but this time they put XXXX in there as well, so I talked to my friend down in XXXX, and he said: "Let me make a few calls". He called up a couple of guys and he got back to me, he said: "Yes, because XXXX supplied [a rebel group]". […] The NATO ally […] didn't want XXXX selling to XXXX as well. […] [It was about ammunition] from XXXX [and it] was not allowed to be bought from [there] […] which surprised myself and also my colleague XXXX who deals a lot with them. […] We found out that this is a XXXX contract. Normally, they [the international authorities] would say: "You're not allowed to buy from Russia, China, Pakistan" and any other countries that are on the XXXX embargo. But they put XXXX in there and we couldn't figure out WHY. So, we called a couple of people in the industry in XXXX. […] They said: "Well, it was because XXXX won a very big arms deal and beat the XXXX with a big deal to the XXXX".

It is through other small-scale arms dealers that he considers colleagues, he receives information on (upcoming) embargoes, arms and ammunition requests and related business. He gives the same information to them in return. For example, his colleagues may provide the arms, and he could provide the ammunition to the same client, from which they would both make money. If either the arms are supplied without ammunition, or the other way around, clients are usually not interested, and therefore an opportunity would be missed out on.

> A colleague of mine approached me yesterday. He said: "I've been approached by a guy in XXXX. He's from XXXX". I said: "XXXX and XXXX are not the same countries, my friend. I'll forgive you because you're XXXX, so you don't really know jack shit about XXXX. What have you got for me?". He said: "I got this company there who's just giving the XXXX police force new pistols and they want to sell their old ones". I said: "What do they have?". He said: "They got the Tokarev", which is a 9x18 pistol. Now, the normal NATO round is 9x19, so the XXXX are changing over to NATO rounds for their police. I said: "How many are there?". He said: "12.000". So, it's 12.000 pistols, so I said: "Alright, let me have a look around and if I can find any ammunition, then if I can find ammo for them, then yes, I'm interested". So, now I have 12.000 XXXX Tokarev pistols for sale, to somebody, whoever, I don't know yet. [...] I'll call my colleague in XXXX and say I've got 12.000 Tokarevs and he'll say: "I've got buyers for those", because he's always got somebody.

There is a professional trust between him and others like him, individuals who operate on their own yet cannot do so entirely. There are three of those collegial small-scale arms dealers whom he works together with closely and frequently. He calls them the White Knights, which is one of the few groups that are active on the legal side of the business, he explained.

> There's me, a colleague of mine in XXXX, one in XXXX, and one in XXXX. So there's four of us altogether. I'm not mentioning [their] names. We've decided, and we've put this down between us, we will not sell under the table, we will not sell knowingly to third parties or end-users that are going sell them onto either terrorists or gangbangers or anybody like that. We control the used arms, I'm talking about stock. At the moment, [there are no] new [arms] that come from factories. If XXXX wanted to go and buy from the factory in XXXX, I'm sure that XXXX export would be more than happy to supply them. Although I'm not so sure that they would. Especially with the situation XXXX in XXXX. So no, we control that market and they didn't get their XX million [rounds]. In the end I know damn well they didn't get it. They tried for smaller quantities, X million, XX million, and they couldn't get it. Which makes my life somewhat difficult sometimes, not just me but the other three of us as well. We are considered, what shall we say, we are the four white knights [...] who don't sell just because we know that they are going to go somewhere that they shouldn't go, and [some clients] don't like us for that. [...] If I stop, there's three others. They won't stop, so as long as they're around, I'm not stopping either. It's the four of us that control that segment. Anybody that wants large quantities of ammunition they have to go through us. [...] We're the only four who control that amount of ammunition. [...] It means that the person in the ministries will not deal with anybody else because they get paid quite a lot of money by us

for making sure that we are the ones that they deal with. [...] From the stock, yes [we have global coverage. [...] And this is stuff that all four of us do, yeah? Because with one person to control that much, you would have to have an ENORMOUS amount of money. For one person alone it's too much. But we have a lot of stock in XXXX. It's in a salt mine, underground in a salt mine, and the salt is there to stop the humidity eating away at the metal.

Whereas large global arms manufacturers are too big to fail, Constantine and his White Knights are too small to succeed separately and fully independently. Some sort of collaboration and trust is important to establish among yourselves, because otherwise you will not make it on your own. Although he does not consider to have any friends in the arms trade, but merely colleagues, Constantine does refer to one of the White Knights as his friend.

I've known one of them, my guy, my friend in XXXX. I've known him since [...] 2008, 2009 when I first started in maritime security because he was also involved in that, and we met in XXXX. We had a chat and we decided we liked each other, and he introduced me to two other people. That was it. We decided then and there: everybody has their own, nobody mixes in anybody else's business, but we'll all work together. [...] If somebody comes to me and [says:] "I need X amount of rifles to go to Africa", I would turn around, I won't say no, I never say no, but I'll turn around and say: "Yeah, I'll get onto that for you, just let me get you a quote". Then I'd send an email to my guy in XXXX and say: "I got this client who wants x amount of whatever, can you do it?" [He would reply:] "Yes", [I would reply:] "Okay give me a price", and [...] he will give me a price and its usually like 15 to 20% mark-up [commission] on there, which is mine. I do the same for him. So everybody is working together, but independently as well, and we don't tread on each other's toes. [...] I think the reason why we teamed up was because we realised that we were a lot stronger together than trying to cut each other's throat as far as prices are concerned. We decided that we would work together. If anybody came to me for something and I couldn't source it, then I would go to them. Each one would use their sources, their resources, whatever it was I wanted. If somebody would come to them and they couldn't find it, well then they would come to me and say: "Do you have any resources for this that and the other?". [...] We do anything [...] we, as in total.

I had to understand that the three others he works with are the only ones who he trusts professionally, but not personally. Moreover, his professional trust in them is not unconditional.

They have a different outlook on life. When we get together, it's only for business. I don't talk personally with them. [...] We're the only ones doing

> it legal, let's put it that way. If I found out anyone of them was doing it black, then I'd probably turn around and kick him in the ass, because we got a pretty good business going and there's no need to be greedy. [...] I'm one of the guys that makes sure that everything I do is on the line, straight down the line. No fucking around, no shady deals under the table.

If there would be disagreement about a deal amongst each other, he would try to have a mediator involved, or some sort of third person and they would discuss

> until I got my way. [...] I don't like losing. I don't like losing, obviously. Who does? Usually it's me trying to hold these other three guys back a bit. It's the other way around. The other ones that want to sell sell sell sell sell. I'm like: "Guys, come one, cool it, let's look at where this shit is going". [...] I have my feet anchored on the ground. I don't like: "Yeah let's get this deal and we can sell here, and do this and do that". I'm like: "Okay, let's take a step back and let's look at this for a moment before you guys start buying airplanes and shit". [...] It's just the way I look at life. [...] I don't like making rash decisions because unless you know every aspect what you're going to do and every facet of the decision that you're making, you don't know what the consequences could be. You have to look at everything, especially in this industry. You have to look at everything under a magnifying glass before you do it. I mean, we've lost deals because of this. Afterwards, in hindsight, I said to the guys: "Okay you were right, we should have done it, we could have done it, and it would have been okay, but imagine if one of those facets had gone the wrong way, then all three of us would have been in the shit". [They'd reply:] "Yeah but we weren't". [I would reply:] "Well then, alright, next time we could have been". It's better to take one step backwards and look through the door instead of just rushing through the door. You don't know what's on the other side until you've opened the door and taken a look. [...] They value mine, as I value theirs. They value my expertise, if I can put it in that way. They value my opinion, they value my professionalism. They haven't said anything otherwise. We have some slagging matches sometimes between us, because somebody wants to do a deal and the others are against it. Even down to where the one guy said: "Can I do this on my own?" and we said together: "You do that, you're out". So, you know, it's a way of making sure that what you're doing is not going to lead to any problems in the future.

However, if there would be done something without his knowing, and of which he finds he should have known about it

> then there will be hell to pay. I would make sure they won't be very long in business. [...] There are many other ways to sabotage somebody's business.

> [...] You just make sure that, for example, one of the shipments you tip off Interpol or Europol, or whoever, and say that they're breaking an embargo or that there's something wrong with the equipment, or whatever, so there's a [...] It's annoying for them. [...] If they still went ahead and sold something to somebody of whom I said: "I wouldn't like this person or this country to be sold to" [...] they haven't done it up until now. As far as I know they wouldn't do it.

What we can see regarding his dealings with other small-scale arms dealers as colleagues, is the fragile line he has to walk in between professional trust and distrust, all to maintain business continuation.

6.4 Conclusion

Constantine brings together people. He deals on a daily basis with and for clients, in-between sellers, and sometimes through and with arms manufacturers together. Moreover, other small-scale arms dealers like himself are parties he works with. Despite never seeing any of his clients, he must trust them professionally. Simultaneously, he also distrusts them regarding whether their 'situation' that they require arms and ammunition for, is steady enough; his business depends on both perpetual war and perpetual peace. He feels like he must survive in competition with global arms manufacturers that dominate the international arms trade and have better means, more offer and are far more connected throughout the world. Luckily, there are a few other small-scale arms dealers left in the killing arena of the arms trade. He works together with them, which only works if there is trust and honesty among them. Together they can deliver the total solutions of arms and ammunition packages to their shared clients. In (dis)trusting and brokering for and between clients, while competing with large arms manufacturers, arms dealing has also become a legal and logistical puzzle (Kruse 2016; Melé 2018) that enforces legal arms dealing business entrepreneurs to comply with certain rules of the arms dealing game, as much as they are subjected to a hypocritical game of the rules, as Chapter 7 will delve into.

References

Engelbrecht HC (1934) The problem of the munitions industry. *The ANNALS of the American Academy of Political and Social Science* 174(1): 121–125.

Eurosatory (2022) The defence & security global event. From: www.eurosatory.com/?lang=en.

Kruse K (2016) What I learned from an international arms dealer. From: www.forbes.com/sites/kevinkruse/2016/09/12/what-i-learned-from-an-international-arms-dealer/?sh=1b929aeb54a0.

Loader I (1999) Consumer culture and the commodification of policing and security. *Sociology* 33(2): 373–392.

Melé A (2018) So you want to be an arms dealer?. From: www.linkedin.com/pulse/so-you-want-arms-dealer-tony-mel%C3%A9/.

Moore M (2010) Arming the embargoed: a supply-side understanding of arms embargo violations. *Journal of Conflict Resolution* 54(4): 593–615.

Raab J & Milward HB (2003) Dark networks as problems. *Journal of Public Administration Research and Theory: J-PART* 13(4): 413–439.

Ritzer G (2013) *The McDonaldization of society*. London: Sage.

SIPRI (2020) Global arms industry: sales by the top 25 companies up 8.5 per cent; Big players active in Global South. From: www.sipri.org/media/press-release/2020/global-arms-industry-sales-top-25-companies-85-cent-big-players-active-global-south.

Zedner L (2006) Liquid security: managing the market for crime control. *Criminology & Criminal Justice* 6(3): 267–288.

7 The rules of the game and the game of the rules

Laws, politics, public opinion and personal morality

> Learn how to construct a bid packet, on time, in full compliance, as the low bidder, competing against the manufacturers who also quoted you. Navigate all of that until you close a deal, asking yourself repeatedly; "So, you want to be an Arms Dealer?"
>
> (Melé 2018 – online source)

The above was publicly shared on LinkedIn by Anthony Melé, a defence trade broker. It shows, and as has been pointed out before about both the illegal and legal international arms trade, how arms dealing has become, if anything, a matter of having to navigate through a difficult logistical puzzle of international relations, legal regulations and management of numerous governmental agencies and private actors (cf. Brogan & Zarca 1983; Kruse 2016; Potter 2012). What will become clear in this chapter as well, is that additionally the public opinion and one's personal morality play an important part in the puzzling rules of the game and the game of the rules.

7.1 Documented control and reaping benefits from laws, licenses and punishments

In brokering his deals, Constantine is required to work within several international arms control laws that are designed to keep the legal arms trade legal and to combat illegal arms dealing. There are several international treaties, rules and regulations Constantine feels subjected to in order to do his job, in particular the Arms Trade Treaty (ATT), certain national trade licenses and the end-user certificate (EUC).

The arms trade was not always as regulated as it is now. For a long time, the arms trade was unregulated and rather lawless; he pities those days are gone.

> Everybody basically did what they wanted. These licences, these [specific licences] that I hold, are actually quite a new thing. They came in afterwards, as a way of the government showing: "We didn't know anything about this! We are now introducing a special licensing system! So that

DOI: 10.4324/9781315148236-8

> we have transparency about who does what". This is bullshit, it's total bullshit.

The arms trade was for him a free-for-all trade that he enjoyed working in before. Before the juridification of the arms trade, and before the controlling, penetrating regulations, it was better, he nostalgically told me.

> I remember the days before arms dealers were licensed [...] that was the beginning of the 80ies. There were people going to the Ukraine buying 'scrap metal' as it was called, selling it to Africa with export licenses from the Ukraine. Officially, the Ukraine was paid off, people would sign an export license for ANYTHING. A lot of these weapons turned up in Africa, turned up in the Homs [Syria], later on in Afghanistan, al Qaeda, African countries [where] there was war, Liberia. The XXXX government started [...] Well, there was a reporter actually. Fucking reporters, they're always making a mess of things. It was an investigative reporter that found out about this, and they did a big exposé and it got into the hands of the left-wing government in XXXX who called for parliamentary inquiry as to who these people were. [...] The results of the inquiry never really came out, but they then decided they would start licensing arms dealers and trader, or brokers, which was where the XXXX department came from. All these weapons from Ukraine were sold anywhere in the world, anywhere and everywhere. "Shop until [you] drop dead in a land far, far away" hahaha! [...] What [arms dealers] were doing after [licensing was introduced], was illegal. Only people [governments] making the law could do it. [...] It was a case of: "This is good for us, and you're not allowed to do it anymore". [...] I'm hoping that [those golden days] come around again. I don't really see it happening, but I hope they do. [...] You knew where you were. It was up to the people themselves who are doing the deals, to have some sense of responsibility and morality as to who they sold to.

The international politics and their governance and laws on the arms trade have taken away the self-regulating and moralising mechanisms of the arms trade, he finds.

Yet he still 'chose to stay in business and do my business my way within the borders of legality'. In doing so, he has to hold different licenses and be in possession of certificates that guarantee the legality of his deals. The most important one is a specific trade license that cannot be specified here due to the safeguarding of Constantine's anonymity. With that trading license of his country, his deals can cover small arms and light weapons as well as the other military goods and so-called dual-usage goods that comprise products and certain technologies that are normally used for civilian purposes but could also have military applications (European Commission 2018). That license allows him to transfer his arms and ammunition to, through and from specified countries.

> I have [a specific SALWs trade license], I have [a specific military goods trade license], and I have dual-use export license. What that means is, if that somebody wants [...] For example, I mentioned the last time: drones to XXXX. The guy asked to me: "Can we put payload on there?". I said: "If you put a payload on there, I'm selling you then military equipment, which is not going to be easy to get an export license for. We'll leave it without the payload. What YOU do with it afterwards, is not my business. You just have to make sure that the ordered one from me has got strong enough motors to be able to carry a payload. It's not my business what you do with it afterwards. You said you were using it for humanitarian purposes, making sure that civilians don't get killed, then this is perfect, it's a good excuse. What you do with it afterwards, then I don't want to know about it".

Besides his licenses, there is one certificate that matters the most to him. International law and European Union (EU) rules specifically demand from buyers to provide an end-user certificate, abbreviated an EUC, to Constantine. By having an EUC, legal arms dealers have a guarantee that the arms and ammunition they delivered to the client are indeed the final recipient and that they will not resell to a third party (Bromley & Griffiths 2010). This way, through legal arms dealers, an overview of the flow of arms is maintained. EUCs are thus important as they 'significantly contribute to preventing the diversion of small arms and light weapons (SALW) to the illicit market', but also 'limit the chances of SALW reaching conflict zones or embargoed destinations' (ibid.: 1). An EUC must be provided, otherwise it becomes impossible for Constantine to broker a deal.

> There was a shopping list, given to me quite some time ago for a lot of hardware [arms and ammo]. Normally, there's an arms embargo on XXXX, but when we asked: "Who's it for?", we were told: "It's for these and these people and the oil companies are paying, and it's sanctioned by the XXXX in XXXX, and the EUCs will be signed off by the European Governments", whichever European government stock that we would be getting. Then I said: "Okay, we'll do it".

He made me understand though that

> [e]nd-user certificates, by the way, can be written by anybody. There are three kinds of end-user certificates. [...] The 1st one is the government-to-government end-user certificate where one government buys, one government sells, technology or arms to another government. The 2nd EUC

> is where a private entity buys from an arms dealer, a private entity in this instance would be the [private] police, which is not a government body, security-related agency, private security, private military companies. [...] The 3rd kind is where a factory, and not many people know this, is where a factory buys or produces or buys from a factory of chemicals. They have to have an end-user certificate, or an end-user understanding that the products are not going to be used for the production of weapons of mass destruction. Lots of people don't know that. I used to write all my own anyway. I still do in fact. Then I get the government of the country that is buying to stamp it up, to get it. Or if they send me an EUC for a quantity of arms. I used to take it to the embassy of the country that they send it from and get it verified. This is how I cover my back. Because I would go into an embassy and say: "I'd like to see somebody in your department. Can you verify this for me?", and if necessary, if it's in Arabic for example, I usually get a certified translated copy.

Given that anyone can write an EUC and can get it signed off, he thinks, shows his frustration about there not being enough control on 'international standards and national practices for the issuing and verification of EUCs and other types of supporting documentation' (Bromley & Griffiths 2010: 1). In fact, the EUC system is rather easily circumvented when the buyer uses documents that have been officially but falsely signed off, according to Constantine. Instead of it being a technique of control, according to research it has become more of

> a tool for the personal enrichment of corrupt officials in the purchasing country, and a means by which selling countries could establish an alibi (the weapons were supposed to go elsewhere) whenever news of a sale to some embargoed or illegal destination leaked out.
>
> (Naylor 2001: 51)

Constantine has several experiences with such an illusion of arms control through EUCs and he detests the fact there are so many loopholes governments have created through EUCs.

> That's the thing, you sell something under humanitarian aid grounds. [...] Let me give you a perfect example. [...] [Before the stricter regulation] you could send various goods that had been taken apart. You could sell the helicopter as a humanitarian aid equipment and you could sell the rocket launchers to another person with a different EUC in the same country. It was like that at one time because nobody was interested in stopping the flow of arms. It's exactly the same. I might sell something and if the person writes on the EUC [...] If the government signs the EUC that says: "It won't be used in connection with [...]" what did they say [...] "the manufacturer [...]" or "conveyance of tactical weapons", we're talking

> about nuclear weapons or WMD. They sign on the EUC that this is what will happen. Now what they do afterwards isn't anybody's business. There's no way of controlling it. The governments make the laws, they make them how they want them. They deliberately leave loopholes in them so that they are able to get around them and people like me are able to get around them, if we know where these loopholes are. Anybody who sold [arms] knows exactly where they are. The fact of the matter is, it's the liberal pussies in XXXX screaming: "You can't do this, you can't do that, it's immoral!". Well unfortunately, they all want free universities and free healthcare, and other shit. They don't seem to realise where that money is coming from. It's all very well to say "Tax the rich, tax the rich", well that's the problem with socialism is that sooner or later you run out of everybody else's money. It doesn't work that way.

Next to the EUC and the specific lists of arms and ammunition he can trade in, lists exist of countries that he can buy from and sell too, but they require a special type of license, which is for a one-off individual trade with them, he explained.

> It means I have to ask an extra permission from the XXXX government who will then look at it […] and say "Hmm" and then depending on where the arms begin to be transported from, which country they're coming from, or which country they're going to, the decision will be made about the countries', for example, human rights situation. For example, I wanted to sell XXXX rifles to XXXX. It was turned down […] because of the human rights delicts. […] It was last year [2015]. […] If the arms or the military equipment was produced in XXXX and I was brokering a deal to the XXXX government, then the chances are that the XXXX government would say: "We will allow you to arrange the deal", because it's good business for the XXXX country. Now, in this case the arms were not being made in XXXX, they were made by XXXX in XXXX, which is a XXXX company. I was turned down [disappointed]. It's the double standards that really make me annoyed […] designed by the XXXX government of course, where money and employment takes priority over human lives.

Following up on his comment on human lives, I wondered whether because of missing licenses and he could not deliver to certain parties 'fighting the good fight', he would still try to get arms and ammunition to them. Basically, would he feel the moral need to somehow help them by supplying arms despite not being allowed to?

> I would get somebody else to do it for me. I wouldn't be involved, but I would still be making money out of it. […] I would pass it onto a colleague of mine who would do the deal, who is in a country where they

> don't have such restrictions that I have on my licenses. He would do it, and we'd talk about the price and then he would say: "Here's your cut, thank you very much". I'd get some commission, of course. […] Why should I give somebody else the business if he is not gonna give me a drink?

As much as he pities the juridification of the arms trade and has difficulties with the loopholes built in laws by governance, he does give meaning to his compliance with the law, making him feel that he is doing the right thing.

> See, I'm an arms dealer with a conscience. […] It says on my licenses. If I even suspect that the arms brokered by me could be used by a person or exported to a third party, then I must not do the business. So? If that's the way that it's got to be, that's the way it's got to be. I don't sell under the table. […] Every movement [of arms and ammo] that I make, has to be recorded and sent to […] Well actually, it doesn't [happen]. It's supposed to. Every movement that I do if I sell to somebody, then I have to, at the end of the year, I have to fill out an online form for the XXXX government, which is [an export department]. I have to say on what occasions I used my licenses for the brokerage or trade and transportations of small arms and light weapons, from and to. Wait, it doesn't say "from", it only says "to". So it doesn't ask me which countries I'm buying from, just where I deliver to. This is military only. So, if I did anything wrong then I might lose my licenses! Which means I wouldn't be able to work and keep my wife and the styles she has become accustomed to hahaha!

Next to his licenses and EUCs, Constantine is confronted with countries being punished by the international community, in particular embargoes and economic sanctions. What an arms embargo does is that it restricts entirely or partially the right to purchase weaponry and dual-use technology and thus serves as a type of sanction to coerce governments and non-governmental actors to comply in accordance with international peace and security (SIPRI 2021). Although the embargo that serves as a sanction is presented as a most effective legal tool to control the legal arms trade, arms exporting states have systemically violated nearly every international arms embargo for a variety of economic and especially political interests (Moore 2010). Embargoes can actually be good for Constantine's business, I had to understand.

> There's a big lead up to [an embargo]. There will be talks of UN sanctions, and talks of arms embargoes. What normally happens before an arms embargo is that the country KNOWS they're in trouble, basically, because they would been warned [by the UN]. What they do is, before there's going to be a war, and before there's any arms embargoes, or before there's any sanctions put on that country, they will buy as much as they can from whoever they can. And that would be legal, because there's no sanctions. […] I would be a very bad businessman if I didn't [keep track of the

embargo talks]. [...] You see the thing is, when countries are gonna be put on an embargo, it's not like it happens overnight. These countries know about it beforehand, so they call every arms dealer on the planet and say: "We NEED arms". I mean obviously the arms dealers know it's gonna be put on an embargo soon as well. [...] What I hope is that I'm gonna find out there's an arms embargo before it happens, so I can sell them shit before they get stopped. [...] The countries wanna buy anything and everything that's on the market. [...] It's like Black Friday! [...] You go well before [a conflict starts and an embargo is effective]. Because they're not stupid, they know what's gonna happen. [...] I keep my ears to the ground, I'm also a geopolitical analyst, yeah? I look at all the countries. I have information on practically every country in the world. Western world and the Africans. [...] That's when you go and say: "I have this this this and this this this on offer. It looks very much like you're gonna need it". The government at the time knows what's going on because they've seen it coming. They may even have experienced it in the past.

Even if a country is embargoed, there are still ways to make money from deals with it, yet indirectly. In particular, proxy-wars are a tactic for larger powerful states, for example, the United States and Russia, to still run their arms trade while circumventing embargos through arms dealers. Altogether, proxy-wars can lead to interesting business opportunities for Constantine.

> Proxy-wars are the best kind of business for arms dealers. Proxy-wars, wars that are made from one government to another country but without the government being involved. [...] When somebody approaches me and asks me to supply certain weapons, certain things to certain groups of people, and they paid me to do it, and I get the papers to do it, and I have the legality to do it, then I'd do it. That's where you make money, that's a proxy war. When the Americans and the Russians started arming the fighters directly, there was no need for third parties like myself.

Alongside the embargos, are the economic sanctions laid upon countries; sanctions he puzzles with on a daily basis. They comprise, for example, trade suspension and export and import restrictions that make it difficult for Constantine to broker deals. Actually, there are no benefits to get from (unexpected) effects of such sanctions, he claimed. For example, the EU put sanctions on trading with Russia, due to the Crimea conflict, which directly limited his capabilities to do trading with Russia.

> The European sanctions on Russia have basically put me out of business, because the majority of my work was done with XXXX. That is a Russian military export company. I can't buy or sell or deal anything with Russia anymore. I'm not even allowed to have communications with them. It even goes so far as BANNING people from sending tourists to the Crimea or

> Sebastopol. I can go to jail for a long, long time. Even for doing that, I am not allowed to make any financial transactions with Russia etc. etc. These are all sanctions from the European Union put on Russia, which basically has made my life extremely hard. Now if I was, shall we say, that way inclined I would tell them to basically go screw themselves, drop my passport, get another nationality, and continue doing it. [...] If the European Union hadn't been so bloody stupid and put sanctions on Russia and Crimea, I could have sold [...] I still have in XXXX about XXX.XXX AK47s and XX.XXX AKMs, a whole bunch of other stuff, and I can't move it legally. So it's stuck there. [...] Before the Russian thing, before Russia got sanctioned, [I had] a lot of armoured trucks, the XXXX and the XXXX armoured personnel carriers. I even have in XXXX at the moment [...] X XXXX battleships, gunships, helicopters.

The sanctioning of Russia is bad for Constantine's business. His critique is not only direct at the EU because of missing out on income. It also reflects his overall frustration with the EU 'where every country agrees to a law being in place, but then individually they can break it. This is something. It just doesn't rub with me. I don't really see how they can do it', he said. So, as long as he reaps the benefits from licenses, the EUC system and punishments such as sanctions and especially embargos, he is okay with the control ineffectiveness and hypocrisy of the arms control. But when they are only causing him trouble, then he becomes critical of (imagined) power politics behind arms treaties, laws, licences and punishments. He then feels the need to uncover the hypocrisy of arms control and its governance.

7.2 Exposing the governmental hypocrisy and the illusion of arms control

The double standard he is blaming governments of is also something Constantine can have himself when he talks about arms laws, licences and sentences as mere legal façades that governments can hide behind to pursue their own goals. He does the same thing.

> Then I hear about XXXX that it sold XX pistols with REAL ammunition to the XXXX Ministry of Defence. They sold XXXX pistols to them. So, here we go again, where you have an arms embargo on XXXX, or had for small arms and things that could be used to repress the population, and one country is sticking to the letter of the law, and the other country's saying: "Well fuck it, I'm going to sell it to them anyway". I mean, you've got law [...] and these laws are made by the EU, but at the same time, the countries, they decide for themselves. So what's the point? [...] If you're going to have laws, then you should have them and they should abide by them. If you [do] not, then they should be open to anybody. [...] They

> give you a license, and they've got all the so-called checks and balances in place to make sure you don't do anything that you shouldn't do. How do they do these checks and balances? Well they send you a form around at the end of the year and it states: "Tell us where you've used your [trade licenses], from where to where?" It's a little like an Excel spreadsheet. Now you can put in there what you want. Do they check on it? In my case they haven't. Nobody ever checked on me. I don't know if I told you in the beginning when I opened the company, they sent me a letter to say that they wanted to do a compliance audit. I said: "Okay, no problem. If you want to come to XXXX". [Auditor replied:] "What do you mean XXXX? Your company is in XXXX". I said: "That's just a registered address". [Auditor replied:] "Where do you keep all your papers?". I said: "I keep them in XXXX". [Auditor replied:] "How can we do a compliance visit?". I said: "That's your problem not mine". In the end we agreed after a long debate and many exchanged emails, that I would tell them when and what is sold to whom.

If anything, embargoes are but a documented reality for him. They have no real effect, as you can also circumvent an embargo rather easily, as seen with the EUC system. As a matter of fact, he explained he could use an EUC from one government to have arms transported from another country to have it imported into the purchasing country that is embargoed.

> It's another one [of those] check the boxes-mentality: "Have you? No! Did you? No. Have you? Yes. Where? There.". So basically you're answering the questions how they want them. Whether a person is actually telling the truth or not, is debatable. I know I do, and I'd put my hand in the fire or on a stack of bibles and swear to the Almighty God, but I can't speak for other people. [...] If people think they can get away with [cheating on paper], and they're unscrupulous, they will. That's my opinion. It's big money. If you have a big order [...] I mean, orders have come to me in the millions. I had one, XXXX million dollars. XXX. HUNDRED. MILLION. DOLLARS! That's a lot of money! This was sanctioned by XXXX. The country they would be going to was under an arms embargo at this time. But it was sanctioned by XXXX. Before all this was going on, in XXXX at the moment, it was starting to going on, I was approached, well, my colleagues and I were approached to supply a very, very large shopping list of equipment. And our first question was: "Where is it going? Oh it's going to XXXX. It's got an arms embargo" [he said to his colleagues]. "Never mind, we will give you an EUC, it will be delivered to XXXX, and from there WE will move it to the area". [He replied:] "Alright, you get me the correct papers from the XXXX and your government saying I'm in the clear and you can have the shit".

Meaning, those who can put an embargo on countries may not comply with the embargo themselves. For him, it is another example of how governments make proper use of

> so many loopholes. These laws allow the XXXX defence industry, for example, to sell bombs to the XXXX that are bombing XXXX. Flying arms to countries that are, shall we say, not politically stable. They left a lot of holes in their [laws]. There are ways and means, I won't say diverting the product. There are legal ways and means of being able to move those things around so that they get where they're supposed to be going without seeming to break the rules. The XXXX defence industry and the XXXX, XXXX and XXXX, which is a British export industry, they're both governmental organisations, they are culpable of rushing through laws on the winds of, what shall we say, parliamentary committees that don't really want to be bound down to say "You can't sell that to them". I mean we're not talking about fighter jets or technology. […] Let me put it this way: those who make the laws, write the laws to suit themselves. […] If you're gonna have laws to sell arms, especially SALW—because they are really the instruments of mass destruction—and if you say "Oh they shouldn't go there", but then later on you find out that the XXXX government has sent via another country […] the arms have gone to the country that [said:] "Oh we shouldn't be selling to these people, because they're naughty boys". It's a little bit, at best, UNETHICAL.

It is unethical and hypocritical according to Constantine who depends himself on that very same (and what he considers) unethical and hypocritical governance. This, while he is trying to run a business as a small-scale arms dealer. The embargoes and the politics behind them are making it harder and harder for Constantine to do his business.

> You know, the loopholes that the governments make when they put embargos on countries, I'm talking generically now […] When governments of the world make laws for arms, they make them in such a way that they can still do business. […] Of course it is [unfair]! The governments make the loopholes so that government companies, big companies, like BAE [British Aerospace Systems], Krauss-Maffei Wegmann, and all of the big, big arms dealers so that government-to-government deals can still go through. The brokers, me for example, can't even get the crumbs off the table. Basically, it's a way of cutting me out of the business. They won't ever cut me out, but the thing is, I feel that it's wrong on one side for them to morally preach that illegal arms are bad, and then on the other side turn around, make laws, that allow them to do exactly the same thing. […] It's money, Yarin, it's all about the dollar. […] It's about the dollar and also about having work in their countries, because a lot of countries are

now only defence product manufacturers. If they can't sell their product, well, people would be out of a job.

He feels betrayed and thinks it has taken away the honesty from legal arms dealing, but it also limits his dealing: 'It's got to the point where an honest arms dealer can't make an honest buck. Let's put it that way. That's the way it's going at the moment, in my opinion'.

Moreover, in relation to the power politics of governments that create the laws and licenses with their loopholes, presenting it as an effective control of arms, he thinks the political agenda of controlling arms violates the right to bear arms and frustrates the ability to defend oneself. He sometimes worries about 'tree hugging leftist politicians' that respond erratically, he finds, to violent events, such as terrorist attacks, and that promise arms-free societies. The example he gave was of a new EU law that was up for debate at the time of interviewing, controlling the total confiscation of semi-automatic rifles by making amendments to the EU's Firearms Directive. It is a direct response to the November 2015 Paris massacres.

> We are seeing governments that will be making laws and taking arms from people, legal arms from legal shooters to satisfy part of the public that doesn't know anything about guns [and] that's not interested in guns. [...] Small arms and semi-automatic rifles will be confiscated from people that legally own them and have licences for them and all they are is sport shooters. This is has been a push by the French and a couple of other European countries [...] for what has happened in Paris. They want to confiscate all the arms from all the legal arms holders in Europe. If they start doing this, now what's gonna happen? The people that have these arms, are gonna buy them from somewhere else, the black arms industry will take off. People will not give their guns. If they have to give up their gun, they will go and buy something from under the table [...] which means that more and more guns will be sold. Basically, all they're doing by introducing this law is creating a[n illegal] market. [...] They just don't see it!

Once more, it is the EU as an unnecessarily patronising, supranational nanny state (cf. Bengtsson & Elgström 2011) he has an issue with, exercising raw power over gun ownership.

> I also own a pistol, I have it locked in my safe here behind me. The only thing that concerns me now is the fact that there's going to be a witch hunt against all of the legal gun holders. I mean, Germany is one of the hardest countries in Europe to get a gun license or at least a license to carry. If you're a member of a shooting club, then obviously you get a license, the same as everywhere in Europe. Last week, there was a motion set forward. Last week was the final decision: the re-categorisation of

> small arms and light weapons. […] This was basically on the books for a long time. Since the Paris Attacks. Basically put forward by the French, rather stupidly. Again, it's about people having their guns taking off them because the powers that be think they know what's good for other people. Just because a terrorist gets hold of a gun or madman gets hold of a gun, they're gonna take the guns of, well, TRYING to take the guns of normal people, which means, in their opinion, nobody would be able to get a gun which is absolutely stupid. […] It's pretty stupid, it doesn't happen. Gun-free zone, put a gun-free zone in the school in the [United] States and you get somebody to go up with a gun, he's not gonna look at the sign and say: "Oh, I'm not allowed in there". He's gonna say: "How nice, I'm not gonna find anybody with a gun inside". You just don't hear about things like that in the mass media where people that are legally armed have actually saved other people by shooting the bad guy. […] Why you don't hear about it? Well it's the agenda of the global elite to get everybody unarmed, or disarmed, so that they can […] I mean […] have you seen the film or read the book by Alduous Huxley? Brave New World? Yeah, well there you go, we're on the way […] It's not paranoia, it's the way I see it.

There was a push by the government he is licensed by to do arms dealing, he explains, to enforce arms dealers to be more transparent about their business. It was a parliamentary committee about transparency in the arms trade.

> Some bright spark came up with the idea of publishing online all the names and addresses of all the arms dealers that were registered in XXXX. […] I wrote to them, and said: "If you do this you're putting my life in danger", which is true! […] They're still talking about that […] I don't think this ever came out in the news. […] They would have my registered business address, but if they have the registered business address they very well find out who the director is and what their private address is. I wrote to them: "If you do something like this, you're putting the lives of a lot of people on the line". I'm not sure whether they cancelled it, or whether it is still in debate, which is why I carry [a] gun with me all the time in XXXX anyway. I carry one all the time. […] I wrote to them and said: "If you do this, the people that you name and list will hand their licenses in, because they will be afraid. They will go underground and you'll have more black arms dealers than before". The arms will still be moved, they [would] just be moved without anybody knowing it. So, in the end they decided, and on the basis of my comments, I'd imagine, and couple of other people that I know, they didn't publish it! Thank God.

Such transparency is dangerous and it has led to Constantine being careful with getting more licenses he may need for his deals. Besides authorities then 'crawling up in every orifice in your body, looking at what you're doing', he thinks that getting more licenses 'brings you too much into the spotlight'.

Plus, he already has enough of them and having to get more would perhaps motivate him to go into the illegal side of arms dealing.

> The different licenses that I have, which is pretty extensive, and then you have to do the background checks and the rest of the crap that goes with it. Then I would turn around and would do it black. I would say: "Thank you very much for the licenses, but I've decided that I'm gonna sell to this country and that country, and any other country that I want to, and I don't really care what you say". If they could catch me, and they would eventually, I'd be put in prison at best. Now why is this not happening to people in government? Now that's the real hypocrisy of it. [...] As I said, the loopholes of the governments, they will always be there. As long as you have people screaming: "Ooooh, the arms trade is bad, you can't do this, you shouldn't be able to do that", the government's gonna go turn around and say: "Okay, let's do something, let's make it better".

The hypocrisy of it all is something he detests, also how widespread the awareness of the loopholes is, according to him, is extra

> frustrating. If I had anything to say about it, I'd like to tear the world in pieces and start all over again, because once again we come down to the military-industrial complex, or the industrial-military complex, however you want to call it, that basically dominates the world where so much money is made from war and suffering of small, of innocent people [...] That it is schizophrenic on the one side to be able to say: "I'm a licensed arms dealer, and by the laws of the country that issued my licenses" and on the other side see what that country is doing for their OWN gain by selling bombs and other mass destruction weapons to countries that have no human rights in their constitution. [...] What we've come to is that governments and big business are only interested in making and selling arms FOR WARS, so that they can keep the politicians in power and keep making money for the factory owners. [...] If you are selling fire wood, you need fire to sell your firewood. If you want to sell guns, you need a war. America has sold to just about every person in America. They all have weapons, practically, they all have a pistol, they all have rifles, possibly even three or four. In Europe it's not so bad. But, once you've sold to your own population, who do you sell to? [...] I will send you a couple of emails with some of the deals that are going on in the world at the moment. These are Raytheon, Northrop Grumman, these companies make billions and billions and billions per year, on government defence contracts. They have people that are dying on the streets, because they got cancer or aids, why don't they use money, to help these people? You see what I mean? It's like there's absolutely no accountability. [...] When you start seeing this process going through, you start to join the dots and you realise that nobody gives a shit about the laws that are being made,

> no government gives a shit. All they're interested in is the politicians keeping their seats, the people being able to work and where the arms go. Doesn't make any difference to them. […] To them it's nothing. The price of human life, is very cheap. […] The major industries in the world today are all based on war. They're all based on war, EVERY SINGLE industry, apart from the motor industry, and perhaps pharmaceutical industry. Well, even they're based on war, because a lot of their products are financed by [a] department of defence, or the ministry of defence. […] The future of the industry is [that] there will always be wars. […] The way I see the industry is just gonna be constant war in one part of the world or another. […] This is why I basically agreed to do this [biography] with you and it's basically to show Joe Public [the truth].

When I asked him why he did not go public before with his frustration and present his ideas about possible conspiracies regarding the military-security-complex that willingly creates legal loopholes, he reacted as if he had given up on it: if he would go public, governments would still get away with their violations of the laws they themselves made.

> I couldn't ever publicly denounce the XXXX government for making laws with loopholes, just so that they could work around them and still make all their money. If you look at what the Americans and the Brits are selling to Saudi Arabia for their bombing campaigns in Yemen, it's all legal. Does it make it right? Not in my opinion. […] Blowing the lid off, I know, I know, I can't. I can't. I would have to go underground, I would have to get a new identity, I would have to move with my family to an island in the XXXX, where nobody would know about anything, and even there I wouldn't be safe. Somebody, be it a government from my country or from another country would want to close my mouth. Yeah? And they would want to close it permanently. This is obviously something that I have to be extremely aware of.

It became apparent to me is that Constantine accepted his position: 'Governments are always involved […] those are the big players. I'm just a small cog in a very, very large wheel'. The politics of it all, the unfairness and the hypocrisy surrounding it – it is here to stay, he thinks, keeping nothing genuine about the arms trade and the wider business of war anymore.

> All people are lovely, all people are lovely! It's just fucking politicians that screw everything up. It's true, come on, let's face it. Let's face it. […] War is a terrible business, don't get me wrong. It's a terrible business, but it is a business. It's the only reason why wars are made now. […] I don't think there's been an honourable war since the Second World War, and even that's debatable. […] I don't make the laws which allow people like me to

> sell their weapons. That's the difference. [...] If they don't want people to sell these things, then they should make it illegal. Full stop. But they do because economies of certain countries run on the defence industry. [...] I am only a product of what these politicians have done, that's the way I see it. [...] I'm just a passive little tool [*sarcastic tone*], jumping at the opportunity to make an honest buck. I'm not so passive about making that buck either. I will go out of my way to sell shit.

Despite his critique on it, he would not want to see the game of the rules on arms control and the hypocritical governance of it disappear. What

> would be quite interesting [however, is] to run a course [...], where you [...] get a grasp on the European export licenses and the export control mechanisms in Europe. [...] *How to become a licensed [arms dealer]*. Yeah, in fact, it could be classified as a new trade! Yeah! An MA in arms dealing! [...] That, or an MSc. [...] It is not impossible. [...] The [authority I am licensed by] have webinars and conferences. [...] They say: "You can't export this, and you can't export that" but they don't tell you how to get around these things. They just say: "You can't do this", but actually you can! You just have to know how to do it.

So, as much as he is against the hypocritical system, in case you have the capacity and capability, and have the right information, you can make the system work for you, he thinks. Therefore, he would not go so far as having an arms trade anarchy, 'because an anarchist is somebody who's for total chaos [...] what you'll then end up within a country is a feudal system, which is pretty stupid'. Such chaos would also be bad for his own business continuation. All in all, despite having a deeply felt aversion to them

> I understand [governments]. Doesn't mean to say that I think it's right. If I didn't understand them I would say this is wrong, totally wrong and they're a bunch of idiots, hypocrites, but I understand them. They're still hypocrites and idiots. It's just the nature of the beast. Governments do what they want to do to make themselves rich, and eventually, at some point in time, look after the people of their country. [...] I've always fought the system. I always have, especially as a teenager. I've always fought the system, but you can't beat the system, the only way to beat the system is from within. It's just not worth it. The people that say: "We're gonna beat the system from within", they get into the system and the system becomes them, well, they become part of the system. [...] I got comfortably numb, let's put it that way. When you start to make a certain amount of money each year, and you're quite comfortable, then you just roll with it. [...] It's just business. It's just business. You don't look at it any other way. [...] Certainly not an excuse! Just the way that things have become.

In remaining 'comfortably numb' and playing by the rules of the game and the game of the rules, he does emphasise he could never become as hypocritical as the powers that be and the politicians wielding them.

> It's very hypocritical, it's double standards. [...] It stinks. [...] I feel disgusted that I as an individual and a person in this business can't [...] I mean if [states] can sell to whom they want, what makes it illegal for me to do the same? [...] It's got to do with my personal feelings where I feel that, you know, one law for me and one law for them. Why? What's good for the goose is good for gander, sort of thing. I mean if they can sell to terrorists, I mean, not that I would, I'm certainly not intended, because I do have a conscience. I'm the only arms dealer in the business that has a conscience. [...] I think that being an arms dealer or trader is certainly a lot more professional than being a lying son of a bitch politician. [...] I wouldn't even go down that road [and become a politician]. I don't have the patience to. I'm not a two-faced person. When I say something, I mean it. If something's pissing me off, I try to change it.

As much as he does not want to be hypocritical and double-faced, he himself manoeuvres along with the hypocrisy of the politics of arms control. That ambiguous position is one that he takes as well regarding the public opinion and debates on (morality of) the arms dealing business.

7.3 Dealing with public opinion, the 'black market' and humanitarian arms dealing

In relation to the game of the rules and the rules of the game, discussing how he 'plays' with laws and politics (that also play with him), often Constantine expressed his unease with the public opinion about arms dealers. Regarding what Pope Francis said about arms dealers after the Brussels terrorist attacks, as cited earlier in this book, how arms manufacturers and the arms traffickers want 'blood, not peace, who want war, not brotherhood' (Democracy Now! 2016 – online source), Constantine said the following:

> Fucking Pope Francis again [on Brussel attacks and the role of the arms trade]! Uggghgh, this guy should keep his [...] I mean, come on man, don't get me started on the Vatican and arms trades. They are some of the biggest, dirtiest people to do business with. You know that the Vatican bank bought a lot, and financed a lot? A lot of arms deals. The Vatican is heavily involved in a lot of arms industries. The Vatican bank was involved in financing many, many deals. They've got [...] That's an act of hypocrisy on his part. It's stupid, he should keep his big mouth shut, because he's making a fool of himself in known circles. [...] This is bullshit because the arms that they're getting, the arms that these people are getting, and not the ones in Belgium or in France, they're not being

> supplied by arms manufacturers or arms dealers. Well, they are being supplied by arms dealers, certainly not legal ones. These are people who turn this up, and it's annoying me. Here you go. [...] This is a stupid thing to say. One because of the Vatican's involvement, the Vatican bank in actual arms manufacturing companies, I think they also have shares in BA systems and possibly Raytheon in the US. Plus, the fact that they're defence forces outside the Vatican as Swiss guards, so that makes them employers of mercenaries. The Holy City is not so Holy, believe you me. There are a lot more deeper things I could go into there, the Vatican is not as [...] is not holier than thou. [...] You don't have to dig very far to find that information. I will send you a couple of links over later on. I can consider this from the pope or any fucking pope to be extremely hypocritical. [...] People have double standards: "Oohhhh guns, for God sake, keep them away from me! But give me the money". [...] The majority of people don't [know anything about arms dealing]. I'm sure there's gonna be a lot of pissed off people when this [biography] comes out. I'm sure about it.

Not only in public debate arms dealers are considered hypocritical and immoral, but also in social psychological studies on morality, the arms industry and arms dealers have been considered morally disengaged (Bandura 1999: 205–206); something I presented to Constantine who did not understand that.

> I don't consider myself hypocritical. [...] No, certainly not. I have my standards. People may think I'm hypocritical, but I don't consider myself to be a hypocrite. [...] They are the biggest fool if they fool themselves, they're the biggest kind of fool. It's logical when you think about it. [...] Ignorance is bliss. If you just go to work from Monday to Friday, go on and watch football on Saturday, and clean your car on Sunday, and then start the whole shit again from Monday to Friday, you go through life living like that, and you'll be none the wiser about anything in the world. It's only when you start to open your eyes and see what's going on you start to question. [...] My eyes have always been open. My eyes have always been open.

He thinks of himself to be awake and not part of the 'sheeple' and instead sees the public as hypocritical itself and uninterested in arms dealers. Otherwise, they would have known, and not stigmatise and falsely lumping together the illegal and legal arms dealing, for example.

> Unfortunately this is a preconceived description, "arms dealer", "dealer of death"! This is all being made out by films, black arms dealers. Arms dealers don't have a good name! Even if they are legal. [...] So, to me, it would be just a question of setting the facts right. When you mention arms dealers to people they automatically think of "dirty deeds done dirt cheap"

> to quote ACDC, and it's not like that, yeah? I like to think myself morally [...] What shall we say, well, moral ENOUGH to be able to say no to a deal if I know I shouldn't, inside myself, I know I shouldn't do that. [...] People are gonna say: "You're a whore! You sold your conscience". No, I haven't, it's my conscience, and if I've done anything wrong [...] When it's my time to die, I'm able to look God in the eye and say: "As far as I'm concerned, I did what I did, if you think I'm wrong, God, then punish me for it". [...] I'll be quite honest with you. I don't give a FUCK what other people think about me. I don't give a flying fuck about what other people think about me. Because I know in my heart that what I am doing for ME, and how I [...] I have to look myself in the mirror every day, and think: "Oh, did I just sell some guns that gonna go and kill people?" I don't know. They're guns. You put a gun in the hand of the wrong person, he's gonna go and shoot somebody. I have to look at myself in the mirror every day when I get up. At the moment, I don't have any problems looking in the mirror. So the critique as far as I'm concerned, are only from people that have preconceptions of what an arms dealer is. [...] If I didn't have any morals, I wouldn't be doing this in the first place.

Constantine detested how the ascribed features of arms dealers being interested in the morale of money, self-interest, short-termism, opportunism and pragmatism (cf. Wiegratz & Cesnulyte 2016) are considered as something evil. It is just the reality of being a business man, according to him.

> Maybe I am one of a kind in the arms trade. I don't know anybody else who even thinks along the same lines as I do. [...] I like to be able to stand out as being honest and straight, stand-up type of guy, who will NOT do anything just for money. I won't sell my soul to the devil. Well, maybe I would, depends on the price. [...] I'm a business man, I told you. Do you think a car dealer goes home every night and worries about how many people his cars are gonna kill because some idiot is drunk and driving? No, no! [...] You may call that immoral or amoral, I don't really give a shit. [...] The first human skeletons were found with spearheads in them. War has been a way of life and has been since the beginning of mankind. It's just that now we don't have pointy sticks. We have pointy bullets. The only difference between a 7.62x51 round and pointed stick is that the bullet goes a lot faster. That's the only difference. Pointy sticks could kill people as well back then. In fact, they did. Bullets kill people now.

The arms and car dealer comparison was one he made frequently. As a matter of fact, that comparison has been made before by late Samuel Cummings, the American small arms dealer as described in Section 2.3 of this book. In December 1980, during an inspection of one of Cummings' arms depots, he said about the business 'It's the same as a car dealer—you must show your products' (Arizona Republic 1980: 29). Not only car dealers, but also any business, as the public should understand, is not any different from Constantine or other arms dealers that want to make money. According to him, making money is business as usual and requires, usually, a specific type of emotionlessness, he pointed out on many occasions. However, if you were to possess such a harsh characteristic, it does not mean he is amoral or immoral per se. In fact

> I wouldn't call any business immoral. I mean, what is it, moral? [...] Let me put it this way, morality [...] As I said, morality is [...] depends on the size of the payee, or the payees' bank account. [...] I always try and make sure that all of the deals that we do fit in with my morals and the morals of the other two guys. [...] I don't think that there would be any criticism from another arms dealer. I would probably be the one criticising them. The only reason they could criticise me is if there's some deals that I didn't do. [...] From the moral side, no arms dealer can criticise me. From the business side, yeah they could criticise me. I could have done some deals that were legal and make money out of them. [...] I can't be criticised for those deals that I didn't make.

Not seldom would I bring up my critique on how he may talk the moral talk, but not always walk the moral walk. I confronted him with how he seems an arms dealer with a conscience when it is most opportune to him. He did not agree, but also not disagree.

> Of course, I'm a businessman as well. You never heard the saying strike when it's hot? [...] [Arms dealing is] a business. Motor dealers, motor cars, you know cars kill more people than guns. I mean there's a difference in buying a car and buying a gun. A lot of people don't buy a gun for war. I have orders from police services around the world, I have orders from security-related government agencies, or for training and arming coastguard. It's not just war. [...] Let me put it this way, if I have enough money, and I see a deal I don't really wanna go through, no matter how much [...] Obviously everybody has their price. This is gonna sound very, very mercenary, but if the price is right, and I was making a big enough cut, then I would let somebody buy my conscience, let's put it that way. But it has to be a very big reward. I mean a very, very, VERY big reward. Of course within the legal framework of the licenses that I have. [...] Obviously I have to be legally justified or otherwise I'm up Shit Creek without a paddle.

The most commonly known public (moral) disgust about arms dealers is that they live off of conflict and therefore of other people's misery and their violence – arms dealing is seen as an obnoxious market, no matter whether it is efficient or not (cf. Kanbur 2001; Satz 2010). In particular conflict, wars and outright mass violence would be necessary to make money as an arms dealer (Maitland 1998). He admitted that

> I live from wars, and I live from people that wanna buy ammunition, and I live from people that wanna buy guns for shooting. [...] Of course it's destructive, if you want to come down to it. I mean, when I sell guns or bullets, or whatever I sell that's military equipment that can kill or it's to be used in war, obviously it's for destruction. A tank is not for driving around in the middle of town. [...] I would say it's destructive, I would say it's destructive. [...] I don't think about it. I can't, because if I did, I wouldn't do it. I couldn't do it.

At one point, we discussed to which extent I could become an arms dealer myself.

ME: Do you think I could do [arms dealing]? Honestly?

CONSTANTINE: If you learned, yeah. Anybody can do it, it's a question of whether you can shut yourself off from thinking about what's gonna happen with the arms, or the rockets, or the grenades, or the bullets, or the whatever it is that you're selling. If you can shut yourself off from thinking about what's gonna happen to them after they left your hands [...] I don't think about it. To me it's another customer, as long as I know it's legal. As I said before, as long it's legal and the papers, I got receipts, the invoices, and the EUC [End-User Certificate] is correct and I'm not in breach with my licenses with the XXXX government then I don't give a monkey's, to be quite honest.

ME: So, again, do you think that I'm able to?

CONSTANTINE: No, I don't. You're too sensitive, yeah? You're too sensitive. Too sensible, no [...] too sensitive, yeah, sensitive. Fragile is probably the word that I'd be looking for in that case. Your soul would not be able to stand the stress.

[...]

ME: Okay, I don't think I'm insulted by that.

CONSTANTINE: No I don't think you could. You would be [...] I think you'd lie awake wondering, especially knowing you because of what you do at the moment. I don't know whether you could do it. I don't know, I would [...] Okay, you're single, which is good. You're young, which is good. You can go knocking on doors [visit potential clients abroad], or rather, go and visit clients, I mean you can do the job. Whether you could live with the fact that you know possibly that your guns are gonna kill people, be it one reason or whatever. I don't know if you could live with that. That's something only you can answer.

I am still not sure whether I actually was insulted or not. What I and what the public opinion fail to see (or do not want to admit to), Constantine explained, is that the business of arms dealing legally is far more nuanced, in that sense that

> I don't NEED a war. It's nice if there is one. No, okay, I am honest. It's nice if there's one, FOR ME. Not the people fighting, but for me it's nice, because it means I can make money, which everybody needs. This unfortunately is the part of the industry that [makes] some people say: "You're a merchant of death, you're a bastard". [...] My sister had this reaction when she found out. She's terribly left wing, she is a silly liberal. She said: "You help fuel the deaths and murders of people in Africa". It's bullshit you know, this is not right. If somebody wants to kill somebody, they will kill them with a knife. [She says:] "You're responsible for the [...]" I won't say "downfall of society" but in those countries. It's not true. The governments of the world, the US, the Brits, the Germans, the French, they sell more in one day than I do in a whole year. Those are the guys that want to have wars. You want to stop the war, so you have to stop the governments from wanting the wars. If there were no more wars, okay, I'd sell baby bottles or contraceptives, because if there's no people fighting they're gonna be fucking!

Despite being agitated by the public disgust about arms dealing, it is due to that disgust he often hides and lies about in what kind of business he is. Meaning, he does seem to care about the negative stereotype that exist about arms dealers, although he does not admit it.

> When people ask me: "Oh what do you do?" I usually say: "Oh I work in the defence industry". [...] It's not that easy, it's not that simple. You have to look at the bigger picture, okay? [...] I'm an arms dealer with a conscience.

And having a conscience, he clarified, means

> being uncompromisable. [...] Never compromising on your own standards [...] by never dealing under the table. [...] By always making sure that what you do is legal, no matter how much morally you might disagree with the deal that you're doing. If it's legal, it's legal, end of story.

So to have a conscience means you do not compromise and that means you will not commit to specifically doing 'black', vis-à-vis illegal arms dealing. You always stick to legal arms dealing (as much as he disagrees with the laws on arms control), he explained.

> I don't sell under the table. I could have been rich a long, long time ago if I wanted to. Or dead in a ditch with a hole in my head. I prefer to be, I won't say poor but I will say I prefer to be [...] With the current

> economic situation, I'd prefer to be alive with the amount that I got, than rich for a few years and then dead in a ditch. No thank you very much! That's like I said. I am an arms dealer with a conscience. I don't sell black arms, I don't do black deals.

Although he never crossed the line from legal into illegal arms dealing, I wondered if he also never flirted with the idea or was tempted to cross the lines just once.

> No. If I was that way inclined, I would certainly know how to do it and NOT get caught. But [...] because I'm [...] What shall we say [...] I believe in somebody higher up than I am, I'm not talking about the police chief in the office, yeah? I believe somebody up there is watching me and watching everybody. I couldn't do it! It would be [...] And I've done a lot of despicable things in my life [...] I certainly wasn't a nice person many years ago. In fact, I must have been a real bastard to some people. In fact I WAS a real bastard to a lot of people. But [...] ehm [...] when you age, you MELLOW [...] And ehm [...] As far as I'm concerned [...] Haha this is gonna be difficult [...] I won't say there is no price that nobody could buy me for. I've never been presented with that ehm [...] dilemma, so I wouldn't know how I would react.

Although not knowing what it would be like to do black arms dealing, it became clear throughout the interviews, he thinks that other people do have a wrong view about arms dealers because of the illegal side of the arms trade. He passionately detests their misconceptions and he blames media for confusing the public.

> Unfortunately this is a preconceived description: arms dealer, dealer of death! This is all being made out by films. Black arms dealers, you know, arms dealers don't have a good name! Even if they are legal, yeah. [...] [The entertainment industry is] about the black arms dealers. [...] It's like calling a private military contractor a mercenary. It makes it more SELLABLE. So if you wanna write a book or make a TV film, or a series: "Oh let's do one about black arms dealers", or "Let's do a film about mercenaries", because everybody has got these preconceived opinions about what they are, and how they do it, and how they live, as opposed to being: "Okay, let's write a book about a legal arms dealer". [People would respond:] "Oh but that's boring, that's never gonna sell. He's legal, we need something about black deals, the girls, and the money and the power, contract killings" and things like that. I mean, come on, it's a preconceived opinion. [...] People have these misconceptions and these ideas in their head of the arms dealer. You know, if you talk to somebody that has absolutely no idea of "an arms dealer", just go up to somebody and ask: "Describe an arms dealer to me", and they would automatically have something between [...] Even if they only read the newspapers, and

> seen *Lord of War*. They would have [imagined] Nicolas Cage and Viktor Bout, and they would have this idea of somebody who didn't give a shit who they sold to as long as they were making money.

The public opinion, he finds, is too focussed on a few infamous and illegal arms dealers. But, as he pointed out, '[t]here are many, many more black arms dealers in the world apart from Viktor Bout, you know?'. He told me a story about an illegal arms dealer who was caught in Italy in a hotel room, with three prostitutes, cocaine, significant amounts of cash money and diamonds. Despite an extravagant lifestyle of black arms dealers, he argued that

> they don't want media attention. [...] They like to be in the eye of those that buy the arms from them, the illegal arms. That's the thing, because [...] if you have illegal arms, then obviously it's all part and parcel of illegal arms, hookers, drugs, blood diamonds, and it all goes in one parcel, and they're inside. Obviously they're surrounded by the people that are involved in these ehm [...] 'business ventures'.

Especially because of the misleading media representations of black arms dealers, he is extremely cautious about giving non-pseudonymised or non-anonymised interviews to media outlets.

> I won't give [journalists] information if I think I'm gonna risk anything myself. [...] The Sun, The Daily Mail, they approached me via [social media]. [...] I was approached on three occasions, by various journalists from UK [news]papers that had somehow got hold of [...] They've gotten into the [social media platform's] group, or they've gotten in by use of a nefarious name, and they sent me a message over [the social media platform]: "Would you like to do an interview? We'd pay you for it". I'm like: "No". That sort of thing has happened before. It's just newspapers that are after a [...] ehm [...] what shall we say [a] headline [stating] "Ex-mercenary packs out over [...]" sort of thing, yeah? Because that's what most of the [...] I mean, newspapers, they want to sell them, and the word "mercenary" sells better than "private military contractor".

As becomes clear, in his struggle with media, for him it is about being staged as legal and running a legitimate business. When we discussed a title for an article I was writing at the time about this biography, he wanted me to make sure that it was made clear in the title and article that he is not an illegal arms dealer.

> "Understanding a Real Lord of War's Personal Morality"?! Oh man! Come on! "A Real Lord of War"?? I don't know if that's a good title. I don't know if I like that. [...] I'm a LEGAL Lord of War, maybe! [...] I find it ehm [...] "Understanding A Real Lord of War's Personal Morality: Considerations for a Criminological Biography". I mean, this

> doesn't say anything about the fact that what I do is legal. [...] I mean it's one thing to say: "He's a black arms dealer, he's lord of war", but when you're legal, you might be a lord of war, but you're a fucking legal lord of war. That's something you may want to look at. That was just the title. I haven't started ripping it into pieces yet, okay?

After he 'ripped it into pieces', Constantine further emphasised his discontent about the initial title.

> It rather incriminates me with that title. I don't sell just for war, I sell for defence. The articles I sell are, I quote: "defence products". [...] [It makes me sound] like a freak. I mean, I guess some people may consider me one for the job that I do. But you know, I don't have three heads and I certainly don't have a black heart. A lot of patches [on it], but not black.

Constantine considers himself to be fair and in the arms dealing business for the right reasons. He is the lesser of two evils, the *illegal* arms dealers being more evil. In fact, by being legal, he feels he prevents the illegal arms dealers from flourishing.

> If I didn't sell these arms, my clients would go black, which means they would buy them from somebody else who doesn't necessarily follow the legal channels. At least I know, and the people that I work with, we know what they bought. It's better to have control over the chaos. [...] If I stop, if I don't do it, somebody else will. I don't see why I should let somebody else make the money? Why shouldn't I? I have to live as well. I would imagine that I am the lesser of two evils.

We discussed some of the most (in)famous arms dealers that were mentioned on a website[1] he shared with me. He knew some of them.

> This guy, XXXX, he's actually quite a respectable arms dealer. The only reason, number X [on the list] yeah, the only reason he's on here is because the XXXX wanted him. [...] His website is still running, in fact, I get offers from him, most of the time if I want to buy anything. He offered me x [amount of] XXXX. They're very big cargo planes, XXXX. He's a nice guy, ex XXXX officer. [...] That newspaper, or that journal, is not positive about anybody dealing in arms. [...] None of [the accusations made on the website] are being proven, because if they were proven they would have been extradited from the XXXX. He spends his time now between XXXX and the south of XXXX, he's free to go wherever he wants, apart from XXXX of course.

I asked him why he is not mentioned on the website and he said that is because he is not operating on the illegal side, after which I asked if the arms dealers mentioned were all illegal.

> Welllllll […] . They are grey, let's put it that way. A lot of them are legal because they had an American government authorisation to do what they were doing. Same as me having a XXXX government okay to do what I'm doing.

As discussed in Section 2.3 of this book, Viktor Bout, the most infamous black arms dealer of the 20th and 21st centuries, and whose biography the movie *Lord of War* was based on (Hamid 2006), was mentioned on the website as well. Regarding Bout, Constantine thinks that he has been wrongly portrayed.

> Viktor Bout is in an American prison, the Americans will not give him up to the Russians. […] I think [Bout] was ripped. I think he was pulled in. He was conned, he was set up [in Thailand]. […] He should never have been allowed to be deported to the States. That's my personal opinion. Because the [arrest] wasn't legal, and the only reason they want him out of the way was because he had too much dirt on the US government. Everybody used him. British MI6 used him, the Americans used him, the French used him, the Germans used him, the Russians used him. Come on, he knew everything about everybody, which is why he would have been either let out or exchanged very, very quickly in the very beginning when he was arrested. Or he will not get out at all. […] They have set him up. Of course [arms dealers, legal and illegal] are used, of course they are used. […] [Bout's] a puppet that was played by both the CIA and the Russians, and MI6 [and who happened to be] at the right place [but] at the wrong time.

He detests the label 'merchant of death', as often is ascribed to Bout and other black arms dealers.

> If someone would call me a 'merchant of death' then I would debate that point with them for many, many, many hours until they know I'm not. I'm NOT a merchant of death. I don't want people killing people with the guns I sell. The guns that I sell or the equipment I sell, obviously, is for killing people. That's what guns do, unless I sell them to hunters and I don't sell shotguns. Obviously, that's what they do, but I don't put a gun in somebody's hand and say: "Go and kill him!". I'm not a merchant of death. The guys using the guns are the merchants of death.

Generally, he thinks that illegal and especially legal arms dealers are misunderstood and misrepresented. He distances himself rigorously from the 'dark side' of the market.

> Obviously there are things that come my way, contracts that I could do but it would be illegal. Then there are contracts that come that are legal and I don't want to do them, because, they're not, as I said, they're not

> to countries that I personally would like those things going to. I want to be able to show that there's a differentiation between what I do, it's not like: "Yeah, give me the money, I'll sell you what you want". This is the big black arms dealer. Driving around, in the boot of your car you lock 50 rifles, and you know, different kinds, and you open the boot of the car, and have a boot sale: "Yeah what do you want? 45, 76.2?". This is not my world. It has to be a very, very clear delineation between the black and the white, and the people aspects of arms selling yeah. It's a product like anything else.

One of the main issues that keeps the black arms dealing business alive is the enormous amount of illegal, unregistered arms that is out there, Constantine explains.

> There are black arms all over the place. I could go into the middle of [my city], and buy AKs if I wanted to. There's enough of them around. The whole of [my country] was flooded with AKs when [a neighbouring country] collapsed. They were brought over in fishing boats from [the neighbouring country] that went into [another city], it's a known fact. It's nothing hidden. In fact, many other people down in [another country], and possibly, well not just possibly, but a lot of other people in [my country] bought AKs from [the neighbouring country]. It's just something […] It's just there. You can't do anything with it. I can't do anything with it. That's up to the police and they deal with it, that's then their thing. In [my country] the police just don't seem to be doing enough. Let's put it that way.

He disagrees with the indifference of his country's authorities towards illegal arms dealing. Illegal arms dealing and the indifferent control of it are problematic and, if anything, actually bad for the legal side of the business. Given that, it would be even more stupid to go from legal arms dealing to illegal arms dealing, Constantine claims.

> If I've crossed that little very, very thin line between one of the good guys to being one of the bad guys, from there, there's no going back, because if the word gets around: "Oh, so and so does deals under the table", then you have every Tom, Dick and Harry in the underworld, or every dictator from Africa knocking on your door and saying "Can you get me these?". [I'd reply:] "Well you know, I can't really sell to you". [They would reply:] "Well, like, here's 25 million [dollar]", yeah? It's a very slippery slope. You do one, you cross over that line between white and black, and you're in a different world.

Constantine understands the temptation to go into black arms dealing, though, it is just not smart to do.

> The dream of making big money and then wandering into the grey areas and then the black areas, has caused the downfall of many people. [...] A lot of people have tried, a lot of people fall by the wayside because they're not prepared to walk the line, toe the line and make sure that their dealings are legal. [...] I could have been rich. Very, very rich a long time ago or dead in a ditch with a hole in my head. I've seen both sides of the business. I know people that have worked on the other side of the fence, so to speak. [...] Of course [I understand], there's a lot of money to be made, but I wouldn't do it. I couldn't do it. I won't deal under the table. If you're gonna do this, this is me. My ethics dictate what I will and what I won't do. It's like if somebody came to me and said: "Okay, we need manpads, missiles, or antitank missiles". [I'd reply:] "Okay, get me an EUC". [They say:] "Oh we don't have one, can you still supply?". [I'd say:] "No". [...] I can't sympathise, [but] I can UNDERSTAND, because the promise of big money is there. It's also big risks, if you get caught, you go to jail for a long time. [...] It's a different kind of lifestyle. You know, black arms dealers, they're mostly not just into black arms. They're into drugs, they're into prostitution, they're into human trafficking, they're into just about anything because it's a criminal enterprise.

Given the intersection of many more illegal activities, he understands the arms dealers that operate in the dark, which also is therefore, he warned me, a one-way trip.

> The best way out is never to get involved. [...] This depends on your upbringing, and the situation [when] you were a child. It denotes your outlook on life and what you intend to get out of it.

He seems to stay away from illegal arms dealing also because of the fear of getting caught, despite the fact that he thinks that actually there is no real control of illegal arms dealing.

> There's no control! There is no proliferation control. If there was proliferation control there would be no black arms being sold anywhere to countries like CAR [Central African Republic] for example, of the Congo, or places like that. They would get no arms, cause if you're on a blacklist then there should be no arms being delivered. They're being delivered all the time! [...] It's the nature of the beast. It's supply and demand. It's: "Can you afford them?". [Client'd say:] "Yes". [I'd say:] "Okay, how many do you want? The higher the risk, the more you pay!".

The lack of control that allows for black arms dealers to exist that affects his legal arms dealing, also makes him want to see illegal arms dealers gone. For him it is unfair that they could get away with dealing without licenses while making more money. It is unfair competition for him, because he does have to be licensed and is scrutinised continuously, while he is not making as much money.

> When governments are involved in open warfare then obviously it's not particularly good for me. That doesn't mean to say that I need illegal business to survive, because I don't work illegally obviously. [...] It's important to stop the illegal arms dealers. [...] It's VERY important for me, because if it wasn't, I would be dealing under the table and saying: "They're making all the money. Why shouldn't I have some cream off the milk as well?". It doesn't work that way. I go to through the trouble getting licenses and then people go and buy the black arms, that's no good for me!

All in all, and as much as he despises black arms dealing and being compared to it, it is crucial for him to be at least be aware of developments of the 'dark side' of the arms markets, I had to understand. It might be unfair, but it is still competition, and actually therefore, serious competition.

> With all this knowledge that I have of the arms industry, and all the knowledge that I have of the BLACK arms industry as well, because obviously [...] Okay, I don't deal under the table. [...] You get to meet and you get to know about things that are going on either side of the line. Now, I walk a line, a very thin line between white and black. My side would always lean to the left side, which is the white side. But you always know what's going on the right hand side, which is the black side. [...] I'm never in the grey, there's no such thing as grey for me. It's white or black. Especially where arms are concerned.

Often he emphasised he wants to stay and will remain legal and stay away from the illegal side. He does have internal struggles with delivering legally to both parties, and especially the governments they represent, he rather would not have to do deal with.

> Honesty to me is where I can decide who and what I want to sell, and not be pressured in having to sell to those I don't really want to sell to. Even though there are lists of countries on my trade licenses, [...] small arms and light weapons, ammunition, military etc., there are lists of countries that I can and cannot sell to. Even in that list of countries that I can sell to, there are some countries that I don't really want to sell to.

Alongside staying away from doing illegal arms deals while trying to make an honest buck, I also sensed a strong wish he has to deliver arms to the suppressed and exploited who try to rise against the oppressive 'system', and who must be weaponised.

> "The best" [deal] includes making as many deals as possible [...] it's quantitative AND qualitative [...] well qualitative[ly the best] would be pro bono, for example, helping groups out, minorities. [...] Helping out people that are being attacked by terrorists, that have not any method of defence, maybe just arranging for the drop of some items for them to learn themselves to defend themselves. [...] I'm a humanitarian person, most definitely, most definitely [...] like I said, I won't sell to regimes that are oppressing their own people, unless it's legal.

In light of his ambition to help out the little man sticking it to the Man, he would even consider, as a matter of speak, a 'good cause discount' by arming oppressed groups.

> I could not sell to terrorists because it would be illegal. Now, but if a government came to me and said: "We want to represent this country's poor farm workers who are fighting for their rights for more land to stop Monsanto, to stop GMO, can you supply?", I'd say: "Yes!". [...] They'd be fighting against the big chemical, big pharmaceutical companies and gene-crop producing companies in the world. I'd give anything to see Monsanto get kicked in the ass! [...] If I had a country and that came to me and said: "We need arms to fight Monsanto", I'd be one of the first in the line to sell 'm, in fact, I'd probably give 'm away [...] Well, when I say "Give them away", I mean at cost-reduced price.

Yet, in his striving to help the oppressed, the law should allow it, as he would not sell illegally to a party fighting for a good cause.

> Remember Boko Haram abducted those 400 female students [...] I was approached by a town, up in the northern area of XXXX. I was asked if I would supply them with arms so that they could fight, defend themselves against XXXX. I was seriously considering flying stuff into them. It would have been illegal, that's the only thing that stopped me in the end. I'm not allowed to sell to XXXX. If I could have found some way of getting somebody to do it, I would have done it. [...] It would have been illegal and you never know what [happens]. Okay, you deliver the arms into this village. The villagers get slaughtered because they're not trained properly, and the arms are taken by XXXX. Basically, you've given them some more arms which would have been a terrible thing to happen. So what do you do? You say: "No I am sorry I can't supply you because it's illegal", but on the other hand you know damn well that if you do supply them they'll get attacked. If you don't supply them they'll get attacked [too].

There is a strong will in him that makes him convinced that there is 'a basic human right which is being able to defend your life and those dear to you.

Not only those dear to you, but those who are repressed', he said to me. In that context, he cited from the Bible at one point: 'He who has no sword should sell his cloak'. With that religious reference, he wanted to emphasise that everybody should be able to defend themselves, which could mean he could and would sell, if no embargoes were laid upon two rivalling parties, to both. Although principally he would not do so, he came around to it and argued that

> if somebody comes to me and says: "I want this", and it's legal: "Here, you can have it". If the person of the other side and comes to me and says: "I want this", but it's also legal, then I will sell to them as well. Unless there is a very sound reason not to sell to them. [...] I wouldn't sell to both parties if there were moral, what shall we say, moral complications as to what one party was doing as opposed to the other party. [...] Arms dealers should never take sides. They should never take sides. I'd sell to both sides. You don't take sides. That's the job of governments. I don't take sides.

Meaning, for him, selling to both sides is not the same as 'taking sides'. These and other morality- and religion-related aspects of his arms dealing and outlook on life will be considered in the following section.

7.4 From Kant to Constantine: Moral neutralisation through religion and the evil human nature

> And we know that we are of God, and the whole world lieth in wickedness.
> (1 John 5:19, *The Holy Bible*, King James Version 2004)

Constantine his (religious and moral) outlook on life and humanity must be understood in relation to his arms dealing. In particular regarding the aspect of how his brokered arms and ammunition could, eventually, end up in the hands of parties who may grossly violate human rights, commit war crimes, or would even be part of genocidal campaigns.

> You're basically asking me: "Constantine, how much of a human are you?" [...] You know, you just haha can't sit there and think: "Oh God I just sent 4000 AKs to a country, those guns are gonna kill people". It's not a job for people with the need for safe spaces and trigger warnings. [...] Anybody can do it, it's a question of whether you can shut yourself off from thinking about what's gonna happen with the arms, or the rockets, or the grenades, or the bullets, or the whatever it is that you're selling. If you can shut yourself off from thinking about what's gonna happen to them after they left your hands [...] I don't think about it. To me it's another customer, as long as I know it's legal, as I said before, as long it's legal and the papers, I got receipts, the invoices, and the EUC is

> correct and I'm not in breach with my licenses with the XXXX government then I don't give a monkey's [ass] to be quite honest.

As long as he lived up to the law (which he despises), he is alright with it. It reveals how he himself just does not like to think too much about it – indirectly implying that he too has moral questions, perhaps, hiding behind the law himself, much like the very politicians and governments do who he demonises. He justifies himself too, because thinking about the moral implications and what it does to you, could spiral him out of sanity.

> It's a very complex situation and the more you try to think about it [...] Have you ever broken a yellow snail in half? Have you actually seen a snail that's being cut in half, the shell? Well it start with this little piece in the middle of this ever widening rings that go round and round, getting bigger and bigger and bigger and bigger and bigger and bigger. If you try and follow that with your thoughts, if you try to follow one thought right down to the essential origin of that thought, you're gonna fuck your head up so much before you get there you're gonna wonder: "What the hell I'm doing on this planet?". You can't do it, you just can't solve every problem. You certainly can't change anybody else, the only thing you can is change yourself first.

Such distancing is required, he thinks, for the job. I asked him whether he has been harsh also because of his work itself, or that he was that way before and applied it in his work.

> No, I think probably my work turned me [...] Possibly, plus all the things that I've seen, working for governments [...] Man's inhumanity to man has hardened me for sure. I wouldn't say it's a case of one influencing the other. I was pretty much like that before I got into the industry. [...] I don't think I'm a pessimist as far as life is concerned. Well, sceptic possibly, but I ENJOY life too much to be able I'm not a pessimist. I'm a REALIST, yeah!

Through his, what he calls, realist perspective, his opinions about human nature and its evil roots would sometimes come up. The religious upbringing he had and his beliefs he holds though have

> got absolutely nothing to do with my job, because I don't see any connection between religion and what I'm doing. You mean selling arms? I'm not selling them to terrorists. [...] How do you separate religion from the arms trade? There's no comparison between the two. They don't interact. They just don't. I can ask you the same question [...] I have a part of me that is very religious. Just because I sell arms, and those arms may be possibly used to kill somebody doesn't disturb me at all and it certainly

> doesn't influence my religion.[…] I mean, you could follow this deeper down the rabbit hole if you want, doesn't religion influence you from the day you are born? If you believe in God, and you believe that everything is mapped out for you in the beginning, and there's just one main road from birth to death, and there's a lot of subsidiary roads that get you to the end destination anyway. Which road you take is entirely up to you, whether you go to the left, which is the bad side, or you go to the right, which is the good side, or you cross over. You still get to the end destination, which is death. […] I would say I'm a self-made man. […] I don't believe, for one thing, that everything is set down for you. I don't believe that the roads that you take are set out for you. You CHOOSE which ones you want to take. That's the difference between us and animals. […] FREE CHOICE. Animals don't have that choice. They do what nature tells them to do. Eat or be eaten. […] In this aspect you can go back as far as the book *Genesis* when God created the world and Adam and Eve. What Eve took was the apple of choice, that was conscience. So with her giving Adam the apple, she awoke his conscience. […] It was only considered evil in the Garden of Eden to eat it, because it gave them the knowledge to discern between good and bad. It gave you the conscience to decide whether your actions were right or not. […] I don't think conscience is a thing of evil. I think conscience is what separates us from the animals. Do you think a lion has a conscience or feels bad when he eats a gazelle? No, he's just like: "That was nice, I filled my stomach. Now what's for dessert?". You know, this to me is like it's your conscience that is what you're doing right or wrong, as far as YOUR conscience is concerned? […] Your conscience guides you. So that's what I'm saying about conscience being that which separates us from the animals, which is conscience that was in the apple that gave Adam, or rather Eve gave to Adam, by symbolically eating the apple. She opened up his conscience which is what God didn't want them to do, which is why the snake said: "Do it!". Otherwise, if she hadn't done it, mankind would just be natural beings, they wouldn't have these tendencies to do evil. They would only be able to do what nature intended them to do.

Having a conscience is thus what leads to evil, Constantine seems to argue here. Philosopher Immanuel Kant argues similarly in his *Religion within the Boundaries of Mere Reason* (1998) that human nature is radically evil. Meaning, we have a habit of being morally weak and impure, perhaps even corrupt. Constantine's views on the human nature echo Kant's idea of 'radical evil' therefore strongly.

> [Evil is] in everybody's nature. […] I know I have a conscience, whether I listen to it all the time, is something else. […] If [I] want to listen to my conscience, my conscience will always tell me what is right and what is wrong. Conscience is just a word. It's a word to describe the feeling that

> we have inside us when we do something bad. [...] I don't think there's something inside you that tells you you're doing something good. I think there's something telling you [...] Like if you have decision to make, then the part of you that will say: "Okay if I do this, it's bad, if I do that, it's good" and you can say it's related to your upbringing, you can say it's related to where you were brought up in school. You can say it's related to the society that we live in. I prefer to take it a lot further back to than that. [...] From way back, to the time of, well, the beginning, basically, of humankind. [...] Kane and Abel, yeah? One of them was jealous and beat the other one to death with a stone. Did his conscience tell him to kill him? His brother? No, his conscience told him afterwards that he had done something wrong which is why he left. He banned himself, God didn't ban him. He banned himself because he'd knew he had broken the law.

For him, given his (contradictory) considerations about evil, it is not arms dealing and making money out of it that is bad – it is money, but also greed and religion itself, that are evil to begin with. Much like how Samuel Cummings once said that '[t]he arms business is based on human folly, and folly has yet to be measured nor its depths plumbed' (Weiner 1998: 29), Constantine indicated arms dealing is not the real issue. For him, it is the human nature of greed on which everything, from our religions to our monetary system, is based. The arms trade is merely a symptom of that evil nature of us and how societies organise themselves based on that nature.

> Money is the root of all evil. It's a very, very old saying. It is true, because money is THE root of all evil. Money and human greed, which unfortunately are human factors, are the root of all evil. The church, religion, catholic church, because the Roman [...] the Greek orthodox church never went on crusades. They never killed people in the name of God, which is one of the reason why I got out of the catholic church and joined the Greek orthodox church. The catholic church was used to [...] I mean the pope for saying this[2] is a hypocrite. He should realise that it is religion that is the driving force, always has been, behind every GENOCIDE in the world. The Tutsi's and Hutu's that was religion. The war in Yugoslavia, that was religion. The crusades, religion. World Wars [...] ehm [...] yeah [...] [...] "God is with us", religion. [...] Only the church [is evil]. The arms trade is a by-product. I certainly wouldn't put arms trade as evil. It's not guns that kill people, it's people that kill people. If I didn't sell guns, I'd sell hammers. They can be used just as deadly. When you sell somebody a gun, you only put the tool in the hand to do good or evil, you're not actually giving them the evil. [...] Let's assume [religion is gone], then you can start the world in chaos which is what evil wants. If you agree there's a devil, there's evil, then you have to agree there's good, and that's God. Just because people say: "God is dead", it means that they've given up

> on themselves and on their […] They've become frustrated in what they see in the world. They say: "With this much going on it can only mean that God is dead, because otherwise God wouldn't allow this to happen". Well, God didn't give us free rights, so that they could take them away from us. I'm getting religious now but I'm also trying to explain by way of an example. Now, if God was dead, which is basically what you're saying when you say religion is dead, God was dead, then evil would be dead as well. Because you can't have dark without light, you can't have light without dark. Now if we all agree that evil is in the world, then everybody has to agree there's good which is God, because evil is represented by the devil, and good is represented by God. If God is dead, then the devil is also dead, then what are you left with? Chaos.

Much like sociologist Zygmunt Bauman who argues evil is not to be clearly divided from 'good' anymore, and vice versa, resulting in 'liquid evil' (Bauman & Donskis 2016), Constantine thinks that

> [n]obody really knows anymore what evil is. […] Everybody knows what evil is, everybody, everybody knows what evil is. BUT, it's become so fluid that it's changing from day to day, from minute to minute. The more a person becomes susceptive to the evil in the world […] it has many tentacles; it has more than an octopus. Evil is everywhere and if you can see it and you don't do anything then you're just as bad, you're just as evil. That's my way of thinking, which is why I like to sit in my office and not go out. […] I think the matter of defeat [against evil] is within the person that's beholding the evil that is, seeing the evil. The thing is, there are so many things that you can use for evil. It depends on the person. If a person is evil, they will use it for evil ways.

Therefore, given that people are inherently evil, we shall always fight and therefore there will always be wars. It is stupid of people to think wars will stop at some point, he explained.

> There are some strange people in the world that think that wars and arms should be done away with and everybody should sing "kumbaya" around the campfire cooking marsh mellows at night. It just doesn't work that way in a modern society, unfortunately. It would be nice if it did.

Wars have been there since the dawn of time and thus arms dealers as well.

> The earliest human skeletons had spearheads in them. It's true, man has always been at war, with himself or against somebody else, but never on a scale such as today, where governments are changed by the snap of a finger by supplying arms to the opposition, armed opposition, proxy wars, terrorism. […] There will always be people selling arms. Always.

> I mean, let's take utopia. Utopia is a world where nobody has to worry about anything. Everybody is safe and happy. It's like the first year liberal students, a perfect safe space. Nobody has to worry about anything. Everything is all warm and fuzzy. The unicorns are free to run where they want. This is utopia! It doesn't fucking exist. The world is a hard place, we are still animals. Just because we're intelligent animals, doesn't mean to say that we're not still animals. In some parts of the world I know animals that are lot more fiercer than we are. It's like when people say to me: "How can you sell those evil people guns?". Well: "Those evil people were the ones you've been exploiting for the past 500 years". So who is the lesser of the evil? Who's the evil one? The people killing their neighbour or the people exploiting them, taking their diamonds, gold, silver and oil?

Whereas we human beings are evil animals, according to Constantine, animals themselves are actually creatures he would like to protect.

> No, I don't sell those kind of rifles [for hunting] and I don't sell that kind of ammunition. If I knew it was going to a hunter, I would go there and shoot the bastard myself. [...] Human beings are not on the edge of extinction. Unfortunately, animals are.

What we can take from the last citation is his appreciation of human beings in comparison to animals. It resembles the Dutch Paul Wilking a.k.a. 'Pistol Paul', a self-pronounced kingpin of the Amsterdam underworld. He received a minor prison sentence and a small fine for trading in illegal arms, supplying arms to aggressors that wanted to overthrow governments and reign through extremely violent oppression of its population, like the Congolese dictator Mobutu (Van Amerongen 1968). At the same time, Wilking founded the 'Organisation for the Fight against Animal Cruelty', because he was a pet lover (Feller 2008). Such ambiguity is reflected too in Constantine's dismay of us as a species. Moreover, he considers mankind to be adjusted by perpetuity of war as a means to retain population control and maintain a 'balance of nature'.

> Nature's always had a way of keeping the population of whatever race, people even, the plague, other things [down]. Now that medicine has taken such great steps, people are living way too long! So it's either you euthanize them, or you have to have a war, and this is nature's way of keeping the population down, I guess. [...] I'm just hypothesising at the moment, but wars will never end. Unfortunately, it's just the way of life.

And as long as there will be wars, there will be arms dealers. Their activities may 'move elsewhere once one failed state has ceased to be a convenient operative base', nevertheless, 'until we are able to eradicate these long-term causes, containment of dark networks is the best choice we may have' (Raab &

Milward 2003: 436). So, as an arms dealer, Constantine will keep on playing a tiny role in wars; wars that he considers as the maintenance of a natural balance in the world.

> [T]he only way to save the world is to get rid of the humans. [...] Come on, what do humans give? Are we in balance with the natural ethos of the world? No we're not. There are too many people, for one thing. [...] Do you know that human beings are the only animals that don't fit on this planet? They don't fit on this planet. Humans just don't fit on this planet. If you look at every other animal, it has a way of reacting with nature around it. Doesn't hurt anything apart from what it wants to for its food, it doesn't destroy anything apart from what it wants. Only humans do this. [...] Look at how many people are starving in the world? From being overpopulated. [...] I mean, is it quicker to die from a bullet or die from hunger? I'd sooner die from a bullet than die from hunger. [...] Unfortunately, the human species as such are a very negative species. [...] Not most people are dumb, they ARE dumb! They ARE dumb, yeah? If they weren't dumb, they wouldn't have wars. [...] Don't you know human flesh is the cheapest on the market? [...] The price of a human life is worth nothing. A pound of beef is more expensive, it's true! As sad as it may sound, it is true. Human life has no value, whatsoever. [...] I'm talking about the majority. Okay, I'm not talking about individuals, don't get me wrong. The species, as a majority, is disgusting, consumer-orientated, and doesn't give a shit about nature. That's the majority of the species that we call ourselves, "humans". That's a joke. I was in a zoo in XXXX once, and I was walking passed all these cages, and the last cage was empty, except for a mirror. On top of the mirror it says: "You're looking at the most dangerous animal in the world". [...] The majority of people are like that. [...] Somebody has to do [arms dealing]. [...] Let's get rid of a few million yeah? I mean, come on, there's too many anyway. War is nature's way of reducing the population. And did you know that the best eras of human technology forthright, where they bound, they'd leap forward in bounds, was in times of war. Penicillin was found during a time of war. [...] It cleans out the gene-pool. I mean let's face it, there are some assholes in the world that shouldn't be here. [...] I don't make wars. [...] The world is a beautiful place, there's just too many fucking assholes. [...] I mean, let's be honest if there were no wars around the world, let's put it quite bluntly and coldly, and clinically, if there were no wars around the world, can you imagine how long it would take for this world to be totally overpopulated? If there were no hungers, and draughts and famines, around the world, can you imagine how long it would take for this world to be so overpopulated that nobody would have anything to eat? Or drink? So basically, I see war, unfortunately, as a fact of life. It sounds cruel, cold and heartless, but it's the way I see it.

Seeing himself as Mother Nature's assistant to maintain the natural order of things caused some ethical unease in me, I noticed. To me, it seemed as if he tried to morally justify his role as an arms dealer by claiming, in a roundabout way, that elimination of larger parts of the global 'dumb' human population is a necessary thing. Perhaps even a morally just thing to do, he seem to imply. It gave me the chills and led to me comparing him with the Nazi-official Adolf Eichmann, who was one of the major organisers of the Holocaust, because he logistically architected the mass deportations of Jews to the death camps (Arendt 2006). Eichmann too saw himself as doing what he did as part of a larger destructive machine that wanted to racially 'improve' the world (ibid.: 104–106). Not unexpectedly, Constantine disagreed with my comparison of him with Eichmann.

> You can't compare him to me man! [...] He should have [had] an approximate idea of what was happening. [...] He must have known: "Why was I sending all these parcels from A to B?", B being 'Arbeit macht Frei' in Auschwitz. He should've known what was going on, and I don't think anyone can say they didn't.

In my response, and much like the international arms trade itself, I pointed out that it is because of the moral blinders Nazi officials wore and the bureaucratic diffusion of responsibility that came along with it, the gravest genocides in history could almost be completed. Constantine then did agree to an extent.

I often wondered if he could morally justify for himself the brokering of deals for an oppressive but non-embargoed regime that is bolstering a genocidal campaign on its own people. As long as the papers turn out to be legitimate, he probably could, was his standard reply. Sometimes those specific replies made me somewhat agitated, unwilling to believe he could make such cold, immoral, perhaps amoral decisions; an infuriation I communicated very clearly with him. At a certain point, I was rather cross and out of anger said to him that the world would be probably better off without a conscience. Constantine disagreed.

> The world would be a fucking mess. [...] The world would be in a mess because nobody would know that what they were doing was right or wrong. Because then you would be amoral. You wouldn't be immoral, you'd be amoral. You'd be doing something wrong that you didn't know was wrong. Amorality. Does that make sense? [...] Amorality is obvious. It's two opposites. It's the same [...] it's [...] one is immorality which means you KNOW you're doing something wrong but you say "fuck it" and do it anyway. The other one, amoral, means you DON'T KNOW you're doing wrong, and you do it and you keep doing it, because nobody has put you in a situation to show you that what you're doing is wrong. There's a very fine line, because who's to prove whether the person is doing, whether he's

> conscience of the fact that he's amoral or immoral? […] I don't have any moral thoughts about selling arms. […] There's no immorality in selling arms. […] It's not immoral and it's certainly not amoral. […] Amoral would be selling of black arms without giving a shit about it because you wouldn't know whether it was wrong or right. There's a big difference there. Immoral would be doing it and saying "Well, I know it's wrong but I'm gonna do it anyway". I'm a morally guided arms dealer, because I only work with governments and people that can supply me with the right kinds of papers. […] Who considers [arms dealing] immoral? […] They don't know what they're thinking. They are brainwashed: "A moral arms dealer? How can you have a moral arms dealer?". Well, here I am, living proof. This is something unfortunately, the world has in their minds [which] is the picture of an arms dealer selling guns out of the back of his car, or whatever. This is not me. I use the system, and I won't say abuse, because I don't abuse it as such. I use the system to allow me to do what is allowed. Okay? You have to think about those words very carefully, because I chose them exactly. I use the system to be allowed to do what is allowed. If somebody finds that immoral, then they have to go and talk to all the governments of the world and say: "You have to change these laws", but then you have people screaming that they are unemployed afterwards.

I argued that immoral is not always illegal and the other way around. As it turned out, he brokered legal arms deals that he considered immoral.

> I'm not gonna mention which countries. One of the XXXX's, okay? […] I had to take a balanced look at myself and look […] pfff […] ehm […] Look and see what my feelings, my internal […] I had to take a deep look at that situation. A deep look at myself and [ask]: "Could I live with myself afterwards?" I made a decision and I followed it through. I don't regret it. […] I didn't even think about it. I was interested in making sure that the product got to where it was supposed to go with the least problems available. That it was LEGAL, at the time. That it was legal. […] Forget the fact that there was an embargo afterwards. At the time it WAS legal and I was paid. Quite handsomely, and for me that was the end of the story. […] I'd probably still do it.

He thinks that it is not up to us to have the final say on what is moral or immoral, on what is acceptable and what not.

> Who are we to say what is inhumane? It's only inhumane in OUR eyes, because we are, what shall we say 'civilised'. […] It's only inhumane in OUR eyes because we find it barbaric that somebody could shoot somebody or kill somebody.

All in all, regarding Constantine's (rather Kantian) considerations of religion and the evil human nature on which his moral (neutralisations) rest(s), we see him as someone changing his morals rather easily and opportunistically, giving the idea there is not a core set of norms or values present (Benjamin 1990; French 1996). However, perhaps it is exactly that (moral) flexibility and fluidity through manoeuvring that troubles us, whereas he seems to have embraced and professionalised it. And maybe, as seen in his manoeuvring through law, politics and public opinion, he deals with a type of legal, political, societal and moral in-betweenness of it all – a certain liminality – we cannot deal with (yet).

7.5 Conclusion

What we have seen in this more elaborate chapter, are Constantine's considerations of and interactions with the game of the rules and rules of the game. His struggles with arms control law, international politics, the public opinion and his personal morality became apparent. In struggling to craft his arms deals, he still is a legal arms dealer that must comply with international laws, despite the fact he does not see any worth in those laws. However, he does enjoy finding loopholes in laws on arms dealing, and he does benefit from the rules and regulations. Only when he experiences he cannot do something legally, he becomes critical of the laws and politics behind them. It is therefore not surprising to see his loath regarding illegal or 'black' arms dealers who cross the line but can get away with their criminal activities, as global governance and control of arms do not function anyway, he thinks. In comparison, he then prefers to be considered a humanitarian arms dealer with an ethical business-man approach to the arms trade, even though the public opinion may think differently about him. In response, he finds that the public opinion is false and rather naïve about arms, war and human nature itself. His views on the public opinion about arms dealers uncovered a specific self-claimed personal morality of realism about doing business, which could be seen as moral, immoral or amoral. He presents as if morality does not matter to him, as long as he can go about and mind his own business legally; doing the very (hypocritical) hiding behind laws and regulation of which he blames governments and politicians.

Notes

1 See www.businesspundit.com/10-most-notorious-arms-dealers-in-modern-history/.

2

> Three days ago, there was a gesture of war, of destruction, in a city of Europe [Brussels] from people who don't want to live in peace. Behind that gesture, there were arms manufacturers, the arms traffickers who want blood, not peace, who want war, not brotherhood.
>
> (Pope Francis, Rome, 24 March 2016)

References

Arendt H (2006) *Eichmann in Jerusalem*. London: Penguin.

Arizona Republic (1980) Gun dealer prepared to sell arms. From: www.newspapers.com/newspage/118073884/.

Bandura A (1999) Moral disengagement in the perpetration of inhumanities. *Personality and Social Psychology Review* 3(3): 193–209.

Bauman Z & Donskis L (2016) *Liquid evil*. Cambridge: Polity Press.

Bengtsson R & Elgström O (2011) Reconsidering the European Union's roles in international relations. In Harnisch S, Frank C & Maull HW (eds) *Role theory in international relations: approaches and analyses*. Oxon: Routledge, pp. 113–130.

Benjamin M (1990) *Splitting the difference: compromise and integrity in ethics and politics*. Lawrence, KS: University Press of Kansas.

Brogan P & Zarca A (1983) *Deadly business: Sam Cummings, Interarms, and the Arms Trade*. New York, NY: W.W. Norton & Company.

Bromley M & Griffiths H (2010). End-user certificates: improving standards to prevent diversion. From: www.sipri.org/sites/default/files/files/insight/SIPRIInsight1003.pdf.

Democracy Now! (2016) Pope Francis points at weapons industry behind Brussels attack. From: www.democracynow.org/2016/3/25/headlines/pope_francis_points_at_weapons_industry_behind_brussels_attack.

European Commission (2018) Dual-use trade controls. From: https://ec.europa.eu/trade/import-and-export-rules/export-from-eu/dual-use-controls/index_en.htm.

Feller P (2008) *Een kleine geschiedenis van de Nederlandse misdaad*. Amsterdam: Carrera.

French PA (1996) Integrity, intentions, and corporations. *American Business Law Journal* 34(2): 141–155.

Hamid R (2006) 'Lord of War' film review. *Cinéaste* 31(2): 52–55.

Kanbur R (2001) Obnoxious markets. Working paper WP 2001–08, July 2001, Department of Applied Economics and Management, Cornell University, Ithaca, New York, NY.

Kant I (1998) *Kant: religion within the boundaries of mere reason: and other writings*. Cambridge: Cambridge University Press.

Kruse K (2016) What I learned from an international arms dealer. From: www.forbes.com/sites/kevinkruse/2016/09/12/what-i-learned-from-an-international-arms-dealer/?sh=1b929aeb54a0.

Maitland G (1998) The ethics of the international arms trade. *Business Ethics: A European Review* 7(4): 200–204.

Melé A (2018) So you want to be an arms dealer?. From: www.linkedin.com/pulse/so-you-want-arms-dealer-tony-mel%C3%A9/.

Moore M (2010) Arming the embargoed: a supply-side understanding of arms embargo violations. *Journal of Conflict Resolution* 54(4): 593–615.

Naylor RT (2001) The rise of the modern black market and the fall of supply-side control. In Williams P & Vlassis D (eds) *Combating transnational crime, concepts, activities and responses*. London: Frank Cass, pp. 209–236.

Potter M (2012) *Outlaws Inc*. London: Pan Books.

Raab J & Milward HB (2003) Dark networks as problems. *Journal of Public Administration Research and Theory: J-PART* 13(4): 413–439.

Satz D (2010) *Why some things should not be for sale: the moral limits of markets*. Oxford: Oxford University Press.

SIPRI (2021) Arms embargoes. From: www.sipri.org/databases/embargoes.

The Holy Bible: King James Version (2004) Dallas, TX: Brown Books Publishing.

Van Amerongen M (1968) *De roerige wereld van Pistolen Paul.* Amsterdam: De Bezige Bij.

Weiner T (1998) Samuel Cummings, 71, trader in weapons on a grand scale. From: www.nytimes.com/1998/05/05/world/samuel-cummings-71-trader-in-weapons-on-a-grand-scale.html.

Wiegratz J & Cesnulyte E (2016) Money talks: moral economies of earning a living in neoliberal East Africa. *New Political Economy* 21(1): 1–25.

8 Wedlock, stock and barrel

Partners, children and stepping down

> Of course [family] plays a part. I'd say a pretty big part yeah. The thing is, when [arms dealing is] your business and you want to provide for your family, then you do whatever is necessary.

When we had our first interviews, Constantine presented himself as a caring husband and a loving father. Yet, he himself does consider himself to be another person when at work.

> When I'm away on business, I'm a totally other, totally different person. I'm not the person you're talking to at the moment. It's not possible. I have to be able to leave all this [family life], what I have, behind. Lock it in a little box in my head, deal with what I have to deal with and then come back [to] open that box again. When I'm away on business, I put all this behind me. It's in the back in my mind, what's foremost in my mind is going on there, doing the business, making sure the client's happy, selling the stuff that they want and then coming back here. Obviously with the money. [...] That money puts steaks in the freezers, as they say.

It is that money to provide for his family that reveals he cares about his loved ones. For Constantine, his everyday family life is

> an entirely different world. [...] That's something close and personal. It's got nothing to do with business. You have to distinguish between what I do for a living and my family life. Never the twain shall meet.

Nevertheless, his family life, he finds, depends on his work and the income he generates with it. Selling arms to someone to kill with, gives him the income that enables him to take care of his family; to live their lives. This chapter, the final substantial one, will present Constantine's family life: his former partners and current partner, his (step)children and grandchildren. This means that in this chapter, the timeline of his life will be picked up again in the past up until recent years. Particular attention will be paid to his love relationships

DOI: 10.4324/9781315148236-9

with his current wife who has three sons who are stepchildren, and his biological daughter who has children of her own and are his grandchildren. These relationships and previous ones have not been unproblematic and still are challenging at times. They have shaped and still shape him, also to the point that they make him doubt whether he should still broker arms deals or not.

8.1 Julia (1972–1974) and Grace (1985–1998), the ex-wives

> That's not short term, that's long term. I'm [in my sixties], I've got to make a lot more money before I leave this world. […] I still have to do it, because I got a wife and three, well four kids, if you count my [biological] daughter. I have a wife and four kids that are still relying on me to do something. Because at the moment we're just living on what my wife brings in. I'm not doing any work at the moment. I'm not employed. I've got no contracts. I've got plenty of stuff to sell but nobody wants to buy it. I got people that want to buy things that I don't have, and neither do any of my contacts. I got other people that want to buy shit that I'm not going to sell them anyway. It's […] It's a hard situation at the moment but it's just the way it is. […] My work has always been […] I got one job and the profit from that allows me a year or two. […] [I never] hide behind my work.

He married three times and at this moment he is together with his wife, Martha, who he heavily depended on financially in recent years. 'The third one [wife] is the one I'm with at the moment. Touch wood, still with her!'. She has three kids of her own and is widowed. Constantine takes care of the three kids, all boys.

Before Martha and he got together though, he was married to and divorced two ex-wives. So, Constantine has met several women who he had an intimate relationship with. These relationships were not trouble-free. In particular his second wife, Grace, was someone we talked about at great length, as she hurt him the most. Whenever he would talk about Julia, his first wife and the mother of his biological daughter Catherine, it was usually with disrespect.

> My first [wife] was 18 years old when we got married. I was 22, she was pregnant with my daughter, and it didn't last. There's not really that much to talk about. It was an unsuccessful relationship where there was a child born out of it. That's basically all there is to say. She was a girl who liked opening her legs to a variety of men. In and out of wedlock. When we split up, she had another six children from different men, so my daughter has a lot of half-brothers and half-sisters, one of which got killed in a car accident, one of her half-brothers. As far as I'm concerned [Julia's] not even worth to mention. […] We never got violent. […] Let me put it this way, to answer quite bluntly, no. I don't think so, I don't think so.

Like in the above quote, in his stories about the early days of Catherine's upbringing that Section 7.3 of this book will look at more in-depth, he claimed to have not done the same thing as his own father did: being violent. However, it became clear to me some of his father's violent behaviour did echo in that of his own. He would not be violent towards Catherine or any of his partners but would, in certain exceptional cases, display violence in front of them.

> Julia had a tendency for sleeping around and I caught her in bed one morning when I came back from working nights, and I was studying and working nights in the factory as well. So I caught her in bed with my best friend. Beat the shit out of him and threw him out of the bedroom window, we had a house one-up, one down, [which] was my house before we even got married. He went out the window naked and I grabbed him by his balls and his hair, and I just threw him out of the window. I just saw red, yeah? I grabbed a knife and ehm […] I was […] I guess I was gonna kill her, but […] the next thing I heard was my daughter screaming in the next room. She'd obviously woken from the [fighting], because I returned home early, I was sick. So, I heard my child screaming in the next room and it just, basically, brought me out of this cloud of red mist, and I just threw the knife at her and it stuck in the head board next to her head. We separated, we divorced. […] I had been told by this former friend of mine, who mentioned [that the man my ex cheated me with] was released from the hospital after they patched him up hahaha! Two broken legs, two broken arms, a shattered vertebrae. Yeah, I was lucky my father saved me from going to jail. I got off quite lightly there, but whatever, we split up. I was under the impression she was going to get married to this guy. I was like: "Okay, if I'm gonna leave", because at the divorce, the judge said: "It's a question of maintenance payments". I said: "I'm not paying anything to this woman. I'm paying my daughter, but I'm not paying anything to this woman. She is responsible for the split up". So we worked it out in the end. My daughter got the house, [which] was in the name of my ex-wife until my daughter became 18. Then my daughter got the house to do with it what she wanted. My ex-wife got half of the money in the bank, which was basically mine anyway, but whatever. My ex-wife got the car, so that she could drive my daughter around, go shopping and things like that. I got my motorbike and I got half of the money in the bank. Yeah, that was it. I asked to the judge: "What about the things in the house?" [The judge said]: "You have to split those up 50/50". I said okay. So after we left the court, I said to my ex-wife: "Okay, just go to the house and split the things up". We got to the house, I got the chainsaw out and cut everything in half. "You can have my half as well" [he said to his ex-wife]. That's the kind of guy I was. […] She didn't keep my daughter away from me. I left. I left because I wanted. […] Why I took the chainsaw and cut everything in half? Yeah […] I was crazy back in those days, believe me.

As negative as he was about his first wife, he never accused her of the lost contact between him and Catherine. He changed since then.

When he left Julia, he moved to another country for his work, where he met and married Grace, his second wife. It was not a perfect relationship but at least better than the relationship with his first wife.

> We never had kids. […] XXXX baroness, that was the second wife. Her father, my ex father in law, because he's long dead, I still remember him. He was an ex-XXXX officer. […] I lived there for quite a while. […] It's a quiet city but I certainly wouldn't call it boring. You got a casino and you got the parks, and there's some hot chicks running around. […] We lived in a very nice area by the police station, with my ex-wife. […] Being married to a XXXX woman, we all […] Even though she was from the XXXX and […] with a title, but no financial means. They lost everything in World War Two. She had her name, which was very respected. […] They're all intermarried […] All the XXXX [people] are all intermingled and related. […] I was not only introduced into that world, I was involved in that world. The place where we lived, in XXXX, XXXX, outside of XXXX, we lived on a place called, it was in XXXX. We lived on XXXX. It's a castle. Country mansion, I suppose you would call it in English. […] A country mansion, I wouldn't call it a castle, it's too small for a castle. A stately home that we rented. That's where we lived. The guy who owned the estate […] was married to a XXXX countess, they bred Icelandic ponies. He had so much land, forests. He and I would go out hunting deer. We'd sit in a crow's nest in the tree and shoot the deer and say: "That one you can shoot, that one you can't". Okay, BANG! Then we'd skin it and I used to eat deer in the wintertime. God, I had about two deer in the deep freezer. It was really nice. Deer and cranberry sauce. Fantastic. Wild boar as well. […] I enjoyed it. Obviously, forget about the personal situation between myself and my ex-wife. At that time there weren't so many problems. They developed later on when we moved to XXXX. […] It was because I was working as a social worker that it got me, basically, buying a small bottle of Jägermeister driving home from work and drinking it in the car. That's how bad the situation was. Then over the weekend we would sit, demolish two bottles of brandy, a couple of bottles of wine. I would get through about another 15 beers over the weekend. […] There wasn't a day that I didn't drink. I always had at least one beer during the day. […] I don't think I was [an alcoholic] because if I was I wouldn't have been able to stop as easy as I did. […] I would call it abuse, certainly, but not as far as alcoholism. Maybe I'm trying to make myself sound better than what I was, I don't know, but that to me was the situation. […] She used to drink A LOT. I guess it was basically her leading me on, me leading her on. We were both depressed in our situation, personal situation, and also the […] It wasn't a financial problem. Neither of us had financial problems. I think we were depressed in our personal

> relationship to a certain extent and also the extent of both being totally stressed out and unsatisfied with the jobs we were doing. [...] I think that there were certain expectations from me that she couldn't fulfil, like a child, which basically, I think, drove a wedge between us. From there it just seemed to rollercoaster snowball, yeah? We would both be over the weekend drinking A LOT. I mean [...] A LOT. That was just if we didn't have guests. If we had guests, we had even a lot more. There wasn't a night I don't think, that the both of us didn't crawl into bed drunk, over the weekend. Sunday was always the day of bringing the alcohol level down to an acceptable level so that you get up on Monday morning and go to work. She had to drive, anyway. She was working for a book publisher. She was a book representative for a very, very famous XXXX publishing house. [...] This is not a good situation. This is one of the reasons why I'm glad that it happened. Well, I'm not glad, but I'm supposed I should be that the situation with my pancreas [attack and cancer] happened, because otherwise I would have never gotten out. I'd probably drunk myself to death. In fact, I was very happy that, in some nights, she didn't make it back home. She would be up in the northern part of XXXX, visiting customers and I would be alone at home with the dog, which for me was perfect. It was a sad situation. We had 12 years together. [...] I won't say twelve years of drinking, but 12 years of being together, and of those twelve years, at least 8 of hard alcohol consumption. [...] She couldn't get [pregnant], unfortunately. [...] She felt guilty about it. She was married before, she couldn't have any kids. She thought it was her ex-husband's fault. Turned out to be her fault. [...] When we decided: "Let's try alternative methods", like artificial insemination, she was too old. She was 8, 9 years older than I am, at that time. So I was middle end of 40ies, so she was middle end of 50ies. It's much too old. I'm glad in many ways that she didn't have a child, because it would have only made the situation worse in the end. A child is not a substitute for a happy relationship. Just because you have a child, doesn't mean to say you're automatically a loving, comfortable happy pair. A child doesn't substitute what you're missing [...] I'm not obviously not in touch [anymore]. My wife, my present wife, would kill me, yeah? They knew each other. They knew each other. We were friends of the family. If I had contact with her again, my present wife would go up the wall. I do know she's living in XXXX, and I do know that's she's now a healer, a homeopathic practitioner, in XXXX. She's got her own surgery, I hope she's doing well. I hold no hard feelings towards her. That's not true. I do actually. When I went off to the XXXX and to the XXXX I gave her the power of attorney over my bank account. She blew a lot of money. [...] Anyway, that was a part of my life.

The work-related stress of being a social worker, as Chapter 4 showed, and the problematic, alcohol-dependent relationship together eventually led to them divorcing. That, plus he had a pancreatic attack in 1996.

> Before that [attack] I was always thinking about others and never about myself. […] [The attack] changed my life. I nearly died. […] I remember sitting, well I don't remember sitting in the hospital, I remember […] afterwards my ex-wife, when she came to visit me and I was in a normal hospital ward, and she said to me: "Do you remember anything about your time in the intensive care?" I said: "Nope, very, very little. I remember being taken down the ward in a bed and screaming: 'You're not getting any fucking spare parts from me', but apart from that […]". She said: "No, no", she said: "When you were in the intensive care ward, the doctor came around to ask you if he could tell me what was wrong with you?". I said: "Yeah, and?" [She replied:] "He asked you if he could tell me what was wrong, and you said: 'Yeah tell me as well', so he explained to me that you might die at any second, and after he told me, you sat straight up in bed and said: 'Okay doc, that's fine, but can I still work?' ", haha! So after that, and after this harrowing experience, I said: "Fuck it. Now I'm going to start looking after number one for a while [myself]". Maybe I became perhaps a little egocentric by putting myself in front of other people, but when you've been that close to death, I mean, really that close to death where you've seen basically the light in front of your eyes […] Okay, maybe it was just imaginary on my part. I don't know. I was in and out of coma's most of the time, and drugged up pretty heavily but it was a harrowing experience. Having to think about the fact of dying, was not something very nice. I thought: "No, I'm not going to fucking die, I got to many things to do still". […] Homeopathic medicine got me through it.

The attack and the divorce also have been influential in his choice to go and do the consultancy work – the work that eventually led him to get acquainted with arms dealing. It was also shortly after he entered the arms trade as a dealer that he met Martha.

8.2 Martha (2000–present), his wife and his stepchildren

> I will do this to the day they nail me down in my coffin, or until somebody decides: "I've had enough of this bugger, I'm gonna end his life". […] I'm not rich enough to retire. If I'd won the lottery, yeah I'd retire. Everybody thinks: "Arms dealers, yeah they make lots of money", [but] those are the black arms dealers. They are the ones who make lots of money. I have a wife and three kids to support, yeah and two kids that aren't working. Two students!

In his current marriage with Martha, Constantine found and still finds peace and love. She was the widow of a good friend of his, and neither of them expected to become involved 'but it just happened', he said. With it, came three stepsons: Jack, Bill and Dennis, 'an instant family', as he referred to. He loves them all deeply. As opposed to his previous marriages, there is mutual respect to be found between Martha and him. It brought him calmness and balance.

> I am trying to keep myself, my wife and my family happy. I try and make sure that bills are paid on time. The same as everybody else. I lead a normal life which is what I never really wanted to do hahaha!

Martha seems to make him more social and caring towards his family, like his parents:

> I haven't rung XXXX, I'll do that as soon as we've finished speaking to say [to my mother]: "Happy Mother's day", which is something I rarely do. In fact, I rarely ever remember even birthdays. If it wasn't for my wife, birthdays of my parents would go [unnoticed].

According to Constantine, Martha is a caring mother and partner and a hard worker.

> My wife has worked since she was 15. She is now 55, so that's 40 years. She managed to get her application for her pension, because we had a young son at the time when she was 50. He was still under 18, so which means she could apply for an early pension, reduced. She gets €330 a month, for a pension, that while she worked so long, which is disgusting! She'll never get a full pension because she took it earlier than she should have done. So, €330 a month, pension, with that a person is supposed to live. [...] She's very intelligent, my wife, even though she never finished gymnasium. [...] But she is also very dumb. If I try to talk her about a situation on the other side of the world, she's like: "You know I got problems at home, I don't have time to listen to other problems". [...] That's this [specific] mentality: "Let's make sure our houses are clean, but throw the junk out of the window".

Something Constantine finds annoying at times is how Martha avoids difficult (political) discussions, because she does not want to be confronted with what he called unnecessary complex discussions and having to think about it.

> People that think too much are often responsible for their own downfalls. This is true. Like my wife, my wife is always thinking. I'd say to her: "What are you thinking about?", [she'd reply:] "Nothing". How to understand men, rule number 48: don't ever say nothing. Because the guy's gonna wonder: "What the FUCK is wrong? Nothing?" She's sitting there with a strange look on her face, and you ask her what's wrong: "Nothing". That's got more men into trouble, "Nothing", than anything else in the world I can imagine. She is always fucking thinking.

It happened often his wife would walk in when Constantine and I had a conversation through Skype. She once came in and gave a piece of cake to Constantine.

> Cake! There you go, homemade strawberry cake with my tea on a Sunday afternoon. My wife's just got up. […] She's probably having a low sugar and decided to eat some cake that would be nice. And she probably wanted to come in and see who the hell I was talking to [over Skype] anyway haha! Because when I told her: "I got this guy who wants to write my biography", [she said] : "Who is it?". I said: "This is a professor in a university in Liverpool". [She replied]: "Yeah right" hahaha! […] [She said:] "Who the hell wants to write a story about YOUR life?". [I replied]: "Oh well, obviously somebody does" haha.

Regarding his work, his wife seems to be accepting, yet does not seem to be interested fully in what he does. They can have a conversation about anything, he told me, but she is not interested in things outside of the immediate sphere of the family.

> The XXXX, XXXX mothers, XXXX women, I imagine the XXXX are pretty much the same. I'm not sure. […] Well, she is the same […] So, you know, it's just one of those things. You just take it as it comes. If she wants to talk, she knows where I am. Or if I wanna talk, I'll see if she's in the mood for talking, if she's not then I just […] Alright [I'd ask:] "You want a coffee?".

She just finds it annoying, apparently, that Constantine is always in his work room, which became clear when we arranged the interviews.

> Sunday is better for me [to be interviewed] to be quite honest. I may try and see if I can take my wife out on Saturday, maybe go for an ice cream. We never get out. I hardly see her anyway. She's always complaining: "You're always in front of that bloody computer". […] My wife said to me: "What the fuck do you do ALL day on the bloody internet?". I said: "You'd be surprised. That's where your new shoes came from". [She replied:] "Oh, alright!".

Constantine thinks that she thinks he is being selfish, whereas he thinks she should not complain about it.

> I always get told by people: "You always […]", especially by my wife at the moment: "You only think of yourself, you don't do anything to help", you know? That's not true. She's got whatever she wants basically, maybe I don't sit and talk with her as much as I should, but this is unfortunately the way I've become. I have my life, my work, and she is not necessarily

> a part of my working sphere, because I told her in the very beginning what I did. She said: "I don't care what you do as long as it's legal". I said: "Okay", and every time I'm working on something, [she says:] "Oh I hope it's legal". [I'd reply:] "Just don't ask me, you told me once, and that's it! So just close the door on the way out of the office please". [...] She's got used to it. I mean we don't spend a lot of time together anyway, I mean, she works in a military factory. She's an electronics technician. She works from 7 in the morning until 4 in the afternoon. She's absolutely wrecked when she gets in. The only thing we have together is the weekends. Saturdays we go shopping, Saturdays afternoons I work. Sunday maybe we'll go out for a drive, or go and get some ice cream, or maybe a small walk, but that's it!

I said to him that it sounds like a pretty normal, 'mediocre' life, meaning, a type of life of which he keeps on saying he never liked it and avoids living: 'Well, it is for her, it's not for me!'. So, despite detesting the 'mediocre' life, through his care for his wife and other 'ordinary gestures' of doing things together and for her, for example, going on a holiday, he reveals he is also enjoying mediocrity.

> My wife is on holiday, so starting from tomorrow, I said: "We'll get up early and go down to the beach", otherwise it will be like: "Where did you spend your holidays?" [she would say] and she will reply: "On the fucking balcony" and I will never live that down when that happens. She said to me last night: "I do not intend on growing roots in this fucking apartment for the three weeks that I'm on holiday". I said: "No, no, no, no".

Eventually, they did stay at home most of the time during the holidays.

> "Al Balconia", as in balcony. No, we didn't go anywhere. We went down to the beach most of the days. [...] We didn't go anywhere. My wife had vacations and we spent practically every day that she wanted to go anyway, we went down to the beach. I'm at home anyway. Yeah, that's it. We went down to the beach, spent a couple of hours swimming and came back. Very relaxed, relaxing time for her. Not for me. I would have liked to have been able to take her away somewhere but this year it's not possible. [...] It's a tough time at the moment. "No money, honey!" haha. I got too much stuff [arms] and can't get rid of it anywhere.

Although he wants and tries to spend quality time with his wife and her sons, it is hard for him to do so because of money shortages, but also because his work itself.

> It's a way of life. You can never turn off. It's not a job from 9–5. You're 24 hours [...] if somebody calls now on that phone and says: "I need this that and the other", and if I know where that stuff is, and can get it like that,

and make maybe 25, 30, 50.000 dollars, I'm gonna say: "Yarin, sent me an invite, I have to hang up". That's the way it is. You can never plan. Even when I used to go on holiday with my wife and the kids. We took Jack and Bill [my stepsons], we never took the oldest one with us, because he always doing his own thing. I would take the laptop with me. They would be in the sea or in the pool in the hotel and I would be sitting at the pool's edge with a computer, emails, telephone calls, wheeling and dealing.

I asked him if he may have neglected his family.

No! At least I would hope that they would agree with me. Obviously my wife is always complaining that I spent too much time on the computer and never talk to her, which is just the way it is, unfortunately. I've told her, many times: "This is what I do. I can turn the computer off, but my head and I can sit and talk with you for half an hour, or an hour, but after a certain time my head is back [thinking] 'make money make money make money'". That's the thing, when you're self-employed, the pressure is on you, on me, the pressure is on me, because I'm talking about me, myself and I, the pressure is on ME to make hay when the sun shines. Make money when you can and at the moment there are not a lot of opportunities. So when an opportunity comes along I have to grab it. The rest of the time I have to look for those opportunities. I'm looking all the time. I scour the internet every day looking for things that people might want.

His wife and he sometimes disagree on how to run the household, financially that is, whereas Constantine is quite calm about the occasional stress of having enough to cover expenses, he thinks his wife is in disagreement.

My wife is exactly the opposite. She's always: "We don't have enough money, we can't pay this, we can't do that". I reply: "Yeah we don't HAVE enough money at the moment so we can't pay this, and we can't pay that. Now be quiet. Stop stressing out". She replies: "How can you THINK like that?". I reply: "It's very simple". She says: "What about all the problems we've got?". I said: "If you think about all the problems all the time you go fucking crazy". She said: "But don't you have anything in your head?". I said: "Yes, and I take it from here, the front, and I put it in a little box at the back and lock it. When I got money, I will open it and say 'now what are we gonna pay'". That's the way I am. I can't change, I'm 6X, getting on 6X now. I know I don't look it, you don't have to compliment me.

Her overthinking, he finds, can cause some frustration and could lead to fights, during which he never crossed the line, he explained.

It's not easy. My wife is also a very strong-willed woman and there have been many occasions where we've basically stood off against each other

> and I had to really bite my tongue and hold my hands so that I wouldn't explode. In the end I just turn around and would walk away, because I KNOW that if […] I can't hit her […] She's a woman. It'd take a lot to make me hit her but she's been very close to it a couple of times haha!

In elaborating on the discussions he can sometimes have with Martha, he explains her behaviour is influenced by her health issues, making him tolerate some of the more erratic moments he thinks she has.

> She's got hyperthyroidism. The thyroid gland in the neck, well, it's called hyperthyroidism. […] Everything just goes haywire. They start feeling agitated, restless, nervous, angry. Basically fucks up the whole [hormonal system]. It's an overproduction of hormones. […] When the thyroid is working overtime, everything gets shot to hell. […] So she's on pills at the moment. We're hoping that's enough to stop the thyroid from producing so many hormones. Hopefully she will be back to normal soon, but at the moment she's got high blood pressure and a very, very fast heart rate. Just have to wait and see. She will be okay, she will be okay.

Martha has three sons, Jack, Bill and Dennis. When they married, Jack was 17, Bill 15 and Dennis 6. They are his stepsons, but Constantine loves them as if they are his own children. For him, it has to do with being a proper family man and a good father. Or at the very least, not trying to be like his own father. He wants to protect his (step)children from any harm possible.

> She said to me in the very beginning: "You marry me, you marry the whole family". I said: "Yeah okay, I'm prepared to do that". […] I've got feelings towards my wife, feelings towards the children who I consider to be mine. […] They've all lived longer with me than what they have with their actual father, because we've been married now 17, getting on 18 years. […] I said to them in the very beginning: "Look I am not going to try and fill the shoes of your father, because I can't. He was too much of a great man, so the only thing I want is that we're friends, and if you have any problems, talk to me about it". But that's how I went into this marriage and relationship, and that's how I am. […] There's a lot of respect there. The oldest one once said: "You know, you're not my father but you're a very good friend, and I love you". The youngest is the same. Now he won't come out and say it, but he shows it by what he does. He's also very closed-in, because like I said, he was 6 years old when his father died. It was a terrible, terrible shock for him. He never got to say goodbye. I imagine that is something that he's gonna have to work on in his future. I hope that when I go I can give him the opportunity to say goodbye. At least that will, perhaps, count to the effects of not being able to be with his real father. […] I acknowledge [to have a father role]. I do.

> [...] But I'm not allowed to say anything to the kids. But I did once. My wife stepped in and said: "They're my children, if they need telling off, I'll do it". I remember one time, when we first started living together, I came home and I saw the kids' shoes here and trousers there, and the socks there. Just everything was a mess. Clothes everywhere. I'd say: "Hey", and their mother wasn't there, she was at work at the time. I said: "Hey guys come on, clean up behind yourself, put your shoes away. If that's dirty, throw it in the wash. Now your mother is not your slave". At the time, all three of them were still living here. They did it grudgingly, they couldn't see that I was right. I said: "Come on your mother is at work. She is working all day. I'm working all day. You gotta respect that your mother, once she's come home from work, the last she wants to do is pick up after you". I tried to explain it to them in the nicest way possible and like I said, grudgingly they did it, but when she got home, the youngest one went and told her, and she came to me afterwards and said: "If you got anything to say to the kids, you talk to me first". From that moment on, I said: "Okay, I won't butt in if there's any arguments".

Although Constantine said he would not get involved in discussions or fights between the boys (and their mother), he does feel the need to correct their bad behaviour. So he has 'butted in' again when Bill, the middle one, raised his hand to his mother, about to hit her. Constantine jumped in the middle.

> It was a very, very bad argument. He was in his puberty at the time. They've been having a REALLY bad argument in the kitchen. I was in the living room, trying to watch TV. They were screaming and shouting at each other as only XXXX can do [...] Yeah, XXXX. He pushed her and took his hand up to hit her, so I jumped up and pushed him away. He faced-off against me, so I just walked up to him and head butted him on the nose. He started screaming: "I'm gonna go to the police". I said: "Yeah, go on, you do that, [say] that you were going to hit your mother". [...] He replied: "You don't have the right to hit me". I said: "No, you don't have the right your mother". He said: "It's MY mother!", and I said: "Yeah and it's my fucking wife". That was the only time. I mean, we've had arguments he and I, but we've always, both of us, backed down, because he knows if he takes me to a certain point and there are no words to be spoken after that point. I'll beat the shit out of him. [...] I love him, and I love them all as if they're mine. They've just been brought up wrong. [...] [Martha] said to me again: "I can take care of myself". I said: "Well, it didn't look much like it". So, since that time, you know, I never butted in any of the arguments. I'd sit and discuss things with them, but mostly it was like: "Okay, if that's the way you want it to do. If you want to scream and shout". As long as it didn't get violent, then I would keep out of it. [...] I can understand the reason why [she told me off]. They're her kids. If I had kids I would probably say to her as well: "Okay listen, they're my

> kids if they're gonna be told off you come to me, I will tell them". That's what I would have done as well, I think. I can understand that! [Violence] just gets me mad and Bill saw [my] reaction. It has never happened since. He was 16 at the time. Had a bad time going through puberty, because of the death of his father. He didn't finish school studies, started becoming bad at school, etc. etc.

He wanted me to understand that he did empathise with Bill *because* he disciplined him. By disciplining, he wanted to show how much he cares for his children, because he could also not be bothered by them. It is to an extent a similar way of love through discipline that he himself experienced when he was younger; however, Constantine refrains from doing so in an abusive way. Besides having arguments with his stepchildren, it is difficult for him to not get involved in parenting Martha's sons due to simply caring about them also by taking care of them and being there when the boys need him. Dennis, 24 at the time of writing, has Crohn's disease, for which Constantine had to go to hospitals with him.

> My youngest son is in a hospital, bit of a hectic time. It is with this Crohn's disease that he has. [...] So, it is sometimes, a little bit exciting when he's sick and we have to rush him into the hospital, because he's bleeding out of just about every orifice on his body.

To see him suffering and then to stay emotionally distant, is difficult. In fact, it brings him closer to Dennis. In sum, in his experience, and in many ways, he is an affectionate and caring father, unlike how his own father was to him.

Such care for his current family also entails keeping away his work from his wife and stepsons, and anyone who he cares about actually.

> In this business you can't get too close to people, because you know, sooner or later [...] I mean, I try and keep my business as close to my chest as possible. There are not very many people who know what I do. That's the way I like it. Not even my wife knows exactly what [...] I mean, she knows I deal in military equipment, she knows that. She doesn't know to what extent. Her kids know, my relations know, my family, and near-relations. As far as that's concerned, that is as far as it goes, because there's always a risk that that information will get out to parties that, shall we say, don't like what you do. You are then at risk yourself. Or I would be at risk, myself and my immediate family.

He also warns his stepchildren for the dangers of arms dealing, were they ever interested to become an arms dealer.

> I basically have raised them, as best as I could. At least they're not junkies or thieves or arms dealers. The youngest one said to me: "I wanna do what you do". I said: "No". He said: "Why?? Teach me!". I said: "No".

> He said: "WHY?". I said: "Because it's not a job". He said: "Yeah but you make lots of money". I said: "Money is not everything. Go to school, keep going to school, finish your studies and then tell me what you want to do afterward". He said: "I know what I wanna do, I wanna do what you do". I said: "You're not gonna do what I do. When you come and see me after you're 18 and say you want to learn the trade, then I might think about teaching you".

As much as he has been a good father for his stepchildren, the following will show how, he thinks, he has lacked such good fatherhood regarding his biological daughter, which is one of the more personal reasons for him to have done this biography.

8.3 Catherine, his biological daughter and his grandchildren

> I think after all that, once we've gone through all this [interviewing and writing the biography], there's not much point in pulling out. If we can sell it, and make something out of it, then why not? Then I can at least leave something for my daughter to read because she doesn't know my life story either. She was six months old when I left. But that's for a next week or whenever. Send me an appointment, okay?

One of the most, if not the most important persons in Constantine's life, is his biological daughter, Catherine. For him, his Catherine is

> a love child. Her mother and I were very briefly married, it didn't work out. [...] I don't remember birthdays well. Well, I remember hers because it's the XX of XXXX, but exactly what year, I don't remember. Let me just work this out [...] 19XX. Just before I left [...] So she was born in 'XX, alright. [...] I was brought up as I was brought up. I have a daughter, my own daughter, I never brought her up. Her grandparents brought her up. My ex-wife, my first ex-wife, we divorced when I was very young. I mean, we were young. I mean, I was like, what, 20, she was 18. She was pregnant, [...] In those day and ages, yeah [you had to marry]. I never brought my daughter up. [...] I never had any responsibility of bringing children up. So I would never know how I would do it. I am almost certain myself, I would certainly do it the opposite to what my father did. [...] I'd make sure there was time for the kids.

When Catherine was about six months old, the incident happened with his ex-wife cheating with his best friend on him and that led to his divorce, as discussed earlier in this chapter.

> Well, I think, maybe [Catherine] just heard a lot of noise, let's put it that way. Anyway, I left, we split up, the divorce came through, and I was under the impression that [...] she'd been brought up with this other guy

> and she'd accept this other guy as her father, and that was one of the reasons why I said I'm not gonna have any contact. I didn't want a psychological impact on her. [...] I swallowed the bitter pill, so to speak, and said: "Okay, if she's gonna be brought up by another guy, then it's best for her, at that age, not to have too many psychological problems. And at a later date, if she wants to find out who she really is [...]", and obviously she would be told. All she has to do is apply for a passport, and it will say my name on there. She will see it on her birth certificate or whatever [...] So that is what happened. She wasn't brought up by my ex-wife or this other guy, she went to her grandparents, which were the parents of my ex-wife, and she was brought up by them. They are good people. I would have preferred to bring her up myself.

The conversations about his daughter were sometimes difficult for Constantine, from what I could notice from the way he spoke about it. In particular, the subject of not having been around for her for so long, was a delicate topic.

> You know, I wasn't [...] what shall we say [...] I wasn't [...] psychologically prepared for [...] and with the way that my life was going, ehm [...] to bring up [...] my life at that time was a little bit up and down with ehm [...] dropping out of the university for a year, taking off in doing what I wanted do [...] then ehm [...] joining the army. I wasn't anywhere [near being] able to bring up a child that small. It would have been, you know [...] It was better she went to her grandparents. Otherwise, if she hadn't gone to anybody, she would probably end up in social services. [...] That's not something [you'd want], because her life would not have turned out the way it is at the moment. It would have turned out something different.

It was difficult for him to not have contact for decades. I was curious about how he managed to do so.

> Did I think of her? [...] Ha [...] You think on other things, you look for other problems, doing. You dig yourself into your work. You put that in a place where it can't hurt you. That's all you can do. [...] Work and alcohol. It's true, I won't deny it. Work and alcohol. I used to be a heavy drinker. I won't deny it. It was nothing for me. Obviously when I was in the forces we didn't go out every night pissing it up. But when I was next day off or a weekend off, then it was party time. But you can never find an answer to anything in the bottom of a bottle. It just doesn't work. It took me a while to find it out, but I found out in the end. It just doesn't work, you can't find anything in the bottom of a bottle, apart from more pain, because you may be able to numb your senses up to a certain point, but in the morning when you wake up, the bottle is empty, you still got the problem. You still got those feelings. So you just lock it up and you put it

> away in a place where it can't hurt you. Occasionally, you take it out, look at it, and see if you can do anything about it.

This does not mean Constantine never felt any guilt, because he regrets how it all went and how he would do it differently now.

> Some guilt? Of course there is! Of course I wish I had been there for her. [...] If I had the chance, what would I do differently? I would undo the amount of years or trying to undo the amount of years that I didn't have contact with my daughter. [...] I'd like to have seen her in her younger years, to have been by her side, when she needed it. Because she was raised by her grandparents, which I knew nothing about. It's a shame, but you know it's something that can't be changed. We have contact with each other now and again, ehm [...] It's just the way it is, there's nothing you can do about it, there's no point in worrying about it. What's done is done. [...] It's like I'm part of her life but I'm not. [...] Well, I never will [be]. Unfortunately that's life. Whether she's got psychological problems with that or not, I don't think so. I don't think so.

For most of her life Constantine was not involved in it, until his brother Arthur, after more than 30 years, approached him, asking him [...]

> "Do you wanna know where your daughter is?". I said: "Yeah, that'd be interesting to know". [...] It was a bit of a shock for me. [...] They found her on a genealogy site, that's what my brothers were into. Well, they still are. They traced our whole family back to 1036, I think it is, not that is really of interest to me. Those guys are all dead, I'm alive still. It's my life, yeah. Okay, it's interesting to know what we did in the past, but it doesn't have any play on what I am now. Anyway, that's how they found her and then my brother wrote to her and said: "I'm so and so, your father's brother, or so we think. This is a picture of your father or who we think might be your father. Do you know [him]?", and she said: "Yeah, that's him". [...] There I was [on that picture], holding her, at the young age of, I think, three months or something.

He told me about how they got back in touch.

> [Through] a lot of emails, a lot of heartbreak, a lot of crying, a lot of self-incrimination. On both parts. In the end we met in XXXX. [...] She was very tearful, me as well. When we first met after so many years. She said: "I don't know whether to cry or beat you up". I said: "Try both, you wanna hit me, you hit me, you'd have every right for it". She didn't. [...] [It was] pretty emotional, pretty emotional, for HER! We'd already have spoken on the phone, we exchanged emails, we exchanged letters, well, letters over email. She said: "I don't hate you". Because she only heard from her

> mother what have happened. She didn't know the true story. Well, she didn't know my side of the story. [...] We'd spoke on the phone, there was a lot of tears, and splattering and crying. I said: "I'm coming to XXXX to see you". So I did, I met her. She met me at the airport. We went back to her house with her partner and I stayed there a couple of days, and then I flew back again. It was a very emotional meeting. She will not EVER call me "dad", which I don't expect. She said: "My dad has brought me up", I said: "I don't have a problem with that". She said: "You might be my biological father but you're not my dad". I said: "Yeah, you know, okay, I can live with that. I'm just happy and it makes me feel proud that you turned out the way you did". [...] At the moment she is a very, very attractive, VERY intelligent, good looking, young lady. Well, young lady, she is XX now. She's got five kids, I'm actually five times a grandfather. My God, I feel old! She lives with her partner. [...] Her first partner died of liver cancer and kidneys. He already had two kidney transplants and that's what he died from. She is very happy. As far as I can tell. [...] She's lost a lot of weight, she's lost [over 75 kilo's]. She's lost a lot of weight. She used to be fat. Now she's slim and damn good looking. Reminds me of me when I was younger hahaha!

After their first meeting, several more followed.

> Every time I try and give her money, because I feel [...] guilty for not being there for her, especially knowing now what I didn't know then. The last time I was over there, I was over there in [2016], I said: "It's your birthday coming up soon on the XX. What do you want". She said: "I don't want to have anything". I said: "Look, you just had little Trevor", which is her youngest son. I said: "You wanna get something for him, what would you like me to bring over?". She said: "Nothing, nothing, it's just enough to see you". I said: "Alright". So when I went over, I cut her a cheque for €230. I said: "Look, I don't know what you want, but here's a cheque for €230, take it. Get yourself something, and get something for the kids". [...] She told me that she never wanted for anything, because I spoke with her once when I was there, I said: "Let me give you some money to buy something, clothes or whatever". She said: "No, I don't want your money. I never wanted for anything when I was a child. I got it all from my dad", because she called her grandparents mum and dad. She's never called me, if she has, once father, how she called me. She never called me dad or father. She's only called me it once. She has only ever called me once father. I went off to XXXX on a day trip, I had an interview up there. I told you, I think. I put it up on [social media] when I came back, because I don't put on [social media] where I'm going and what I'm doing. It's rather stupid, operational security. I've put up there afterwards, and she said [...] She also speaks XXXX, she went to XXXX and studied XXXX in school. She wrote in XXXX: "I hope you had a nice trip, my father",

> which made me feel good. She never called me dad, or father or anything […] It was the day after I came back from XXXX.

It becomes clear, given how she called him father once, that since their first meeting they have established

> an on-and-off sort of relationship […] friends, that's it. I obviously feel more for her than I think she feels for me, because I was never in her life. It's always very nice when we meet and when we talk on the phone. Or when we chat on Skype, or on [social media]. It's always very enjoyable. She is always happy. […] We've moved on from that uncomfortable situation of "I'm the abandoned […] I'm your father"-sort of thing. I mean, there was a show on XXXX TV, this reality show "I miss […] my father left me 15 years ago, I only met him last week"-sort of thing. Catherine said to me: "Should we put in for that?". I said: "No". Hahahaha no! That's not what I'm about. […] She is very intelligent, she speaks XXXX. She went to XXXX on holiday with the school, she was very well-brought up, she never had […] she never missed anything out of her life. […] It makes me happy that she had all of the things that she materially needed. I guess she had the love of her grandparents. But her real parents, well, her mother, not only did she have a child, two children by the guy, by that ex-friend of mine. She also had a child by his brother. Then by three or four other guys. And now she is living with some black guy.

As we saw at the beginning of this chapter, Constantine was and still is not very positive about Catherine's mother, Julia. Catherine herself was not either, according to him.

> She thinks she's a slut. I didn't say anything, and she said: "As far as I'm concerned, she is a slut, she is an alcoholic, and she should keep her legs closed" hahahaha […] She said: "I've got some lovely half-sisters, got some lovely half-brothers, but as far as I'm concerned", Julia, which is […] what she calls her, she won't ever call her mother.

As Catherine means the world to Constantine, I wonder to which extent her opinion about his arms dealing matters to him as well.

> She knows what I do. […] No [she does not have an opinion about it]. If she does, she certainly told […] She certainly hasn't said anything to me. […] I don't think it bothers her, I'll be quite honest. […] Well, the only thing is, she said to me, when we were talking about the company and she asked me what I did, and she said: "Oh that's interesting" and she sort of just changed the subject, and we started to talk about other things. She is not really interested.

Whereas he might think his arms dealing career might not mean a lot to her, for Constantine it means a lot what the arms dealing business could possibly mean for her safety.

> I wouldn't want to even think about it. […] As I said, I think I've said a 1000 times up till now. I could either be extremely rich or dead in a ditch in Africa somewhere with bullet hole in the back of my head. […] I wouldn't have thought about the consequences, I would have taken a totally different path in life. I would have cut myself off from EVERYBODY that knew me and that I knew, and become basically another person. […] Obviously I don't know that I would have cut myself off from my daughter but at that time, I wasn't connected with my daughter again. […] Even though I'm working in a white area, for lack of better words, there are obviously people that get annoyed about me selling guns. If they knew that my daughter was in any way connected [to me] they may well decide to take it out on her because they couldn't get to me. […] [If something would happen to her, I would] KILL 'M! Yeah? Wouldn't have any second thoughts about it.

Clearly, he would kill for her. And so would he for his five grandchildren, all Catherine's – three girls, Christie, Rosie and Tracy, and two boys, Arnold and Trevor. When he speaks about them, similar to how he talked about his daughter, Constantine would light up and become cheerful. He remembers when he first met his grandchildren.

> They were a little bit confused to begin with, because when my daughter introduced me to them as their granddad. They said: "How many granddads do we have?" So she had to explain to the oldest one, and the oldest one explained to the next one down, and so on. But now I'm just "Constantine" or "granddad Cons". […] I said to them: "Don't call me granddad, yeah? You wanna talk with me with, it is Cons or Constantine. Granddad? I'm not granddad, makes me feel old". They said: "Well you are". I said: "I may be to you, but I'm not to me". […] They don't need to know [what I do for a living] and there's no reason for them to know. […] I don't wanna go putting ideas in their head. […] [It's] about preconception. […] You can imagine them going to school and saying: "We met our new granddad, he's an arms dealer", saying that in school, that would get around, and this, that and the other, and then it'd come back to my daughter, [people asking:] "What does your father do? Are the kids safe?"

The aspect of protecting them, as well as his current wife and three stepsons, from danger (including the arms dealing business itself) is absolutely crucial for Constantine. As important is what people might think of him as an arms dealer and what people's thinking does in terms of the harm it could inflict upon his loved ones. These and other worries he has, have started to make him consider whether to step out of the arms dealing business. Yet, such stepping out is more difficult than expected, as became clear.

8.4 Between quitting the job, retirement and death

When we were heading towards the end of the interviewing sessions, Constantine expressed his concern about struggling with brokering deals and with generating enough income to provide for his family.

> I was offered a job in XXXX to go and work for XXXX as a crisis-management advisor. But I turned them down, it would have meant moving to XXXX. My wife didn't want to move. I don't particularly want to move. She said: "There's no quality of life over there, you just work, house, work, house, the weather is shitty" haha and she doesn't speak XXXX. [...] I turned them down. I took a job here in XXXX at the moment, because my companies are not going so well. Since the Americans and the Russians are supplying directly, there is no need for people like me hahaha [...] That's been now six to nine months.

It matters to Constantine that if a new job opportunity would present itself, it should not be outside of the country he is currently living, and that is because of his wife. He is indeed in wedlock, stock and barrel. Still, occasionally he did think about moving away from the arms dealing business. It would not mean he would move away entirely though. He would still be doing something with arms, as his expertise knowledge is attractive for employers in the military-security industry.

> I'd find something to do, probably make knives or something, or sell knives and axes, other killing weapons. [...] There are two head-hunters that have approached me. Two positions are in XXXX. One is for a company making armoured vehicles [...] weapons, and the other one is for a company making bullet proof vests, which doesn't really interest me at all. I'll be quite honest, I'm not really interested in selling tanks. It's not fun. I can't drive a tank, and I like to shoot the products that I sell. [...] If I have to get a job, working for somebody, instead of working for myself, I thought perhaps I might apply, with the knowledge that I have in this industry, and possibly work for an NGO. For the counter-proliferation of small arms. Exactly the opposite! From one extreme to the other! I sell arms, now I chase people that sell arms!

When I brought up the subject of retirement as a way out of arms dealing, it became clear he did not truly have thought about it enough. On the one hand, he would really like to be able to do so though, also being financially able to do so. However, that is difficult to do as he did not build up a pension.

> I won't retire, I won't get a pension ever. For one thing, I don't think I will live that long, and secondly, I haven't paid enough pension payments. I'm self-employed. [...] Maybe if they ever change the law that says that every XXXX person gets a minimum pension, then okay, I might get through, €460 euro a month. It'd be enough to buy a couple of packages of spaghetti and packet of Nescafe or something. [...] I guess as long as I'm alive and I can still type and talk on the phone, and over Skype, then I'm going to be working. You don't get a pension in this business. I don't work for XXXX systems or any of the big guys. Unfortunately, it would be nice to have a job, a steady job with a real arms company, and just sell the products for them. I'd be an employee because then you don't have to worry about licensing. Then you have somebody above your head and says "Ts ts ts, you can't do that" hahaha. Then you get a pension as well after you're 65.

What he hopes for is to have one big final deal, from which he can live off of: 'From 500 million our profit would have been [...] around about 55 million. That would be split in three ways. [...] I only need one like that in a year and I can retire'. I wondered if he really could ever leave arms dealing as a profession, and not work at all actually, to which he replied: 'I'm not afraid of idleness'.

Even if he would retire, it would not be a joyride, because he is also severely ill. He has pancreatic cancer since 1996 and it is worsening. It was one of the reasons to do this biography. In fact, he often made sure I stayed aware of his poor health and the approaching finality of his life, saying things such as 'send me an email, make an appointment. I'm hoping that I will still be hanging around'. While being a main motivator, his health condition was also blocking this biography, because sometimes we had to rearrange interviews because of check-ups and his overall exhaustion due to the treatment. He truly hated if that had to happen:

> If my wife didn't wake me up at 11am today [...] What time did she wake me up? Two o'clock? If she hadn't woke me up, I'd still be in bed until half past six to get up in time and talk with you.

The condition of his health was usually the topic we would start off small talk with before interviewing, but not too long because he did not feel comfortable talking about it. He simply does not want to think about it.

> Obviously when I go in for the radiation therapy, which is [...] The third one has happened now, ehm [...] Obviously it kicks in and you start to think but then on the other hand I just say: "Fuck it", yeah? [...] What's gonna happen is gonna happen and [...] Whatever this is [...] Master plan of the universe is [...] That they put me into, well, then I'm just gonna have to ride it out and accept whatever comes. Because that's all I can

> do. I'm a very pragmatic person, Yarin. [...] I try not to [think about it], I always put on a brave face so to speak, and you know, tears of a clown where the clown has always got to smile. You can never see what's going on inside. I got a very, very hard exterior, but inside [...] once somebody gets to the inside of me, it's pretty soft. [...] It's just, you know, that's life man. People get killed at fourteen in a car crash, others get blown-up with a bomb. Some get shot in Munich.

At the time, the 2016 Munich shooting took place in a shopping centre, taking ten lives, including the perpetrator's life. Deflecting from the subject by discussing catastrophic events or something similar, was his way of dealing with the severity of his cancer and the treatments involved; a cancer that has been a part for almost a third of his life.

> I had a pancreatitis in 1996, which is now twenty years ago. Normally, people who have had pancreatitis and lost a third of the pancreatitis, like I have, are usually dead within ten years of pancreatic cancer. So, basically for the last ten years I've been living on borrowed time. [...] I knew about the pancreatic cancer, I knew that when they discharged me from the hospital in XXXX. [...] It's 20 years, so ehm [...] I'm still going hahaha, I'm still going, I'm still going. I'm still doing what I want, basically. [...] I can't travel as much as I want. I have to be close to the hospital, just in case. Taking a whole bunch of medication every day. On top of what I was taking before, blood pressure, aspirin, pills for stress, things like that, yeah? Whatever. But [...] You know [...] it's nothing [...] there's no point in talking about it, because you can't change anything. [...] I nearly died, I came out of the hospital after a very short time and amazed all the doctors that I was still alive. I said to myself: "I'm gonna turn my life around, because now there's no point in living on what's gone. Look forwards". That's the way I am.

Whereas he thinks he is an exception in how he is surviving cancer, he thinks he deserved it at the same time due to his unhealthy lifestyle, especially his drinking with his second wife.

> If this is what shall we say the fine [...] Not the fine, but the punishment that's been thrown on me for doing what I do, or for doing what I've done in the past, some people would agree with that I've just said. Some people would say: "That's a load of bullshit", but if this is the punishment that's been thrown on me by some superior being, then so be it. It's not much I can do about that to change it, yeah? So, fuck it, I just have to roll with it, yeah? [...] That maybe I'm responsible for my illness? [...] Well let me put it this way. Obviously [...] pfff [...] [...] No I don't [...] Think so, I've never put that in my head. Like: "Oh you're responsible for your own illness", nope. Okay, so I smoke, I used to drink A LOT. I'm certainly not

> responsible [...] Well, then again [...] Perhaps. I'm certainly responsible for the pancreatitis that I had, but nobody knew that I had this blood disorder which caused the triglycerides to go up very high, which in the end my pancreas dissolved one third of it. So, there again, you know, it's a question of how deep do you want to dig? How far down the rabbit hole do you wanna go? Because if you start doing things like that "Oh my God I'm responsible for my own illnesses", in a year, you'll get really fucked up in the head once you start thinking like that. You become a hypochondriac: "What have I done to cause this flu that I have?" I mean, come on! [...] I stopped [smoking] once for six months, then I started again. You know, I've forgotten who it was that said it, but they said: "Stop smoking is the easiest thing in the world, I've done it at least 10.000 times". [...] I don't drink, so I smoke more. [...] It goes with the beer, I mean, if you're in a pub and you have a beer, you got the glass in one hand, you do need something in your other hand. It's usually a cigarette.

The effects on his body are severe, caused by pancreatic cancer, which is

> what they call diverticulitis, which is [...] in your gut. It's like polyps in your gut but on the outside. Polyps, it's like [...] It's not polyps exactly, and it's on the outside of the gut not inside, which makes it a little bit interesting. It's where the gut has gotten weak inside, and it's [...] like a bubble on the outside. It fills up with excrement sometimes and it's extremely painful.

Next to the effects of the cancer itself, there are the different therapies he undergoes, the check-ups he has to get and the variety of medicines he must take, that are severely affecting his quality of life. Perhaps even more so than the polycythaemia vera cancer itself.

> Now I started on radiation therapy, I don't know if I told you? [...] Fucking radiation treatment, and shit like that. It's just another fucking hill to climb man. I'm just trying not to think about it, trying to keep myself busy, which is at the moment, extremely difficult. We'll see how it goes, so anyway. Let's get this book finished, otherwise it might be published posthumously, hahahaha! Well, you never know, I could walk out the door tomorrow and get hit by a crazy XXXX driver. There are enough of them on the roads. [...] I have to go in for phlebotomy, that's to take blood out. Also they want to do ehm [...] an MRI from the stomach and the pancreas, and the lots. Well the thing is with the [...] well this [...] obviously they suspect it's the pancreas. I'm getting a lot of pain in that area, because I only have two-thirds of the pancreas. [...] We're looking at ways to deal with that. It's possibly through the chemo, ehm [...] Nobody really seems to know where it's from. I'm on a special diet, etc. etc. etc. Still on the chemotherapy, which I have to take for the fucking red blood cells, ehm [...] Pfffff [...] Don't get me started, yeah? [...] I got a loose tooth, which is

> a pain in the butt. A loose tooth, a tooth that waggles. It's all the fucking chemo, it's starting to make my teeth drop out. I gotta go to the dentist, they'll probably pull it. I don't know what I'll do, I'll probably just get […] I probably will just tell them: "Pull 'm all and put me a couple of plaques in, screw-ins" hahaha "and make one a bottle-cap opener" hahaha. […] I'm on tablets, chemo every day still. Every day that will go on till the day I […] Till the day the good Lord takes me, or the day He says: "Okay, it's time, I want you". […] It's every day, 500 milligram tablets every day. […] You never get used to that poison. It's hydroxyurea, which is basically uric acid, which is basically what's in that pill, and some other things. […] Hydroxi is acid and urea would be uric, so highly concentrated uric acid. That's supposed to, well, what it does do, at the moment […] I don't know whether it's successful or not, because I still have to go into hospital every two months for them to take a litre blood out. What it's supposed to do is kill off some of the red blood cells. It won't ever cure, it can't be cured. Myelofibrosis […] it's part of a MPN, if you google that under "myelofibrosis neural system". It's to do with the DNA, it is a corruption of the jak-2 DNA which produces red blood cells in the body. It's cancer! Yeah. I've been forewarned that the tablets will make me grow older a lot quicker. So, it's just another fucking hill to climb.

The different and rather severe therapeutic and medicinal interferences have made his work less interesting. It takes the fun out of arms dealing ever since he got cancer, making him desk-bound.

> Yeah I feel old haha! I'm getting the medication and the shit they're giving me makes me feel old. […] [Treatment is] not so good. I've been in for a couple of radiation therapies and ehm […] looks like I may well have diabetes as well, so. Yeah, it's just another fucking hill to climb. Never mind, excuse my French. […] [I'm] tired. I had to go and get some new chemo tablets today, which is a bastard, run around. Like my normal chemist shop, he usually has them because he knows, when I'm gonna buy a packet it's gonna last me so long. Three months. Then he forgot to order a new one, so I had to run around the town, looking for somebody who got it. Nobody got it, so I had to get them to order it. It came in today so […] I took that, earlier this afternoon, just before lunch. Really, really tired. This chemo […] I mean I […] it's basically poison. I mean they don't even know how it works against cancer, but it does, so they say […] No, it's not very satisfactory. […] It's difficult to do stuff, because I don't have the energy that I used to have, obviously. […] I can't travel, not as much as I want to and the only contact I have with my clients now are either over the phone or through the internet. […] I used to travel a lot, I used to travel a lot more than I do now. Obviously, because ehm […] Okay, chemo I could take with me, tablets, for wherever I go. But I have to be around, every two weeks for blood tests. I have to be stable, in a place, I mean not

> stable condition, I have to be in a place where I can get to a hospital and take blood out of me, if ehm, if the red blood cells, if the blood is too muddy [...] to thick [...] I used to travel four or five months of the year. The Africans, sub-Sahara regions, Mozambique, Tanzania, Djibouti, I used to travel to all of these places. Knocking on doors, talking to the army colonels, taking them out for dinner. You know [...] just basically [...] it's like [...] it's a salesman job! "Real road warrior" as the Americans would say. But now it's basically telephone and a laptop. In my case a telephone and my tablet, or my telephone and a desktop.

Usually, he would end the short conversations about the status of his cancer, treatments, medicines and overall health with a joke.

> Somebody might put a fucking bullet in my head hahahaha which is, which may well be a blessing!

Or

> I'm an old car, it's time it went in for an exchange. I need a new body! hahaha If I had the money of the Rolling Stones and I could go to Switzerland and get a blood wash haha and get new organs put in! Hahaha! [...] I laugh! That's the best medicine. Laughing, laughter is the best medicine. It's the only way you can deal with life.

And the need to deal with life is important for him. Actually, it is a need to deal *for* life. Meaning, he needs his job to pay for medication, next to providing for his family as the main breadwinner.

> Not a lot [business] going on at the moment, just trying to keep myself busy. Got a couple of training courses out at the moment to some XXXX countries. [...] Waiting for them to get back and accept my price. [...] As soon as possible [hopefully]. As soon as possible, because it's getting tight. My health costs are costing me a bloody fortune. With the insurance [...] Okay, it doesn't pay everything. [...] I'm insured through my wife and I get the basic, basic shall we say, therapy, which is not the optimal one, and I've chosen to go for something a little bit better and I have to pay the difference. Which is quite a lot. [...] I have a whole stack of medical bills to pay [as well], but you know, I just take every day as it comes.

Moreover, besides it paying for his medical bills, his daily work distracts him from his cancer. Work gives him energy to live his life and to beat the exhaustion of medicine, chemotherapy and radiation therapy.

> Sometimes, maybe it's the illness, cancer [...] Sometimes, I am very tired. I don't have any energy. I prefer [...] And at the moment there's lots of

> stress as well, because businesses is not going well, so money is obviously a factor. I am sometimes able to go to sleep at night. Get up the next morning, take my wife to work and then go back to bed for six hours, possibly even longer. It's a way of release for me to forget about the problems and with no opportunities coming for such a long time until now. With those Tokarov pistols, I suddenly find [...] And also the weapons management system [...] I suddenly find that I have energy to do things that I didn't have before. I guess you could say it's a kind of depression.

Whether it is a depression for him or not, he has accepted his faith, his cancer and the severe treatment of it, and, eventually, he has embraced death.

> What else can the good Lord throw at me, Yarin? Only thing above that is death, yeah? You know, that comes to all of us, so what the heck, yeah? Hahaha! I've lived my life to the fullest, and ehm [...] I mean [...] If I could, there'd many things that I would undo. If I could [...] well, I can't, so there's no point in worrying about them. You know, what's done, is done, unfortunately. Just have to make my peace, and that's it, yeah? So, what the heck. [...] I take full responsibility for my actions. I just don't wanna make any more mistakes. As for my health [...] Let's put it this way. Some people die of old age, some people die of a road accident, some people die of a building falling on their heads. Some people die in car bombing accidents, some people get hit by rocket shells, some people even get hit by lightning! Some people die of illnesses. Unfortunately that, by the way I'm going, that's what it looks like. Unless something happens to me on the roads that I'm driving or I drop dead sometime from a heart attack from smoking too many cigarettes, I don't know. But death is a part of life! As far as I am concerned. Okay, I'm 6X years old, I've had a good life. I would like to live a few more years but if the oil in my lamp has run out, then it's run out. [...] You see the thing is, there's no point in being scared of death. Because if you're scared of death, then you're scared of living. This is my motto, this is my feeling.

8.5 Conclusion

Whenever he is at work, he is a different person than at home. Yet his family life and beating cancer, he finds, depend on his work and the income he generates with it. Selling arms to someone to kill with gives him the income that enables him to take care of his family, to live their lives. It could be considered a contradiction: monetising on people's ambition for death and destruction, in order to sustain the life of your loved ones and yourself. During his stories about his former relationships and family life, he emerges as someone who struggled with romantic partners to the extent he has willingly remained an absentee father for a long time. Yet, he also is someone who is friendly and caring in well-functioning relationships, as was seen in how he keeps his work away from his family and friends. That is not to say he does not trust them, because he does, but it is to protect them. He would like to quit the job, perhaps even retire, but besides not being able to do nothing, he also cannot quit because of his family situation and because of his own health. His work gives him the means to provide for his family and himself, as well as that it gives him the last bit of meaning and purpose in order to live with his cancer.

9 All is fair in love and war

A criminological imagination of the arms dealer Constantine

'Art is never finished, only abandoned', as claimed Leonardo Da Vinci once (n.d.). The same may go for this biography of the arms dealer Constantine. This biography is finished, but his life moves on. A life that is like any other life: incoherently coherent and structurally fragmented. Seen through his own eyes, this book has tried to bring together Constantine's life that is full of ambiguities. Still, this book is but a limited story of a man's life and, by all means, not the entire story. It is neither finished, nor all-encompassing. Nevertheless, a criminological imagination can be provided here of Constantine's life as a child, as a young man, as a father and grandfather, as a husband, as a brother, as a diving instructor, as a social worker and, of course, as an arms dealer. It is a criminological imagination that is based on his biography in which there are no misinterpretations, only understandings.

However, it should not lead to putting Constantine, or arms dealers in general, into a theoretical category. When deducting a criminology, or criminological theory, to explain 'the experiences of the main character', 'the biographer is confronted with a serious issue', because 'it is almost impossible to let the extent and variety of the data flourish fully in a report' (Van Gemert 2011: 209–210). At the same time, understanding is not about reducing a rich life into abstract concepts that damage someone's life story (ibid.). It does aim at retrieving theoretical ideas to relate 'to everyday lived reality' through which criminologists 'should not obstruct the evolution of theory' (Mythen & Walklate 2006: 394). Understanding an individual and theorising together will lead to an understanding here – a criminological imagination – of the arms dealer Constantine. Such an imagination is given, living up to lessons about biography as key ingredient for a sociological and criminological imagination (Mills 2000 [1959]; Young 2011). As such, and 'no matter how high the flight of theory, no matter how painstaking the crawl among detail' (Mills 2000 [1959]: 128), that imagination is crafted by ideas yet disciplined by biographical fact and vice versa. That means that the criminological imagination here will be based on the biographical insights delivered in previous chapters, but contrasted by (theoretical) ideas. In this case, these will be existential and critical socio-criminological ideas on the post-war nuclear family, boarding school, university, craftsmanship, neoliberalism and liminality.

DOI: 10.4324/9781315148236-10

First and foremost, Constantine is a Jack of all trades, yet master to none and also mastered by none. He has lived a life of adversity and of adventure, of danger and of dullness, of professionally making money out of war and of personally embracing peace and quiet. Regarding his childhood, it became clear he had a very problematic relationship with his parents, specifically his father. The relationship with his mother was more respectful but often still problematic. Opening up about his troublesome childhood was hard to do. He did do so, nevertheless. Rather similarly to the biography on Jan Hoolwerf, a most violent man (Van Gemert 2011), Constantine had an authoritarian and abusive father with a military background. Whereas Hoolwerf became a hardened prison gangster, Constantine became an arms dealer. His childhood has been abusive but Constantine did not speak in those terms and he put it into perspective, showing an understanding for how he was treated and, indirectly, for how his father did it. He would never become the same though, which is one of his life lessons. His father's line of work not only disciplined Constantine in military fashion, but it also limited him to escape and have friends, except for his brother Arthur.

His childhood story, as problematic as it may have been, is not unique. In being raised with an iron fist in a post-war nuclear family, Constantine had a typical upbringing through which he embodies the social changes that were going on at the time (Honch 2012). What perhaps makes his childhood even more prototypical, is the fact that he was raised by an air force police officer nearby an air force compound. Constantine's father fulfilled a representative role in the rising military-industrial(-suburban) complex, unconsciously being militarised by it, while militarising himself the relationships with his wife and children, including Constantine, as head of that nuclear family. So, although the post-war decade has frequently been characterised by the shifting of focus from war and discontent to peace and 'happy' family life, family men were still motivated to assist in defence industry and its war efforts. The nuclear family lifestyle, as Constantine's upbringing reveals, benefitted from his father's job in defence and comprised a 'lifestyle [that] was ingrained within a larger military-industrial-suburban complex' (ibid.: 29). The abusive treatment by his father was normal given the era of his childhood, which was in a post-war society (Black & Pemberton 2017; Hague & Wilson 1996; Young 2011). The militarised childhood was laid upon by his parents who envisioned a certain shaping of Constantine into conformity with the then prevailing social norms (Jenkins 1998), that of masculinity and rigid order. They did so in a very punitive way, disciplining in a 'shock and awe' manner through physical violence, fear and shame.

Those post-war times are also characterised by decline, new complexities revolving around consumerism, shifting sociocultural and political-economic values and popular culture (Black & Pemberton 2017). Constantine's military upbringing forms the opposite of that social progress and of the welfare state developments. Simultaneously his childhood is typical of the relative deprivation that came along with the post-World War II Golden Age of prosperity, often causing the domestic violence he and his contemporaries underwent; violence that generally was silenced while it slithered during those decades (Hague & Wilson 1996). The normality of such militarised, abusive parenting echoed later on in his life and that of his entire generation (cf. Brownfield 2010). Constantine has not ignored but embraced that past though. It not only brought him trauma, but also discipline, respect and 'reality checks' regarding (fake) friendship. These are features and skills that are much needed in arms dealing, while reaping benefits from the military-industrial(-suburban) complex as a legal arms dealer. Meaning, it is his very 'normal' militarised upbringing that early on gave him experiences and nurtured the skills and career goals required for being a successful arms dealer later on.

His teenage years in boarding school, his university life and the early career path he walked are rather alike to his early youth. By being sent off to boarding school, Constantine went from a rough and abusive childhood to teenage years spent in perceived privilege and the best preparation for worldly success in later adult life (Duffell 2000; Gaztambide-Fernández 2009; Schaverien 2015). However, his boarding school life was not free from socio-psychological and physical costs, as he was more often than not subjected to bullying and violence, while being far away from home. Not that his home was any better. It means that boarding school brought about further trauma that can emerge later on in adulthood, including stress related disease, difficulty in establishing and sustaining meaningful (intimate) relationships, but also becoming a workaholic to the point of burnout, serious health issues and drug and alcohol misuse (Duffell 2000). These effects of especially drug and alcohol abuse most definitely occurred in his later life. Therefore, Constantine seemed to have suffered from 'boarding school syndrome' and probably adopted, unconsciously, several coping mechanisms that have caused difficulties in intimate relationships later on in adult life (Schaverien 2015), that indeed unfolded themselves his love relationships and role as a parent and grandparent. To an extent, Constantine is a classic example of a boarding school survivor that was forced into

> [t]he development of the pseudo-adult, the strategic survival personality, [that] cloaks the loss of original innocence and wholeness. We have all donned many cloaks but the boarding school survivor puts his or hers on very securely, and very early. It can be a long hard job taking them off again.
>
> (Duffell 2000: 295)

Yet, what became clear as well, is how Constantine resisted boarding school doctrine by fighting with other pupils, for which he received, once more, military-like punishment. Commonly, classical sociological analyses of elite boarding schools reveal how they often institutionalise traditions of the elite and acculturate members of the younger generations into upper-class lifestyles (Baltzell 1958; Mills 1956), by pushing young adults through different 'rites of passage' to make them loyal to elites by stripping them of their sense of self (Cookson & Persell 1985). They make them part of the reproduction and enforcement of oppressive social structures (Giroux 2001). Based on those ideas, it is understandable that by being defiant against the boarding school regime, Constantine therefore, albeit indirectly, resisted the dominant hegemonic structures of society. That also testifies to his own notion of himself being anti-establishment. All the while having been in the establishment, he therefore manoeuvred through it by embodying, to an extent, a critique from within.

The similar can be said about his studies in IT at university. He did not want to study IT, yet his father pushed him to, to which he eventually gave in. At university though, he soon realised he did not fit in. It was the place where he did drugs and became religious. It is also where he discovered his interest in counterterrorism and security-related themes. Moreover, he realised from there onward he does not like the 'fake', intellectualist and elitist world of the Ivory Tower (Benwell & Stokoe 2005; Lexier 2019; Willis 1977). In a way, he started his opposition to academic institutionalism already before neoliberalisation of academia started and to which critical scholars, including myself, are rising up against by forming a resistance against the neoliberal Ivory Tower (Lexier 2019). Students refusing to perform academic tasks and avoided shaping an academic identity, as Constantine did, is then a type of resistance, commonly associated with masculinity (Benwell & Stokoe 2005). Given Constantine's nuclear family background, being an 'army brat', who transcended out of that family into upper-middle class through an academic career has been and still is rather common today (Hollingshead 1950; Reay et al. 2009; Willis 1977). As opposed to complying with upper-middle class cultures and structures, we see Constantine at university adopting and developing 'counter-culture specific working class themes' instead, such as 'resistance; subversion of authority; informal penetration of the weaknesses and fallibilities of the formal; and an independent ability to create diversion and enjoyment' (Willis 1977: 115). In resisting (upper-)middle class, even elitist norms and values of the university, he moved (back) towards the working class, as well as to the (socio-)religious norms and values his parents descended from.

After having finished university, he committed himself to different lines of work with a common red thread: sticking it to the Man. From being a diving instructor to training dogs, and from being social worker to doing government consultancy work to advise on counterterrorism and even counterproliferation of illegal arms, he presents himself as an excelling, professional non-conformist, much like he did when going to boarding school and university, protecting the – in his eyes – weak. Whenever he sensed an oppressor would appear that affected him and the ones he is responsible for, he felt the need to become defiant. Especially as a social worker at the end of the 1980s, he was duty-bound to protect his mentally ill clients as they were being suppressed. He rose against the neoliberal exploitation of 'emancipatory elements of social work' and the consequential struggle of social workers to 'become a more powerful voice for social justice' that is 'inherently resistant to neoliberalism' (Hyslop 2018: 20).

Constantine's coming of (r)age and early career-building was filled with all too human moments of gratification through resistance and disillusionment through being oppressed. He wanted to fight certain larger social structures while conforming with others, operating inside powerful societal institutions themselves (e.g. boarding school, university and governmental positions). It unpacks his very normal his wish to stand out. We all want to be unique, which makes it anything but unique. In his career ambition to be a thorn in the flesh of concentrations of neoliberal power and authority, he did what he thought was best. The (perhaps unconsciously) resisting of neoliberal governmentality led him to combatting the illegal arms market that, eventually, got him interested in legal arms dealing. In other words, his educational and professional early-career of being anti-establishment and against neoliberalism prepared him to become a legal entrepreneur that reaps the benefits from the international arms trade and war industry. In his coming of age, he thus emerges as rebellious, while being introduced to the cut-throat international arms trade. A trade that is part of a larger international shadow market that is fed by and feeds into global neoliberalism itself (Castells 1998; Galemba 2008; Nordstrom 2004). It means that, out of resisting neoliberalism, he got dropped right in the middle of the archetypical neoliberal arms dealing profession, something he previously so fiercely and proudly resisted. However, he still seems to be able to resist, or at least wishes to do so from within, but this time he is closer to that heart of neoliberal darkness.

Given how Constantine sees himself as an arms dealer before and nowadays, he seems to be motivated by a certain will to firepower, consisting of enjoying arms aesthetically and of being a mastermind in the chess game of the arms dealing logistical challenges. He also enjoyed the fast but unhealthy life involved. It is a life from days gone by though, as it all has changed since he got ill. He does not go out to see his clients anymore, neither does he ever see or possess the arms and ammunition physically. Interesting to observe, is how he emphasises being a small businessman and craftsman, who is 'not just a gun runner', as he often would tell, and definitely not an illegal, 'black' arms dealer. In fact, dealing under the table would be professional suicide. Besides having to stay at home, as arms and ammunition themselves are not as wanted as they used to be, the nature of arms dealing changed as well because he feels the need to specialise himself in delivering tailor-made solutions, consultancy and other services, including risk-assessments and geopolitical analyses, and training courses on combat, ethical behaviour and cybersecurity. His goal is to give a unique customer experience of his arms dealing craftsmanship and create a type of brand loyalty, through which he sells his products and services. This way, he can compete on the basis of quality and diversity instead of 'dump-pricing' and extreme advertising, like the large global arms manufacturers seem to do in his experience.

Much like a craft beer microbrewery that offers 'rebellious' beverages – that are capitalised on by the larger craft beer industry – Constantine wants to craft quality arms deals and related services (Morris 2016; Murray & Overton 2021). In doing so, he exercises his resistance against large manufacturers, and thus once more, against 'oppressive' forces. Yet he is not the only one. In fact he is 'part of a broader evolution of experiential "more-than-commodity" sectors that extend product life cycles and add competitive advantages' (Murray & Overton 2021: 81). It means that, through his craftsmanship for which he wants to offer originality and quality and 'where craft is framed as an act of resistance, couched in the language of rebellion', he draws 'upon an intractable yet mythical narrative in which craft is synonymous with altruism, morality, resistance, and self-determination' (Morris 2016: 5). He thus is trying to be a craftsman who speaks to arms-purchasing audiences that wish to identify as more than just gun consumers; all done so within the global neoliberal context of large arms manufacturers. By it, he gives meaning to his 'citizenship and social responsibility, advocating rebellion yet ensuring its impotence' (ibid.). Seen from that point of view, Constantine's crafting of arms deals is just another 'mode of cultural capitalism' that can be 'a persuasive—albeit illusory—counterpoint to neoliberal capitalism', letting him preserve 'the conditions of the late capitalist state rather than destabilise them, underscoring power inequity, cultural hegemony, and rebellion as commodity' (ibid.). Hence, as much as he wants to be (seen as) a rebellious arms dealing craftsman that offers an exceptional experience, he unconsciously sustains the global neoliberal order that feeds into and off of the international arms trade.

It is somewhat remarkable that he sustains it, because he is aware of the fact of how arms dealing has become a neoliberalised trade that is dominated by multinational arms manufacturers, untrustworthy clients and a couple of small-scale small arms and light weapons (SALW) dealing kindred spirits. These parties sometimes are brought together by him in his role as brokering arms dealer, however, and much like his offered arms and ammunition, he almost never meets his clients or any of his contacts physically anymore. Usually, he is approached by clients or in-between parties that represent governments. If you want to get his serious attention as a client, you must guarantee to have some sort of stable situation, whether that is peaceful or hostile. It means that Constantine will only invest his time and energy in potential deals that comprise clients that are in an ongoing conflict and perpetual war. Or, in case of perpetual peace, if you are in policing and security in which arms and ammunition are required for training purposes, then he is also interested. Next to having to trust the level of stability of the client's situation, warring or not, he must trust that the client will not resell his arms and ammo. Geopolitical analyses as business intelligence help him decide and also gain a client's trust. Regarding those analyses, it is important not to instil fear into his clients, as fear-mongering works counterproductive, which counters the idea of it being profitable for security markets (cf. Loader 1999). It could actually lead to clients distrusting him in case his analysis that 'promised' war and conflict eventually did not happen. It would be bad for his business continuation. So, whatever he does, he will not betray his clients despite that they can betray and have betrayed him – those are his business ethics. As long as they can show an End-User Certificate (EUC), he can trust them. He would even sell to both parties if both would have an EUC (cf. Brogan & Zarca 1983).

Constantine struggles with large arms manufacturers that are fake and do not care about clients like he does, he finds. They have more capacity to reach out to clients than he has; an incapacity of his that threatens his business. In comparison to these manufacturers, he presents himself, once more, as genuine and trustworthy, and as a craft arms dealer. In his eyes, they provide cheap, tasteless, mass-produced 'burger'-arms deals, whereas he resists such McDonaldization (Ritzer 2013) of the international arms trade. He instead delivers high-quality, artisanal and customer-fit 'burger'-arms deals. In fact, he is convinced that because of that quality, his company and that of similar small-scale arms dealers cannot ever cease to exist. He works together with a few of those small-scale arms dealers, where, once again, trust plays an important role – professional trust that is. They need each other and get information from each other for their own geopolitical analyses and business intelligence, and for their own client base. Also, combined they can offer total arms and ammunition packages to their shared clients, much like arms manufacturers can do on their own. It is a type of collaboration that entails co-dependency, because only together they make a chance in the cut-throat competitive world of the international arms trade that is ruled by multinational arms manufacturers. This also means Constantine and other small-scale arms dealers, like his White Knights, cannot betray each other; if one does, they all fail. If that happens though, Constantine has no trouble to be disloyal to them and betray them. All in all, and given previous research on brokering (dis)trust and leadership (cf. Halevy et al. 2020), Constantine stages himself as an emergent but silent leader that prides himself with being able to spot complex issues between involved parties. He ameliorates those complexities through balancing professional trust and distrust, self-awareness and a having adopted a chameleon-like style of interacting with and between clients, with large arms manufacturers and with small-scale arms dealers. And he does so while trying not to lose face as a professional who crafts his arms deals.

In delivering that craft and by staging himself as an entrepreneurial arms dealer with an anti-corporate attitude, and because he is a legal arms dealer, he must comply with (inter)national laws, despite that he does not see any worth in them. It gives him a sense of purpose to be able to find loopholes in the legal bureaucracy of the – he considers – over-regulated international governance of arms. In doing so, he is embodying a commercial resistance against a perceived 'big government', having to be part of a resurgence of the free market against global legal regulation (Truong 2006: 337). At the same time, he uses that system of loopholes as well to succeed. As long as he reaps the benefits from licenses, the EUC system and punishments such as sanctions and especially embargos, he is okay with the ineffectiveness and hypocrisy of the arms control. But when rules and regulations are causing him trouble, then he becomes critical of power politics behind the arms treaties, laws, licences and penalties, making him feel the need to uncover and vilify the hypocrisy of arms control and its governance. His conspiratorial thinking towards the politics of arms control 'law and order' as an oppressive regime, and from which he deducts his resistant conspiracy theories, mirrors the increasing prevalence of conspirationalism (cf. Cohnitz 2017; Hellinger 2018; Imhoff & Ruder 2014; Mancosu et al. 2021). That thinking as such, fits the idea of how conspiratorial belief ought to be seen as a generalised political attitude of anti-authoritarianism, while being yourself slightly authoritarian in convincing others of your belief (Imhoff & Ruder 2014). Moreover, given how easily accessible uncontrolled information has become that stimulates us to think we have alternative and 'truer' information to be anti-establishment, we rather only reconfigure previous stereotypes and prejudices (Mancosu et al. 2021). It means that his conspiratorial attitude primarily uncovers his own somewhat hypocritical stance on arms control. Still, conspiratorial thinkers are considered to be often more critical and better informed than average citizens, and although they make grave mistakes in their reasoning (Cohnitz 2017: 18), their '[c]onspiracy theory, appropriately developed, can make erosion more perceptible and stop the erosion' of a system (Hellinger 2018: 284). The system in this case would be the international arms control laws, treaties and politics behind them. Therefore, in criminologically imagining Constantine, his frustration about the arms trade should not be fully accepted but also not simply dismissed as mere conspiracy thinking.

This also goes for the taken for granted imaginaries that exist about the arms trade and arms dealers, as discussed in Chapter 1. In fact, due to discussing those imaginaries, Constantine's presented his refined business morality, how he is not a 'black' arms dealer and that he in fact despises them. In fact, he considers himself a humanitarian arms dealer. Instead of having bulldozed over such refined intricacies, as is done by the public opinion that demonises arms dealers, it is exactly those refinements that matter to him and thus matters in understanding him. The same goes for his moral outlook on religion and the evil nature of mankind, from which he rises as a 'moral chameleon' who can quickly 'modify or abandon previously avowed principles in order to placate others' (Benjamin 1990: 47). He then ought to be understood as someone that may not possess a core set of values they stand for (French 1996: 142), which seems to be required when being an arms dealer.

Shifting in between morals and principles is also something he does regarding his family life. He points out that he is a different person at home compared to 'at work'. However, he brokers arms deals so that someone purchases arms to kill with; deals over which he receives commissions that enable him to take care of his family and himself to live their lives. It seems a contradiction to commoditise people's ambition for death and destruction to sustain the life of your loved ones and yourself. But for him it is a way of life.

A life that is under threat by pancreatic cancer that has brought him closer to death, and simultaneously, makes him appreciate life more. In fact, it has made him appreciate *his* life, with all of its mistakes and merits, not all too different from what Nietzsche once wrote.

> In the face of tragedy, the warlike part of our souls celebrates its saturnalia; whoever is used to suffering, who seeks out suffering, the *heroic* human being exalts his existence with tragedy—to him alone does the tragedian present this cup of sweetest cruelty.
>
> (Nietzsche 1997: 65)

Heralding Constantine here with heroism shall be avoided. He is not a hero, nor does he wish to be considered as such. However, he is used to suffering, he does not avoid it and as a matter of fact, he uses it to live. In finalising the criminological imagination of this somewhat Nietzschean Jack of all trades, yet master to none, is that Constantine acts as a broker not only in arms dealing. He has done so his entire life, which he realises himself very well, I discovered when he said the following to me:

> You ever heard of something called the chameleon syndrome? That's me. I'm your original chameleon. [...] The chameleon syndrome is where I'm in a strange environment and when I have to fit in with the others, then I fit in. I make myself unseen. I do not draw attention to myself, that's what I meant by chameleon.

It has been argued that 'in playing out many roles as a "social chameleon," the sense of an obdurate, core self is compromised' (Harter 1997: 87). However, *that* compromising seems to be his self. He is chameleonic, manoeuvring through resistance and compliance, which he seems to have embraced and professionalised. For him, it is not about being a fast living, mischievous arms dealer or being a serious businessman merely interested in logistics. Neither is it about trusting and being trustworthy on the one side, nor about distrusting and being untrustworthy on the other. It is also not just about playing by the rules of the game or merely dismaying the game of the rules. It is for him not only about being an arms dealer or simply being a husband and (grand)father. And it is not about life or death.

No, to understand him is to accept that he is all of it and none – he is somewhere in between: an original chameleon which he has embraced. It is that in-betweenness, or liminality, which is required in imagining him criminologically. It is about understanding the arms dealer Constantine as neither the one nor the other, yet whose life somehow denotes all of those simultaneously while also distinguishing between them, without actually doing so (Thomassen 2016: 103). The person that – also in his arms dealing 'reality' itself – can be shaped and shifted in different directions (ibid.: 104). He is then also to be understood as someone who is not truly committed to leave such a chameleonic situation, he might only simply pretend to (ibid.). In fact, Constantine seems to reside just fine in preserving the confusing (moral) ambivalence he has, while he is mimicking a certain charisma of being resistant and rebellious. In (unconsciously) representing *and* ignoring that ambivalence and fluidity, nothing can be to taken away from him (ibid.: 105). That is exactly Constantine's own way of remaining solid and indestructible, which is one of the greatest accomplishments in a world that is constantly changing and trying to change you (see Waldo in Hewlin 2015: 53). If anything, Constantine is his own tower of strength. He is his own rock.

References

Baltzell ED (1958) *Philadelphia gentlemen: the making of a national upper class*. Glencoe, IL: Free Press.

Benjamin M (1990) *Splitting the difference: compromise and integrity in ethics and politics*. Lawrence, KS: University Press of Kansas.

Benwell B & Stokoe E (2005) University students resisting academic identity. In Richards IK & Paul Seedhouse P (eds) *Applying conversation analysis*. London: Palgrave Macmillan, pp. 124–139.

Black L & Pemberton H (2017) *An affluent society?: Britain's post-war 'golden age' revisited*. London: Routledge.

Brogan P & Zarca A (1983) *Deadly business: Sam Cummings, Interarms, and the Arms Trade*. New York, NY: W.W. Norton & Company.

Brownfield C (2010) *My nuclear family: a coming-of-age in America's twenty-first century military*. New York, NY: Knopf.

Castells M (1998) *End of millennium, vol. 3 of the information age: economy, society, and culture*. Malden, MA: Blackwell Publishers.

Cohnitz D (2017) Critical citizens or paranoid nutcases?: on the epistemology of conspiracy theories. Retrieved from: www.uu.nl/sites/default/files/oratie-cohnitz-2017.pdf.

Cookson PW & Persell CH (1985) *Preparing for power: America's elite boarding schools*. London: Basic Books.

Duffell N (2000) *The making of them: the British attitude to children and the boarding school system*. London: Lone Arrow Press.

Elias N (2000) *The civilizing process: sociogenetic and psychogenetic investigations*. Hoboken, NJ: Wiley-Blackwell.

French PA (1996) Integrity, intentions, and corporations. *American Business Law Journal* 34(2): 141–155.

Galemba RB (2008) Informal and illicit entrepreneurs: fighting for a place in the neoliberal economic order. *Anthropology of Work Review* 29(2): 19–25.

Gaztambide-Fernández R (2009) What is an elite boarding school?. *Review of Educational Research* 79(3): 1090–1128.

Giroux HA (2001) *Theory and resistance in education: towards a pedagogy for the opposition*. Westport, CT: Greenwood Publishing Group.

Hague G & Wilson C (1996) *The silenced pain: domestic violence, 1945–1970*. Bristol: Policy Press.

Halevy N, Halali E & Cohen TR (2020) Brokering orientations and social capital: influencing others' relationships shapes status and trust. *Journal of Personality and Social Psychology* 119(2): 293–316.

Harter S (1997) The personal self in social context. In Ashmore RD & Jussim L (eds) *Self and identity: fundamental issues*. Oxford: Oxford University Press, pp. 81–105.

Hellinger DC (2018) *Conspiracies and conspiracy theories in the age of Trump*. Dordrecht: Springer.

Hewlin PF (2015) Authenticity on one's own terms. In Roberts LM, Wooten LP & Davidson MN (eds) *Positive organizing in a global society*. London: Routledge, pp. 53–57.

Hollingshead AB (1950) Class differences in family stability. *The Annals of the American Academy of Political and Social Science* 272(1): 39–46.

Honch M (2012) The military-industrial-suburban complex: the race for nuclear arms and nuclear families in southern California. From: www.pugetsound.edu/files/resources/2012honch_hist400thesis.pdf.

Hyslop I (2018) Neoliberalism and social work identity. *European Journal of Social Work* 21(1): 20–31.

Imhoff R & Bruder M (2014) Speaking (un–) truth to power: conspiracy mentality as a generalised political attitude. *European Journal of Personality* 28(1): 25–43.

Jenkins H (1998) *The children's culture reader*. New York, NY: NYU Press.

Lexier R (2019) Resisting the Ivory Tower: liberal education and social change. In Dharamsi K & James Zimmer J (eds) *Liberal education and the idea of the university: arguments and reflections on theory and practice*. Malaga: Vernon Press, pp. 179–192.

Loader I (1999) Consumer culture and the commodification of policing and security. *Sociology* 33(2): 373–392.

Mancosu M, Ladini R & Vassallo S (2021) Political consequences of conspiratorial thinking: evidence from 2016 Italian constitutional referendum. *Acta Politica* 56(1): 69–88.

Mills CW (1956) *The power elite*. Oxford: Oxford University Press.

Mills CW (2000 [1959]) *The sociological imagination*. Oxford: Oxford University Press.

Morris K (2016) You are not a lemming: the imagined resistance of craft citizenship. *The Journal of Modern Craft* 9(1): 5–14.

Murray WE & Overton J (2021) Sites of consumption and sights of production: brew bars and craft beer in the city. In Capitello R & Maehle N (eds) *Case studies in the beer sector*. Sawston: Woodhead Publishing, pp. 81–103.

Mythen G & Walklate S (2006) Criminology and terrorism: which thesis? Risk society or governmentality?. *British Journal of Criminology* 46(3): 379–398.

Nietzsche FW (1997) *Twilight of the idols, or, how to philosophize with the hammer*. Indianapolis, IN: Hackett Pub.

Nordstrom C (2004) *Shadows of war: violence, power, and international profiteering in the twenty-first century*. Berkeley, CA: University of California Press.

Reay D, Crozier G & Clayton J (2009) 'Strangers in paradise'? Working-class students in elite universities. *Sociology* 43(6): 1103–1121.

Ritzer G (2013) *The McDonaldization of society*. London: Sage.

Schaverien J (2015) *Boarding school syndrome: the psychological trauma of the 'privileged' child*. London: Routledge.

Thomassen B (2016) *Liminality and the modern: living through the in-between*. London: Routledge.

Truong TD (2006) Human security and the governmentality of neo-liberal mobility. *ISS Working Paper Series/General Series* 432: 1–22.

Van Gemert F (2011) *Van prison gang tot TBS; biografie van een gewelddadig man*. Meppel: Just Publishers.

Willis P (1977) *Learning to labour—how working class kids get working class jobs*. Farnborough: Saxon House.

Young J (2011) *The criminological imagination*. Cambridge: Polity Press.

Epilogue

A bittersweet criminological aftertaste

Perhaps the criminological imagination of an arms dealer as a self-reliant human being and not as an evil, immoral creature that depends on feeding off of human suffering in war and conflict tastes bittersweet. Because it requires a certain 'scepticism that refuses to treat at face value the categories, assumptions and self-understandings that make up "common sense" about [arms dealing – YE] and its control' (Loader & Sparks 2010: 130). It is a bittersweet criminological aftertaste that will be epilogised here. Constantine and I will be leaving from Vaihinger's philosophical assumption (1935) 'as if' it is possible not only to imagine his life and understand him, but also to subtract *from* a single life a story about our society. It is, if anything, a criminological afterthought about a society 'to provide an instrument for finding our way about more easily in the world' (Vaihinger 1935: 15). Thus, Constantine's textual afterlife should be seen *as if* it can narrate a story about the wider, macro, sociocultural forces that a normal, everyday legal arms dealer and all of us are subjected to. The criminological afterthought here is then, in its most humble form, a critique of society and its nature (Restivo 2018). Meaning, Constantine's biography tells something all of our lives' all too human liminality and its contradictions. This might be hard to acknowledge, as it would mean we can (and perhaps should) relate to Constantine and his life (choices). And that is scary, because it means he and all of us are not that different; we resemble the arms dealer that we commonly demonise. This epilogue therefore echoes what Hannah Arendt observed on Nazi official Adolf Eichmann (2006), how understandable his actions were and what that says about all of us. We all can commit evil as well. However, when Arendt's analysis of Eichmann as an ordinary man was published

> Arendt's phrase about the banality of evil outraged people because it removed from monstrous crimes the depth and darkness to which we usually consign them; it gave them no depth but merely surface. To say that evil is banal has the consequence of taking the supposed depth and profundity out of it and levelling it: it is then supposed to be widespread, commonplace.
>
> (Donoghue 1979: 283–284)

DOI: 10.4324/9781315148236-11

The same may go for Constantine's life and how we do not want to relate to arms dealers as evil. It is for us hard to deal with the idea there is no specific darkness of an arms dealer to be found, because if there is, it is commonplace and we therefore may all possess it. We could very well have become an arms dealer ourselves, were we to have been taken in a different direction through life. And that means Constantine's biography also is to an extent a biography of you, the reading audience. You probably have recognised (yourself in) the stories he shared with us here: a problematic youth, resisting teachers and classmates, career ambitions, wanting to professionally excel, loving your partner and children (despising exes), retirement plans and facing death in the eyes because of being ill. These are stories that tell an exceptional tale about a life of rather banal and recognisable attitudes, choices, behaviour and events.

The fact that we are most likely not that different from Constantine by acknowledging that his arms dealing and entire life are ordinary, should then make us wonder why we demonise arms dealers to begin with. Why *do* we consider them extraordinary sinful geniuses, moral degenerates, key drivers of human suffering, merchants of death and all in all evil incarnate (cf. Bromley et al. 2012; Hornaday 2021; Theodoulou 2009; UN Security Councel 2019; Wechsler 2016)? What does that demonisation tell us about ourselves? To answer that, let us return to Ivan Karamazov, as cited at the start of Chapter 1. Ivan, a main character in Fyodor Dostoevsky's last novel *The Brothers Karamazov* (1992), explained something about evil to his younger brother. To imagine people as evil that is separate from being human is wrongful. That is the point Dostoevsky makes, along with the idea that as soon as someone dehumanises someone else into being evil or the devil, evil is actually created in their own image; it reveals something about one's self. Our wrongful imaginations of arms dealers therefore say something about what is wrong about ourselves. Such a process of demonising the other reveals a story about our own demons, about our Self (cf. Said 1978), without necessarily wanting to learn about the demonised person or phenomenon itself. We require evil to herald ourselves, to romanticise and idealise our lives. According to Nietzsche, we are actually in desperate need of an enemy to escape the real world of the sometimes violent nature and horrific history that accommodates pain and hostility, fleeing into an alternative, imaginary reality (1974: 282). Constantine argued something similar when he said that as a society we need 'moral pick-me ups', which we receive by demonising arms dealers, because then 'you feel a bit more refreshed so you don't feel so bad what they're responsible [for] through their consumer lives'.

By demonising arms dealers for societal moral pick-me ups, as a society we re-establish what the sociologist Émile Durkheim referred to as a collective conscience of society (Durkheim 1982: 98–102). He argued how such a conscience keeps a society together. Now, he based his sociology of cohesion on the industrial, capitalist society and its culture of the late 19th century (1964). However, we live in the first quarter of the 21st century. It is an overly digital age, in which various societies exist, with each having their different and merging cultures, and one in which an aspirational class emerges – a novel class that strives towards inclusion, diversity and overall cosmopolitanism (Curid-Halkett 2017; Hochschild 2016). Our collective conscience is thus one of aspirationalism: world peace, ending global hunger, everything green, becoming more tolerant, more diverse, more 'woke', more virtuous and thus more emancipatory – in themselves 'bright' things. However, in that collective striving, we hypocritically continue the very conflict, prejudice, bigotry, monoculturalism and inequality we want to eradicate. It is a specific abstract form of emancipatory evil that is preserved by a aspirational, cosmopolitan class that aspires to fight concrete violent evil such as war and arms dealers. But it feeds the invisible, structural violence that goes behind that concrete evil, such as the defence industry and its economical role in society (cf. Bauman & Donskis 2016; Currid-Halkett 2017; Hochschild 2016; Žižek 2009).

Such an aspirational hegemony tells people to be educated and it requires people to strive towards a more egalitarian society but that is only possible if you can afford it. So, aspirationalism is enabled by inconspicuous consumption, residing in the 'top echelon of the new world order [...] reliant on acquisition of knowledge, not birthright, not property held for generations' (Currid-Halkett 2017: 17). At face value, there is nothing wrong with aspirationalism spreading across the global West. There seems to be a genuine cosmopolitan interest to 'save the world'. However, aspirationalism puts on moral blinders and it makes people ignorant of the growing inequality they (re)create themselves without blaming themselves (ibid.: 22–23). Aspirational decision-making and establishing of norms have a far more malicious impact on society than previous elites had (ibid.: 185). Aspirationalism therefore may appear to embody the morality of global righteousness, social justice and cosmopolitanism. However, people improve their own quality of life and upward mobility, while stratifying themselves further from the real, everyday hardships of the middle- and lower-income strata (ibid.: 186–189). They risk becoming unable, or perhaps they willingly stay comfortable numb to even be able to 'imagine (let alone solve) the pervasive problems of their poorer fellow citizens' (ibid.: 189). Such a collective conscience to keep together society, then means to remain 'willfully ignorant that many of these decisions, veiled in morality, are practical and realistic outcomes of socioeconomic position' (ibid.: 196).

In that sense, aspirationalism keeps intact an invisible but structural evil violence that is forgotten about, due to visible aggressive acts of crime, terror and war (Bauman & Donskis 2016; Žižek 2009). We do not want to look at ourselves and our structural role in the arms dealing business by looking, for example, at investments in the arms trade made by large (healthcare) insurance companies we are all insured at, such Aegon, Allianz en NN Group (PAX 2020). We instead prefer to merely distance ourselves further from the invisible systemic violence brought upon society, of which Žižek says that

> [t]he exemplary figures of evil today are not ordinary consumers who pollute the environment and live in a violent world of disintegrating social links, but those who, while fully engaged in creating conditions for such universal devastation and pollution, buy their way out of their own activity, living in gated communities, eating organic food, taking holidays in wildlife preserves, and so on.
>
> (2009: 23)

Our aspirational evil is not dressed as 'grey and uniformed Orwellian "totalitarian" bureaucrats, but [as] enlightened, democratic administrators, cultured, each with his or her own "life style"' (ibid.: 24). The fact that we remain comfortably numb in our celebrated and expressed aspirationalism dims actual passionate commitment to truly bring about actual change for which we maybe even must sacrifice our life (ibid.: 25), violently. Instead, we rather commit ourselves to the 'endorsement of emancipatory violence', as Žižek refers to it (ibid.: 174). It comprises the fight against visible, sporadic violence, such as wars and evildoers, such as the demonised arms dealers, while we sustain the invisible structural violence and evil that actually drive war and the arms trade. Aspirational evil is therefore a liquidised evil, hard if not impossible to catch, floating and flowing around, posing a considerably more dangerous and venomous threat than its earlier versions (Bauman & Donskis 2016). It is capable of disguising itself 'for recruiting human – all-too-human – concerns and desires to its service under false – yet exceedingly difficult to debunk and falsify – pretences' (ibid.: viii).

It is a type of vicious, global hypocrisy ingrained in aspirationalism that spawns such liquid evil. Not just are we hypocritical towards the arms trade, arms dealers, war and our own role. Consider the creation of online communities about awareness of Facebook's privacy rights violations, on Facebook (Hull 2015). Or think about online crowdfunding to support projects that help refugees who fled ongoing war crimes and human rights violations by, for example, armed militia in the Democratic Republic of Congo; Congolese militia that control one of the world's largest natural resources of cobalt and coltan and the involved mining industry (Henleben 2020). Cobalt and coltan are vital components in manufacturing mobile phones, computers and other electronic equipment (Danso 2021); the very equipment via which make online donations to such crowdfunding initiatives. Or what about the vegetarian and vegan lifestyles that promote ecological awareness and advocate a halt to animal products by replacing it with tofu; tofu that depends on the intensive mass-farming of soybeans by powerful global conglomerates, such as Monsanto, that operate in an anything but eco-friendly manner (Gruen & Jones 2016: 164).

Such aspirational evil we all (unconsciously) take part in and that silently slithers through our collective aspirational consciousness (perhaps collective delusion) is revealed – and with it, our hypocrisy – whenever arms dealers appear. Because, as this biography has shown, Constantine is not unlike any of us. But to acknowledge that, is to admit we are part of such aspirational evil whereas we do not want to be confronted with it. Hence, we *must* demonise arms dealers and anyone who reminds us of that hypocrisy and its evil to prevent the confrontation with ourselves. Therefore, aspirational evil reflects to an extent Arendt's banality of evil (Arendt 2006), but it manifests itself 'so much neater, smoother, more trouble-free [...] and more proficient', while 'disabling moral resistance against the committing of immoral deeds' (Bauman & Lyon 2013: 82). In (actively) veiling aspirational evil, we demonise those phenomena that might remind society of such evil. Demonising the arms dealer is then merely a small part of far bigger and necessary (ideological) veiling to keep together a collective conscience that wants to appear moral, cosmopolitan and emancipatory. Nietzsche considered such ideological veiling as widespread ignorance of the often self-destructive tendencies of deeply rooted structures of society itself. In being aspirational, our collective conscience ignores and detaches itself from those structures, whereas instead it ought to acknowledge and embrace them as a symptom of our own 'sickness' (1911). It would be interesting for criminology to consider aspirational evil as itself *criminal* or *criminogenic* for the structural violence we bring about while thinking – or pretending – we are fighting (observable) 'evil'. In that case, there lies a task, which is to venture more often into studies that comprise *a criminology of society*,[1] possible through the life story of one single individual, like Constantine's biography. A biography that is a mirror to widespread aspirational hypocrisy and its evil. Or, as Constantine himself said so eloquently, 'when this [biography] comes out, there is going to be a shit storm in certain circles'.

So, whereas Chapter 9 has criminologically imagined the arms dealer, the epilogised bittersweet criminological aftertaste here, is one in which the arms dealer is a reminder of how not all of us live in a world of perpetual peace, love and harmony. And that in our aspirations of trying to get to that blissful state of being for everyone, we actually sustain the very wars, hate and evil we want to eradicate and escape from. The arms dealer is then the perfect enemy of the aspirational class, and thus also a perfect reminder of how we are our own worst enemy in the most mundane and banal aspects of our lives. Therefore, to an extent, this biography could be considered another biographical report on the banality of evil (Arendt 2006), specifically about the banality of aspirational evil of and, unconsciously, by us all. And the more we try to structurally distance ourselves from arms dealers and demonise them as evil, the more we uphold the very aspirational evil structures. Perhaps we could start to accept such evil, especially because, as this biography depicts, the arms dealer Constantine is a person like everyone else and goes about in his professional and social lives the same way we all do. And like all of us, he would like to live in a world where everyone can get along. But unlike most of us, he has seen war, the darker milieus of banal evil, and the amorality of a cut-throat global trade. And still, he remains hopeful, because, he said:

> [w]ithout hope there's nothing. Without hope you just don't get up in the morning, without hope you might just well dig a hole, lie down in it, put a bullet in your head and then ask somebody to cover the hole over. Humans have to have hope. They have to hope for better times, they have to hope for more money. They have to hope for better weather! There's always hope. If you ask somebody what their biggest hope is, they'll say: "World peace". You ever think that's gonna happen? No, but it's still hope. [...] My hope would be that it wasn't necessary to have guns. This is me personally. This is my deepest, most personal hope, [my] wish that there was no need for guns. But this would be impossible, because to do this, it would mean you'd have to have everybody on the same page all over the world, everybody in the same socio-economic status as everybody else. There would have to be no wants, no fears, and no worries. To stop arms trading, everything else would have to be sorted out, first of all. [...] My hope, my most secret desire, even though I'm an arms dealer [...] My most secret desire would be that there would be no need for guns. Okay? Because with no guns, it would also mean there's no worries, no fears, everybody was on the same socio-economic status, there would be no jealousy. All of the other sins in the world would have been rotted out, which is impossible, but there's still hope. [...] Hope is the last thing to die, because with no hope, everything else is dead.

Perhaps the hope Constantine holds out is a far more realistic hope than most of us have. A type of genuine hope by which one does not deny one's own potential to commit or be part of evil structures; a single person's hope in which, ironically, may lie an antidote to structural evil.

Note

1 At the time of writing, Google gave zero results for 'a criminology of society'.

References

Arendt H (2006) *Eichmann in Jerusalem*. London: Penguin.

Bauman Z & Donskis L (2016) *Liquid evil*. Cambridge: Polity Press.

Bauman Z & Lyon D (2013) *Liquid surveillance: a conversation*. Cambridge: Polity.

Bromley M, Cooper N & Holtom P (2012) The UN Arms Trade Treaty: arms export controls, the human security agenda and the lessons of history. *International Affairs* 88(5): 1029–1048.

Currid-Halkett E (2017) *The sum of small things: a theory of the aspirational class*. Princeton, NJ: Princeton University Press.

Danso K (2021) The link between the phone in your hand & bloodiest conflict in modern human history. From: https://grassrootsthinking.com/2021/01/23/the-link-between-the-phone-in-your-hand-bloodiest-conflict-in-modern-human-history/.

Donoghue D (1979) Review of Hannah Arendt's *The Life of the Mind*. *The Hudson Review* 32(2): 281–288.

Dostoyevsky F (1992) *The Brothers Karamazov*. New York, NY: Vintage Books.

Durkheim E (1964) *The division of labor in society*. New York: Free Press.

Durkheim E (1982) *The rules of sociological method: and selected texts on sociology and its method*. London: Macmillan.

Gruen L & Jones RC (2016) Veganism as an aspiration. In Bramble B & Fischer B (eds) *The moral complexities of eating meat*. Oxford: Oxford University Press, pp. 153–171.

Henleben C (2020) The Kimberley Process' Legacy: how the 2000 certification process for conflict-free diamonds can help solve contemporary human rights violations within the cobalt & coltan mining industries. *Loyola University Chicago International Law Review* 16: 115–128.

Hochschild AR (2016) *Strangers in their own land: anger and mourning on the American right*. New York, NY: The New Press.

Hornaday A (2021) While Hollywood looked for perfect villains, they were hiding in plain sight. From: www.washingtonpost.com/entertainment/white-supremacy-hollywood-villains/2021/01/15/515f5386-5696-11eb-a08b-f1381ef3d207_story.html.

Hull G (2015) Successful failure: what Foucault can teach us about privacy self-management in a world of Facebook and big data. *Ethics and Information Technology* 17(2): 89–101.

Loader I & Sparks R (2010) *Public criminology?*. London: Routledge.

Nietzsche FW (1911) *The case of Wagner, Nietzsche Contra Wagner and selected aphorisms*. London: TN Foulis.

Nietzsche FW (1974) The gay science: with a prelude in rhymes and an appendix of songs. New York: Vintage Books.

PAX (2020) Controversial arms trade and investments of insurers. From: https://eerlijkegeldwijzer.nl/media/496454/2020-12-praktijkonderzoek-controversial-arms-trade.pdf.

Restivo S (2018) *The age of the social: the discovery of society and the ascendance of a new episteme*. London: Routledge.

Said E (1978) *Orientalism*. New York, NY: Pantheon Books.

Theodoulou M (2009) The bizarre double life of Latif Yahia. From: www.thenationalnews.com/world/mena/the-bizarre-double-life-of-latif-yahia-1.571406.

UN Security Council (2019) Small arms and light weapons: report of the Secretary-General. From: https://undocs.org/en/S/2019/1011.

Vaihinger H (1935) *The philosophy of 'as if'*. London: Routledge.

Wechsler M (2016) 'Merchant of death' or victim of an international sting?. From: www.thebigchilli.com/feature-stories/merchant-of-death-or-victim-of-an-international-sting.

Žižek S (2009) *Violence*. London: Profile Books.

Index

For Product Safety Concerns and Information please contact our EU representative GPSR@taylorandfrancis.com
Taylor & Francis Verlag GmbH, Kaufingerstraße 24, 80331 München, Germany

www.ingramcontent.com/pod-product-compliance
Ingram Content Group UK Ltd.
Pitfield, Milton Keynes, MK11 3LW, UK
UKHW020148200926
475702UK00016B/2607
9781032189024